Checklists in the Text

Third Edition

WRITING
RESEARCH PAPERS

Third Edition

WRITING

RESEARCH PAPERS

A NORTON GUIDE

MELISSA WALKER Emory University

W · W · NORTON & COMPANY · NEW YORK · LONDON

Copyright © 1993, 1987, 1984 by Melissa Walker
All rights reserved
Printed in the United States of America

The text of this book is composed in Meridien.
Composition by ComCom
Manufacturing by Courier
Book design by Jack Meserole

Library of Congress Cataloging-in-Publication Data
Walker, Melissa.
    Writing research papers : a Norton guide / Melissa Walker.—3rd
ed.
        p. cm.
    Includes index.
    1. Report writing. 2. Research. I. Title.
LB2369.W25 1993
808'.02—dc20
92-14009

ISBN 0-393-95943-0

W. W. Norton & Company, Inc., 500 Fifth Avenue, New York, NY 10110
W. W. Norton & Company, Ltd., 10 Coptic Street, London WC1A 1PU

1 2 3 4 5 6 7 8 9

CONTENTS

6 RECORDING INFORMATION   114

7 ORGANIZING MATERIAL   139

PREFACE TO THE THIRD EDITION

Writing Research Papers: A Norton Guide provides all the necessary guidance and information for students to do research and produce satisfactory research papers; but it goes beyond that. To counter the notion some students bring with them to college that research is a senseless exercise having to do with footnotes and index cards, this book teaches the spirit and value of independent learning. It helps students appreciate that learning to do research on their own can be an exciting part of their college experience and that the skills acquired can serve them in other academic endeavors and throughout their lives.

This text contains instruction in basic research skills: narrowing a topic, using library sources, recording information, and organizing material. It provides guidance in the process of writing and documenting a research paper: writing rough drafts, revising, preparing a bibliography, integrating sources, and producing a final accurate copy. While much of the book is concerned with teaching library research skills, it also contains substantial information on research activities beyond the library. Students will learn how to contact people who can give them information not available in published materials and how to conduct an effective interview. There are new sample letters that show students how to ask for information or for an interview, as well as a new interview, with Professor Peter Vitousek of Stanford University, demonstrating that students can request and get information from experts. In addition to general instruction appropriate to research in all disciplines, there are clear examples for reporting and documenting according to three styles commonly used in undergraduate assignments: the styles of the Modern Language Association (1988), the American Psychological Association (1983), and the citation-sequence system used in many technical and scientific papers and endorsed by the new style manual of the Council of Biology Editors (1993).

The third edition of *Writing Research Papers* includes substantial new material. The significant revision of the science chapter includes updating the scientific documentary style to be consistent with the style of the Council of Biology Editors, an expanded discussion of scientific research, and an exciting new sample paper on seed dispersal in tropical rain forests. There is a new chapter on doing research about literature, with two sample papers—a documented essay on Alice Walker's *The Color Purple* and a documented argumentative paper on the controversies surrounding Mark Twain's *Adventures of Huckleberry Finn*.

The book now contains six sample research papers: Linda Orton's short paper in chapter 8 provides students with an easy, accessible example of an original approach to research findings reported in a straightforward, readable way. Michael Gold's paper, "Conflict and Cooperation: The Making of *Rebel Without a Cause*" (ch. 11), is the result of a carefully planned search for materials followed by innovative use of various kinds of sources as Michael pieces together the story of how that film was made; in chapter 12, David Harris's paper, "The Need for Education to Combat the Psychological Effects of the Nuclear Threat on Children," illustrates the development of a strong persuasive argument. Lisa Lee's paper (ch. 13), "The Fate of Seeds in Tropical Forests: Determining Factors," exemplifies a straightforward presentation of research findings following a commonly used format of scientific writing, including an abstract, an introduction, methods, discussion, and conclusion. In chapter 14, Carla Medina's "Always Trouble: Huck Finn and American Social Values" is also an argumentative paper, as Carla takes a position about this novel, the controversies it generates, and the social values that feed it. She presents her findings in a way that makes her position clear. Carla's other paper, "The Voices of *The Color Purple*," demonstrates a way to combine analysis of a literary work with critical responses of others to the work. In addition to a narrative of the students' research, chapters 11–14 contain not only a sample paper (or papers), but step-by-step summaries of the processes that culminated in the papers.

Each of these papers uses the appropriate documentation style. The short paper on Eleanor Roosevelt, the paper on *Rebel Without a Cause,* and the two literary papers use the most up-to-date MLA style of parenthetical documentation with a "Works Cited" list; the paper on the psychological effects of the nuclear threat is documented with the revised APA style; and the science paper uses the updated citation-sequence system of the 1993 manual published by the Council of Biology Editors. Instructions for documenting sources in these three disciplines were prepared with the assistance of the editors of the style manuals, Walter Achtert of the MLA, Leslie Cameron of the APA, and Robert Huth of the CBE.

For the convenience of teachers who want their students to document their papers with endnotes or footnotes based on the approved MLA format, appendix A includes instructions for citing sources with notes, an expanded list of sample citations, and pages from a paper documented with endnotes.

Since the last edition of this book was published, the advent of electronic information has transformed many libraries. Computer terminals that read directly from on-line catalogs have replaced many card catalogs, traditional indexes are now available in a CD-ROM format and on-line, and some students are now more comfortable doing an electronic search than they are using bound volumes. Yet numerous libraries have not adopted extensive electronic equipment and materials.

This edition is designed to be helpful to students using computerized sources as well as to those who still depend largely on traditional materials; it encourages students to use the appropriate references, rather than the most convenient. There are sections throughout the text that advise students to find out what computer-read materials are available in their libraries. There are descriptions of these new materials and suggestions about how to use them. The sections on the research that led to the new sample papers include discussion of the computer sources that the students actually used as well as alternatives for students who do not have access to such sources.

The annotated bibliography in appendix B has been expanded and updated. It includes new reference books, new editions of old favorites, and a description of those indexes available on-line and on CD-ROM.

In the past few years, the number of students who use computers for all aspects of the research process has greatly increased. While many do not go to a computer lab until they are ready to type, revise, and print the final copy, others use a computer from the beginning—for recording and arranging sources, taking notes, composing a first draft, printing drafts for revision, making final corrections, and preparing and printing the final copy. This new edition provides instruction and encouragement in special sections throughout the text for students who want to use a computer whenever possible. Lisa Lee's experience also serves as a model for such students.

Of course not all students have access to computers or know how to use a word-processing program. To ensure that those students have what they need, this text retains detailed guidelines for students who complete the entire project using pencils, paper, cards, notebooks, legal pads, and finally a typewriter.

Other new features have been introduced into the third edition of *Writing Research Papers* to enhance the book's usefulness for students.

Checklists, deployed throughout the text and clearly indexed inside the front cover, summarize essential points, help students avoid pitfalls, and make it easy for them to review what they most need to know about research. General example boxes get students thinking about research outside their areas of interest.

Activities at the end of each chapter are now divided into two categories: general activities that help build research skills across the disciplines, and project activities that directly apply to the student's own research.

The new design highlights the research processes of Michael Gold, David Harris, Lisa Lee, Carla Medina, and Linda Orton so that students can easily follow their progress from beginning to end. Detailed lists preceding the sample papers summarize and clarify the step-by-step process that leads to the completed projects.

ACKNOWLEDGMENTS

I would like to thank the many people who contributed to the preparation of the first two editions of this book and who have continued to offer support, encouragement, and suggestions while I prepared the third edition: my husband, children, parents, and friends who have made many positive suggestions; my colleagues at Mercer University and now at Emory University who have used the book and have helped me make it better; and my students, who continue to help me understand what they need to know and who have used the book and proved its usefulness by completing exciting research projects of their own.

I would especially like to thank my students at Emory University this term who have taken on their research projects with enthusiasm and energy and have produced a set of papers that have been a joy to read, reminding me how much I have always learned from my students.

Others made it possible for me to have the time and quiet needed to write. I am grateful to Mercer University for giving me leave for a term to begin the work and to Eleanor West of the Ossabaw Island Foundation for providing a retreat from other responsibilities.

For their many suggestions and encouragement, I thank Jerome Beaty, Richard Bondi, Roberta Bondi, David Goldsmith, Jay Knopf, and Marjorie Shostak (all of Emory University); Elizabeth Penfield and Ann Torcson (University of New Orleans); Blanche Gelfant (Dartmouth College); Paul Hunter (University of Chicago); and Michael Lund (Longwood College). I am grateful to those who read the manuscript at various stages and offered helpful advice: Adra Bogle (North Texas State University); Rosa B. Calvet (Broward Community College); Peter Dusenbery (Bradley University); Richard Felnagle (Mesa Community College); Constance Gefvert (Virginia Polytechnic Institute and State University); Richard Meyer (Western Oregon College); Kathryn Van Spanckeren (The University of Tampa); and David Yerkes (Columbia University).

For their contributions to the new science chapter, I thank Jack Ewell of the University of Florida; Randy Hayes of the Rainforest Action Network in San Francisco; Amy James of Washington University in St. Louis and the La Selva research station in Costa Rica; Terri Matalson of the Monteverde Conservation League in Costa Rica; Ronald Suarez, Deborah Clark, and David Clark, directors of the La Selva station of the Organization for Tropical Studies in Costa Rica; and Richard Walker, freelance writer.

Many colleagues around the country have taken the time to write and relate their experiences using the book with their students and to provide guidance for this revision. For their evaluations and suggestions, I thank Dennis Eddings (Western Oregon State University), Peter Peterson (Shasta College), Norma Rudinsky (Oregon State University), and Laura Zlogar (University of Wisconsin).

For their advice about students' needs and experiences using electronic information retrieval and computers, I thank Brenda Ameter (Troy State University System); Jennifer Berne Ginsberg (Northeastern University); and Melinda Kramer (Prince George's Community College).

Many librarians have helped me along the way. I wish to express special thanks to Virginia Tiefel, head of the undergraduate libraries at Ohio State University, who read the chapters on library sources and offered valuable suggestions; I am also indebted to her 1982 article, "Libraries and Librarians as Depicted in Freshman English Texts," in *College English*. I also appreciate the patient explanations about new electronic information retrieval systems provided by Bob Williams, director of the library of Kennesaw College, and Jim Dodd from the reference staff of the library at the Georgia Institute of Technology. I would like to thank the reference staff at Woodruff Library at Emory University—particularly Greta Boers, Nancy Books, Alan Clark, Luella Davis, Eric and Marie Nitschke, Elizabeth Patterson, and Mary Ellen Templeton. I especially appreciate Elaine Wagner and Bob Greene for answering endless questions about using reference materials in the natural sciences. John Brandt and Elizabeth McBride have cheerfully answered reference questions, and Marie Hansen and Margaret Whittier were extremely helpful in obtaining materials from other libraries.

I am particularly grateful to Walter Achtert, the director of Book Publications and Research Programs of the Modern Language Association, for his very careful attention to the chapters that illustrate or use the style of the 1985 *MLA Style Manual* and the 1988 *MLA Handbook* and for keeping me up-to-date about corrections and changes since then. His patience and good humor during several late-afternoon telephone calls helped immeasurably. I also thank Joseph Gibaldi and Carol Zuses for clarifying the current status of the MLA style for this edition. David Uchitelle of the MLA was also helpful.

During the writing of the first edition, the American Psychological Association also revised its style manual. I would like to thank Leslie Cameron of the APA for helping ensure that the format and citations of the psychology paper conform to the current authorized style.

The new sample paper on a scientific topic is documented with the latest style recommended by the Council of Biology Editors. Professor Edward Huth, chairman of the CBE Style Manual Committee, provided me with advance copy of the newly revised manual to ensure that the format and citations of the science paper are correct. I deeply appreciate his cooperation.

All these people have contributed their knowledge to this book but are not, of course, responsible for any errors that may be in the text.

Barry Wade, my editor at W. W. Norton, was involved in every aspect of the creation of the first edition and has shown the same care and thoroughness with subsequent revisions. I am extremely grateful for all he has taught me and for the countless ways he has helped. John Mardirosian has provided rigorous attention to the details of this revision as well as many positive suggestions that have made a difference. I wish to thank others in and around Norton: the late John Benedict for his encouragement and for those flashes of insight that he contributed whenever we talked; Allen Clawson for suggestions about the new chapter on research about literature; Libby Miles for helpful brainstorming sessions; Justine Trubey and Johanna Vondeling for their work in handling details that moved the revision forward; Marian Johnson and Patricia Peltekos for their splendid copyediting; Jack Meserole for his beautiful new design; and Roy Tedoff and Diane O'Connor for their meticulous and creative work in turning my manuscript into an attractive, easy-to-use text.

UNDERSTANDING
WHAT RESEARCH IS

1

An Introduction to Research

You may think of research as something you do in laboratories and libraries, usually as a requirement for a college course. But think for a minute. When you or your parents or friends are in the market for a new car, what do you do? You probably read consumer guides, visit car dealers, and talk to other people about their cars. When you look for a job, you may study the want ads, check bulletin boards, and ask around among your friends. Choosing a college or academic major or graduate school, deciding on a career, settling on a place to live, buying a house—all these activities require research.

While the word *research* has come to mean a serious, systematic activity, one requiring hard work, dedication, and perseverance, it once referred to a man's effort to win a woman in love or marriage, rarely a systematic business. The common element, however, in a lover's suit and a scholarly inquiry is found in the first two letters of the word. The prefix *re-* has the general sense of "back" or "again" and suggests repetition. The struggle to obtain what is personally desirable, socially good, or intellectually true is usually a matter of searching again and again.

To try again and again to understand other people, the natural world, and social and political structures is a significant step toward living consciously and deliberately. Researching has probably already played an important part in determining what you think and what you do. The skill with which you conduct research in the future can have a significant impact on the quality of your life, influencing how you perceive the world and what choices you make.

EXPLORING

Before setting out to investigate a subject systematically, it is helpful to recall that you are a natural investigator. You have been conducting informal research all your life. As an infant you conducted research primarily through your hands and mouth, often grasping, dropping, and grasping the same object again and again, until one day you were able to hold it and make it your own. As a two-year-old you probably discovered the nature of a dog by feeling it; perhaps you learned an unforgettable lesson about canine behavior by examining its teeth or pulling its tail.

As soon as you could talk, you discovered that there are shortcuts to knowledge, and so you began to ask questions: Does that dog bite? Is the stove hot? What is that thing? You probably never stopped asking questions, although the nature of those questions may have changed: What is inflation? How does a camera work? What did Martin Luther King accomplish? What are genes?

By the time you enroll in college, your success as a student depends on how much responsibility you take for your own learning, particularly on how you try to answer questions. Following through on questions can help develop habits that will make learning a part of your daily life, not just as a student, but in the years to come. Questions have a way of leading both to answers and to other questions, and the search for answers can help you keep alive—or recapture—the curiosity that comes so naturally to a child.

As an adult—particularly as a student and researcher—it is important that you learn to discriminate, to choose which questions seem the most important. It is not a good idea to look up every word you do not recognize in a difficult text, to ask professors to clarify every statement that you do not understand in a long lecture, or to go to the library for information on every subject about which you would like to know more. Rather, it is more productive to look up those definitions that you need to understand an author's main ideas, to ask a professor for clarification when independent study of the text still leaves you baffled, and to select topics of particular interest to explore in the library.

The issue is not *whether* you will need to conduct research, but *how well* you want to do it. The success you will have in finding information is dependent on both your attitude and your skills.

The first step in good research is gathering the available facts. Whether you are trying to discover the best way to go from one place to another on public transportation or a politician's stand on particular issues, you want to begin with the facts. If you consult a published bus schedule or a campaign brochure, you may only have just begun. To verify the reliability of the bus schedule and the campaign brochure, you may need to talk with people who actually ride a particular bus route in the first case and to consult the senator's voting record in the second. Does the bus actually run on time? Are the candidate's campaign promises reflected in his or her voting record?

Getting at the truth of what has actually happened is perhaps one of the most challenging of human efforts, and often the more we know about a subject the more we are aware of the difficulty of achieving absolute knowledge. Consider the physician who is asked to bring relief to a patient suffering from the most common of human ailments: a headache. To really help, the doctor must consider the possible causes of pain: Is there stress in the patient's life or some chemical imbalance in the patient's body? Has the patient had too much to drink or eaten food containing monosodium glutamate or other substances that cause headaches? There is no way to be certain what has happened in the body to cause pain, but a careful physician will consider the evidence for each of the possibilities and make a judgment about the best treatment and the best way to prevent future headaches. In daily life, people frequently have to gather evidence, reach conclusions, and take action without having reached absolute certainty; but conclusions are more likely to be valid if they are based on evidence that has been carefully collected.

Once the evidence has been gathered, the researcher must learn to understand and evaluate it. The first step in this process is learning when to trust and when to doubt the validity of sources. A book on the wonders of marine life by a skin-diving instructor probably does not contain the most reliable information about sharks; a study of cholesterol funded by the egg industry would not have the same authority as one conducted by objective researchers. A general biologist who personally opposes the development of procedures for creating test tube babies may overemphasize the dangers, while another who has a grant to do genetic research may understate the risks of such procedures.

But the unreliability of sources, or at least the fact that they present material from a particular perspective alone, is not always obvious, and you may sometimes need to investigate the author to make that judgment. Learning to identify a person's special interests and prejudices can help you determine if that person is likely to slant a presentation of facts to lead to a particular interpretation. Of course you will not always be able to judge the authority of a text or a person's oral statements, but you can ask

Evaluating Sources: A Checklist

Before deciding to use a book, article, or other source, consider the following questions:

1. Is the source up-to-date?
2. What are the author's credentials?
3. In the case of a journal or newspaper, is it known to be slanted to support a particular point of view?
4. Does the author have a special interest in the topic that might affect the reliability of the source?
5. Is the source adequately documented so that readers can determine what authorities the author uses as supporting evidence?
6. In the case of controversial subjects, does the source give a balanced view, acknowledging both sides of the argument?
7. Is the language vague or nonspecific? Is it discriminatory? Are percentages misleading?
8. Is the book published by a respected publishing house?
9. How was the book reviewed?

(See pp. 87–90 for more information.)

yourself what assumptions are behind what you read or hear. It is a good idea to suspend judgment and to get a balanced view of any subject before you reach conclusions, before you take a stand on controversial ethical issues, assume a political position, adopt a theory of human personality, or accept a set of standards for judging a work of art or literature.

There may be issues in these areas about which you keep an open mind all of your life and about which you never feel that you have reached final conclusions. There will be many times, however, both in school and in everyday life, when you will ask questions that have definite answers, when it will be reasonably clear what processes are at work and what events produce certain results. You will be able to study and determine how the heart functions to pump blood through the body, how the sun is used to heat water, what diseases have been linked to cigarette smoking, how a computer stores information, and how certain tax laws favor the rich.

As a student researcher, you will mainly be concerned with discovering for yourself what other people have already studied more exhaustively than you will be able to do, and one of your tasks will be to distinguish between what is known and what is still open to further research. At times you may want to conduct original research to test the conclusions of others (as in interviews, polls, and surveys), and occasionally you may wish to design an original research project (such as correlating the eating and exercise habits of a group of students with their academic achievements). Though most of the time you will be researching what is known, your research report will still be original: You will be the one to make sense of the facts and to arrive at your own conclusions.

REPORTING

When you do research, you ask questions and look for answers; you find some answers and identify questions that you cannot answer; and usually, even when you are doing informal research, you make some kind of record of what you find. You record an address, write down a memorable quotation, jot down figures, or take notes from what you read. When you conduct a systematic and sustained research project, you may not be sure of what you have learned until you organize and try to make sense of what you have found. Writing a formal research paper is a way of making connections and reaching conclusions. By outlining your findings, writing

---

Probable Cause

Some research projects may lead to the discovery that the ultimate cause of events is difficult if not impossible to determine. Historians may always debate the various theories about whether the assassination of John Kennedy was the result of a conspiracy, and if so, who planned it. While as a student researcher you are not likely to reach a conclusion about this subject, you might study the evidence and arguments used by proponents of one or more theory. Similarly, you could learn much about the attempt to overthrow Gorbachev in the summer of 1991 and about some theories of what led to the failed coup, but the causes that led to that last attempt to take over the former Soviet Union may never be known. Other events with causes that may remain unclear are the war between Croats and Serbs that began in 1991 and the crash of Pan Am flight 103 above Lockerbie, Scotland, in 1988.

a first draft, revising, documenting your sources, and producing a polished final paper, not only will you try to make sense of your research, but you will also try to communicate what you have found as clearly as possible to others.

The requirements for writing research papers depend on the purpose of a given assignment. The kind of topic (assigned or selected), the time allotted for researching it, the number and kinds of sources consulted, the methods used to record information—these may vary from one research project to another. The purpose of a particular assignment will dictate the organization, the length, and the style of documentation of a final paper.

In all cases, however, you want to report your research in a paper that is organized, clear, readable, and interesting. The real value of a research report depends on what you as a researcher have discovered and how well you tell others about it. The outline, title, list of sources, and notes are details that can help you record and communicate the conclusions of your research so that how you arrived at those conclusions will be perfectly clear to your reader. A good research paper will reflect your best effort to make what you have discovered understandable to others.

An Introduction to Resources

An unusually large number of resources for satisfying your curiosity are available to you in college. You probably have more sources of information and more experiences than you have time to use. Even in a small college community there are more people with experiences different from yours than you will be able to talk to, and there are more books even in a small college library than you can read in a lifetime. Learning to find and tap the resources around you is an important skill both in formal education and in everyday life.

The research resource that most people think of first is the library, and it is the place on a college campus where you will find the largest concentration of sources. But there may be other academic resources for you to explore, such as the bookstore, the computer center, or a museum. Beyond every college is a town or city with public establishments, businesses, and even shops and restaurants that may serve as resources for learning. Finally, the people you already know—family members, classmates, teachers, friends, and acquaintances—as well as those you can arrange to meet—other professors, experts from the community, specialists in one field or another—will prove to be living sources of information and opinion.

THE LIBRARY

A college library is an inexhaustible and ever-changing storehouse of information. New books, periodicals, databases, and other sources of information are constantly being added to the collection. An academic library benefits from the knowledge of many people on the college campus, since faculty members from all disciplines keep up with the latest books, magazines, journals, and other information sources so that they can select the best ones for the library.

Of course not all college libraries are the same; each reflects the institution it is part of—the courses in the curriculum and the interests of the faculty and students. A school of technology will certainly have much more information on technological and scientific subjects than will a general liberal arts college, while a university with a business school will provide a full range of books and periodicals on economics and the various aspects of business. Libraries use computers to catalog their collections, to provide access to databases, and to read indexes stored in mainframes or on compact discs. Learning to use a library's computer-based information retrieval systems is a requirement for effective use of library sources.

You will discover the valuable resources of your own library only by spending time there, so take a few minutes to explore: find the periodicals, the reference books, the stacks, the circulation desk. You can easily find your favorite magazines, but if you look further you may discover many other journals and newspapers that you will enjoy reading. You can probably find books by your favorite authors that you have never read, as well as books containing information that is new to you on a subject you know well. Locate the computer terminals that you may use for finding articles in periodicals or books in the collection.

OTHER ACADEMIC RESOURCES

The main college library is the most obvious research resource on the college campus. But there are many others. Some institutions have more than one library, and most have other resources for independent learning. To find them you might begin by asking the following questions: Is the library collection all in one place, or is it spread out in several locations? How many libraries are there? Is there a museum? an art gallery? Does your institution publish a newspaper? a magazine? an academic journal? Is there a computer center? a theater? a lecture series? Some of these questions can be answered by studying your catalog or by talking with other students. Others may require some investigation.

For example, what does your college bookstore have to offer? To answer this you may want to go there and spend some time. Browsing among the shelves and skimming texts can help you choose your courses more carefully and learn something about the many courses you will not be able to take; and, when you are trying to decide on a major, you will want to survey carefully the texts used in the discipline that interests you. Finally, when you choose a research topic, you may want to find out if your topic is being studied in a course on your campus; you may want to examine the assigned books and in some cases consult the course instructor.

THE COMMUNITY

Your college is part of a larger community—whether a small town, a huge metropolis, or something in between. Often there is an exchange arrangement between the services of a college and those of the greater community. You may be able to use the public library, borrow materials from public organizations, or attend meetings or lectures at other institutions. Each community has its own individuality: its traditions, civic organizations, political climate, cultural and social identity, businesses, and public services. It is a good idea for you to know something about the greater community in which your college is located and to find out which of its institutions are available for your use. Again you will want to ask questions: Is there a theater? a museum? an art gallery? (In large cities, you will want to ask how many such places there are and whether there are specialized ones.) What cultural events are there? What is the ethnic makeup of the population? Are there many people from other countries? Are there consulates to serve them? What about public libraries, other academic institutions, social services, historical associations, religious organizations, institutes, and foundations? What is the economic base of the community—its trade, manufacturing, and management organizations? What kinds of shops and restaurants are there?

If there are commercial bookstores in your community, you may want to begin there. When you visit such a store, you will usually find books that reflect the interests of a town or a particular neighborhood. It is a good idea to learn how the books are classified before you begin to explore the shelves. If you plan to spend any time browsing in a bookstore, you will probably be able to discover for yourself how the books are organized. If not, people who work in bookstores usually will help, and they typically like to talk about the books they sell. Remember also to look for used-book stores and those that specialize in certain types of books, since these stores can often help you find hard-to-get or unusual materials for your research.

PEOPLE

Learning what people have to teach us may be more difficult than learning the content of a book or the holdings of a library. People we meet do not provide us with a table of contents, an index, or a card catalog, nor can we punch a button to receive a printout of their interests. Rather, we have to ask questions: What kind of work do you do? What are your hobbies? Have you traveled very much? Where have you lived? Simply by chatting with your classmates, you may discover that some are citizens of other countries, some have intriguing hobbies, and others have special

---

Talking

Some people are very reluctant to talk about themselves, and you may have to work hard to learn what they have to teach you; others welcome the opportunity to talk about their interests and will usually do so without much prodding. You may be surprised to discover that you know very old people who remember World War I, the Russian Revolution, and the founding of the Soviet Union. You could easily meet people over seventy who could tell you about the Great Depression, Prohibition, or Babe Ruth. People you know who are about forty-five will probably have fairly detailed memories of the civil rights movement, the Vietnam War, the early space program, the first moon landing, and the assassinations of John and Robert Kennedy, Malcolm X, and Martin Luther King, Jr.

Americans will of course have a very different set of memories from individuals who grew up in other countries. Ask yourself whom you know from Yugoslavia, Vietnam, Russia, Israel, Saudi Arabia, Nigeria, Liberia, Indonesia, Australia, or Chile. If you grew up somewhere other than the United States, then you've had the experience of learning about a new culture, and you may have found that people are in some cases more valuable resources than many books.

---

skills. Making such discoveries often requires that you listen carefully to what other people have to say and that you resist talking too much about yourself.

Research as a Vocation

Many professional researchers are busy answering questions that are not likely to affect the quality of life on earth:

1. Will the American public buy colorless cola drinks?
2. Will red covers sell more books at Christmas than blue ones?
3. Do people spend more money in hamburger restaurants with orange-and-yellow decorations than in those decorated with cool colors?
4. Are people more likely to buy tuna that is caught without killing dolphins?
5. Do shoppers buy more in stores that smell like cookies baking?

Though these questions may seem trivial, they are important to people concerned with marketing strategies.

There are people in many fields whose full-time job is to address the stubborn questions that continue to plague human beings. By considering these questions, we get a sense of the huge challenges facing researchers and the extent to which research is necessary to the quality of life and even the survival of life on the planet. Consider the following challenges:

1. Confronting the AIDS epidemic
2. Searching for renewable energy sources
3. Building sustainable societies
4. Understanding the environmental consequences of fossil fuels
5. Comprehending the consequences of illiteracy
6. Deterring nuclear proliferation
7. Stopping deforestation
8. Controlling population growth
9. Preventing heart disease
10. Feeding the hungry

Each of these pressing concerns is engaging the energies of people around the globe, and the chances are that at some point your life will be affected very personally by the extent to which they succeed or fail in these areas.

LISA LEE

Lisa intends to major in biology and perhaps go to graduate school in environmental studies or forestry. Growing up in a rural area of northern California, Lisa had teachers and friends who were concerned about the misuse of forests in her own state. It was not until she came to college, however, that she learned that many people are concerned about the fate of forests all over the world. After attending a lecture on life in the rain forests of Central America, Lisa brainstorms on the subject of rain forests (p. 20), reads a book the lecturer recommended, Adrian Forsyth and Ken Miyata's *Tropical Nature,* and becomes fascinated by the amazing ways plants and animals have adapted to their environment. Lisa's research project may be the first step leading to her vocation.

Activities

A. Suppose a hospital is considering building a fitness and preventative medicine facility. What kinds of questions might marketing researchers ask to determine if such a center is feasible?

B. If you were planning to open a bookstore in a suburban shopping mall, what would you need to know about the people who live nearby?

C. Choose one of the ten challenges listed on p. 10 and make a list of questions that you think researchers are attempting to answer. For example, for decades people have explored the factors affecting heart disease and have in fact reached certain conclusions, but questions remain: How much fat in the diet is too much? Is moderate use of alcohol helpful? If so, is red wine better than white wine? Do people who know how to relax or who meditate have less heart disease than those who don't?

CHOOSING A TOPIC 2

Doing independent research is a valuable way to enrich your study of the courses you take in college. What you learn in class or from assigned textbooks will probably be more enjoyable and meaningful if you also explore aspects of the subject on your own. Once you learn research techniques, you will be able to go to the library or to appropriate experts to learn more about the topics in your courses that particularly interest you. Some courses include assignments specifically designed to teach you how to do research and to write a paper based on what you have found. The first step in that process is to find a topic—a specific aspect of a general subject—or to adapt an assigned topic to the resources available to you.

The choice of a research topic, like the choice of a friend, is not usually made after a systematic investigation; rather, it is the consequence of circumstances and actions involving both conscious effort and luck. The professional writer deciding on a subject for a new book, the graduate student choosing a thesis, and the college student selecting a topic for a limited research project all have the same general set of resources: where they live and where they have been; the people they know and those they have known; what books they have read and what they have done. The particular details of people's lives determine their existing interests as well as what new subjects they are able to learn about.

Five Important Activities

Whether your instructor assigns a topic or asks you to select your own, there is a process you need to go through to adapt a topic to your own interests and abilities. The early stages of any research project should include the following five activities:

1. Budgeting time
2. Following and developing interests
3. Letting ideas brew
4. Asking the right questions
5. Making a commitment

BUDGETING TIME

Throughout your project, you will need to budget your time. While this is not always easy, since you may not know how long particular activities will take, it is important that you plan from the beginning how to use the time you have. Begin by making lists. If you have four weeks set aside for a research project, then decide what you hope to accomplish each week. Your first decision will be to decide how many hours or days you can allot for choosing a topic. Remember that if you exceed your budget at one stage, you will have less time for other tasks; and you may need to revise your budget every few days. It is also a good idea to coordinate your research project with your other responsibilities. For example, do not schedule the final writing of your paper the day before you have a major test for another course.

FOLLOWING INTERESTS

Once you stop and think, you will probably find that there are many subjects you would like to explore. One way to begin to choose a subject for research is to recall what interests you already have, to think about what you already know, and to consider how to build on what you know.

In choosing a subject for research, you will want first to think about what you already know and what you have to build on. The next step is to consider those subjects that you think you want to learn about.

A carefully chosen research topic can contribute to your educational goals whether you are exploring possibilities for a course of study and a career or you know for certain what you plan to do with your life. Imagine that you are trying to decide between two majors: biology and psychology. Conducting research in one of these two areas might help you make that decision. If you are still considering a number of different possibilities among subjects you don't know much about, a research assignment is an opportunity to investigate a new discipline.

You may already know of several subjects that you have an interest in and would like to research. There may also be subjects suggested in your classes, by your instructor, or in this book about which you are curious enough to want to learn more. Before you commit yourself, it is wise to take time to consider the possibilities. You may want to make three lists:

What You Know

Perhaps you already have one or more strong interests. You have played the guitar, the piano, or the drums for years; you have read science fiction, mysteries, or contemporary novels; you have raced bicycles, participated in swim meets, played soccer or football; you are an expert on cars, movies, rock and roll, or batting averages; you have operated computers, worked in a business, or cared for small children; you have worked in a community organization, for a political group, or for a newspaper; you have spent time in the wilderness, traveled, or lived in another country. You may be able to use what you already know as a context for new knowledge. For example, the student who has raced bicycles for years will already have some of the background necessary to study the most famous bicycle race, the Tour de France; a student who is interested in computers and in music would be prepared to study the development of electronic synthesizers; and another who has lived in Brazil may want to study the movements to save the rain forests in that country.

What You Don't Know

Perhaps you would like to take up painting, photography, or organic gardening; you would like to learn more about alcoholism, drug rehabilitation, or weight reduction programs; you are considering studying psychology and would like to know something about Sigmund Freud, B. F. Skinner, or Carol Gilligan; you would like to be more physically fit and to learn about speed walking, nutrition, and yoga. Perhaps you are planning to take a course in anthropology next month, and you get a head start by doing research on the bushmen of the Kalahari Desert, or you are already taking a course in biology that provokes you to learn more about how plants attract pollinators. Ideally you choose your college courses because you are interested in the material, you want to know about a subject, and/or because studying a subject is a prerequisite for further study. A research topic will work best for you if your choice is based on the same criteria. Choose a topic, then, because it interests you, supports something else you are learning, or helps you realize certain goals.

1. A list of subjects that you already know something about
2. A list of new subjects that you would like to explore
3. A list of those items on the first two lists that are appropriate for your assignment

LETTING IDEAS BREW

By now you probably have many ideas, and it will be good if you can take the time to think about each of them. Discuss your ideas—even seemingly trivial or fleeting ones—with as many people as possible: friends, family, faculty, or others who may know something about the subject that interests you. Other people—your teachers or the reference librarian—may discourage you from pursuing some ideas because of the difficulty of finding materials or simply because a subject is not compatible with the goals of a given class. Once you have arrived at a subject that is acceptable to your instructor, give yourself time to determine whether it is one you want to pursue for three weeks, a month, six weeks, or in some cases more. Live with your ideas for a while; let them brew.

LISA LEE·

In preparation for choosing a research paper topic, Lisa's instructor asks the students to think of a large subject they already know something about and to break it into subheadings by making a branching diagram like the one below:

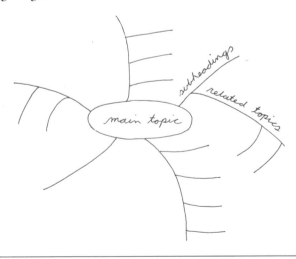

Since she has taken a course in ecology and is already interested in the environment, Lisa readily breaks down that large subject using a branching diagram:

(Branching is the right-brain alternative to outlining. An outline is a list of points usually arranged under headings and subheadings, and it can show exactly the sequence of development that an essay will follow. [For more on this see pp. 147–56.] But unless you already know how your essay will develop its points, you can't very well list them in sequential order. What you can do, however, is put them on branches radiating from a single idea, and make the branches sprout more ideas. You can thus generate a picture of the ideas in your mind—a pattern of connections to look at.)

Next you will want to explore possibilities by asking questions: You may ask your classmates, your instructors, or other people what they can tell you about the possibilities you are considering. You may want to look up several items on your list in encyclopedias or other general reference books. If you decide in advance how much time you can give to exploring possibilities, you will find it easier to draw the line at the appropriate point and say, "I must decide now."

Often the final decision about a topic can be made simply by jotting down questions to which you would like to know the answers. Each of the questions below could lead to interesting research:

1. How do space probes "know" how to get to another planet?
2. How did the civil rights movement change life in Selma, Alabama?
3. What are possible substitutes for products (such as styrofoam and freon) that are known to harm the environment?
4. What can a potential employer or creditor find out about a person's financial or medical history?
5. What legal recourse do women have when they are sexually harassed by an employer?
6. Can diet improve mental functioning?
7. How do diet, exercise, and/or stress affect the risk of heart disease?
8. What drugs can be used to lower cholesterol?
9. What explanations can you find for the recent worldwide increase in nationalism?
10. Is the Ku Klux Klan a significant force in American politics in the 1990s?

This technique is particularly helpful if you have identified a general subject area and broken it into a number of particular topics. The questions above, for example, result from breaking down general subject areas like space exploration, civil rights, or the environment. The best topic sometimes emerges when you study such questions and think about how they might be answered.

It will be easy to choose your topic if there is one thing in particular you want to know more about. Look at the list of questions you have made about possible topics and see if there is one that you would most like to be able to answer. When several questions interest you, ask yourself which is the most important, the most relevant to your studies, the most challenging, or the most suited to your resources.

Once Lisa has decided that she wants to focus on some aspect of tropical rain forests, she further narrows her topic by making the following list of questions:

1. What kinds of rain forests are there?
2. Where are they located on the globe?
3. Who is destroying them?
4. Why are they being destroyed?
5. Will the trees grow back?
6. Can the cleared land be used for farms? for grazing?
7. What happens to such land after a few years?
8. What do the animals do when the trees they live in are destroyed?
9. How will the loss of animal life affect regrowth?
10. In what ways are animals and plants interdependent?

Lisa is not yet sure how she will focus her topic, but the list of questions reflects her growing interest in animal/plant interaction.

MAKING A COMMITMENT

After you have selected a subject, done a little background reading, and talked to your instructor and others about it, you will probably be ready to make a commitment. Remember that you will live with a research topic for several weeks, and so you should stop and ask yourself if you have a sincere interest in the subject. If the answer is yes, then proceed with the conviction that you will not change your mind. You are now ready to begin your research by focusing on a limited, manageable topic.

DECIDING WHETHER TO USE A COMPUTER

If you have experience using a word processor and have a computer that is available to you and convenient to use, then you will certainly want to take advantage of this technology that will make your work easier and more fun. Study the suggestions on pages 159–60 of chapter 8 to determine if you are ready to use a word processor from the beginning.

If, on the other hand, you are not comfortable using a word processor, you must plan ahead if you intend at least to use it for the final paper. Begin now to explore possibilities. Visit the computer lab on your campus, find out what is available there, and ask someone to help you get started. If you have a friend who uses a computer frequently, ask for help. Ask permission to sit and watch someone you know use a computer. Ask questions. Find out about the advantages and disadvantages of different word-processing systems. Experiment. After you have chosen a program, study the manual, practice using the program, and when you have trouble talk to others who use it.

Most students are able to learn what they need to know about word processing in a few hours. The early stage of a research project, before you are under the pressure of a deadline, is a good time to learn and practice the basic skills of this helpful technology. Even if you do not know how to type, you can still learn to use a word processor, and with a little more effort you can learn touch typing by using one of the widely available computer programs that teach typing. A few minutes a day beginning when you are choosing a research topic is sufficient for you to develop good typing skills before you finish your research.

Using a Word Processor: A Checklist

Before you begin using a word processor for your own work, make sure you know how to do the following:

1. Move cursor up or down, and to the beginning or end of your document
2. Indent for paragraphs, set margins, and set off blocks of text
3. Delete words, lines, or blocks of text
4. Insert words or passages into your text
5. Move a block of text from one part of a file to another
6. Search for a word or passage
7. Move part of a file or an entire file into another file
8. Use the split screen or window feature
9. Save, delete, copy, and backup files
10. Format for printing—underlining, numbering pages, etc.
11. Print part of a file or the whole file

Once you are able to do these tasks comfortably, you are ready to use a word processor for a research project.

During the period when you are collecting ideas for research topics, keep a small notebook or note cards with you at all times so that when interesting topics come up in class or in conversation, you can write them down and later add them to your file of possibilities. A word processor can be very helpful for storing and ordering ideas.

LISA LEE

After attending the lecture about rain forests, Lisa comes back to her room, turns on her computer, and opens a file. She has already narrowed her topic with a list of questions; now she brainstorms on the subject of rain forests before discussing possible topics with her English teacher. The following list is the result:

```
Forests endangered
Rapid deforestation in Costa Rica
Massive loss of forests in Brazil
Animals in peril from forest fires
Many species will be lost
Plants with possible medicinal value are lost everyday
Why animals are important to health of the forest
Loss of one species threatens others
Animals and plants need each other
Forest dynamics
The fate of forests without birds and mammals
Pollinators and seed dispersers
```

Following Lisa's progress, you will see that the kernel of her research project is present in this original brainstorming list, even though she did not know it at the time. Keeping and adding to such a list will make a very valuable record of the process of exploring and learning about a large topic.

Exploring a Broad Subject

Some research projects focus on the achievements of individual people. If you are going to study a prominent person, for example, you will want to consider some particular aspect of their lives. While it is a good idea to inform yourself of the general outline of a person's life, your paper need not include a summary of the life. Anyone can find a summary of the lives of famous people in an encyclopedia or other reference work. A meaningful research project will combine material from different sources in an original way.

LINDA ORTON

Linda is enrolled in an English composition class in which she is asked to write a short research paper of approximately one thousand words, or four typed pages. The assignment is to explore a particular aspect of the work of a person on the following list:

Jacques Cousteau	Ralph Nader
Angela Davis	Sandra Day O'Connor
Amelia Earhart	Eleanor Roosevelt
Jane Goodall	Gloria Steinem
Mikhail Gorbachev	Norman Schwarzkopf
Lee Iacocca	Clarence Thomas
Norman Mailer	Ted Turner

Linda begins by checking the index to the *Encyclopedia Americana,* where she finds articles on most of the people on this list. She turns first to the article on Eleanor Roosevelt and identifies the following aspects of her life as possible topics for research:

1. Activities during World War I
2. Work in women's organizations in the 1920s
3. Career as an educator: The Todhunter School
4. Radio program
5. The furniture factory at Hyde Park
6. Syndicated newspaper column, "My Day"
7. War work: World War II
8. Role in the formation of the United Nations
9. The United Nations Declaration of Human Rights
10. Fighting for the underprivileged and racial minorities
11. Contribution to Adlai Stevenson's campaign

Each of these topics, suggested by a general encyclopedia article, is appropriate for student research. There are other aspects of Eleanor

Roosevelt's life—her childhood, her struggles with her mother-in-law, and her personal suffering—that may be interesting but that Linda will not be able to research as thoroughly as her role in public life. It is, after all, people's accomplishments and their roles in society that are reported in newspapers; studied by scholars; witnessed by observers; and, finally, recorded and analyzed in periodicals, books, and films. The events of private lives are often obscure, rarely recorded accurately, and seldom accessible to researchers.

Once you start reading about an individual's life and accomplishments, you may, like Linda, find several possible topics, but of course you will soon have to focus on one such as those below:

1. Jacques Cousteau's work with sharks
2. Angela Davis and the struggle for economic equality
3. Amelia Earhart's 1937 attempt to fly around the world
4. Jane Goodall's study of social rejection among chimpanzees
5. Mikhail Gorbachev and the early days of perestroika
6. Lee Iacocca and the transformation of American industry
7. Norman Mailer and World War II
8. Ralph Nader's work to improve auto safety
9. Sandra Day O'Connor (or Clarence Thomas) and the abortion issue
10. Gloria Steinem and the National Women's Political Caucus
11. Norman Schwarzkopf and the Persian Gulf War
12. Ted Turner and the rise of cable television

Focusing a Subject

Once you have committed yourself to a subject, you will want to take some time to explore possible ways to focus your study: talking to people about it, doing some background reading, and thinking about what aspects of the subject most appeal to you. Again, decide on how much time you can afford to spend before you begin concentrated research.

It can be helpful to see how other students break down large subjects and finally focus on a particular topic. Consider the progress of two students who start with general subjects and arrive at manageable, limited topics.

When Michael was growing up in New York, his father regularly took him to the movies on Saturday afternoons, and at a very early age, Michael became interested in old movies, especially those of the fifties and sixties. During their high school years, he and his sister frequently rented videos to watch on weekends. By the time he enrolls in college, Michael has watched hundreds of movies, some of them several times. Studying his college catalog, he is surprised to discover that academic courses are offered in film history, film appreciation, and film theory. When Michael is asked to choose a topic for a research project as part of his freshman English course, he immediately thinks that he would like to learn more about the history of film. Michael first goes to the library and consults the *Encyclopedia Americana*. He looks up "film" and "movies" and finally finds an article entitled "Motion Picture." (It would have been quicker to use the index, but Michael enjoys browsing in encyclopedias.) After reading the article, he concludes that one way to approach the subject is to break it down into different types of movies. Michael then visits his college bookstore and examines the textbooks that are used for film courses. Skimming through one book, David Cook's *History of Narrative Film,* he soon discovers that there is much more to learn about film than he had thought. At lunch one day, he talks with a student who is taking a film course. He asks her a few questions about the course and discovers that she is studying films that have influenced film making. By asking more specific questions, Michael learns the titles of important films he has never seen and of those that have attracted a cult following of fans who see them over and over again.

Based on what he already knew about movies and what he has learned from a little preliminary research, Michael begins to jot down ideas. The subject is so broad that he finds it helpful to divide it into rough categories. In a few minutes, he has produced this:

TYPES OF FILM

Comedy	Fantasy	Spy
Western	Gangster	History
Spectacle	Horror	Musical
Social realism	Thriller	War
Political propaganda	Detective	

```
                     TYPES BY NATIONALITY
  American         German           Swedish           Soviet
  French           Italian          Japanese


                        OTHER TYPES
  Feature films         Documentaries          Animated films
  Shorts                Blockbusters


                       LANDMARK FILMS
  The Great Train Robbery (1903)    Citizen Kane (1941)
  Birth of a Nation (1915)          Rebel Without a Cause (1956)
  The Battleship Potemkin (1925)    2001: A Space Odyssey (1968)
  The Jazz Singer (1927)


             TECHNIQUES AND SKILLS OF FILM MAKING
  Editing                  Dubbing
  Processing               Special effects
  Adapting music           Scriptwriting
  Sound                    Adapting scripts from other media


                      OTHER APPROACHES
  Great actors             Equipment
  Great directors          Industry vs. art
  The star system          The economics of film
                              production


                     FILM AND SOCIETY
  Censorship               Political propaganda
  Cult films               Social values on film
  Violence and film
```

Michael looks at the lists he has made, somewhat amazed at the
possible approaches to a subject that he thought he knew something
about. He considers researching a particular film genre, such as the
Western or the musical, but after some background reading in Cook's
History of Narrative Film, he realizes that the Western has really
spanned almost the entire history of film and the musical began with
the first talking movies. Not quite sure how to limit such broad
subjects, Michael considers other possibilities. In doing so, he
checks the topics that interest him and consolidates them in another
list:

```
American films
Social realism
Social values
Great actors
Feature films
Cult films
Rebel Without a Cause
```

A little baffled about how to limit his topic, Michael puts his list aside and decides to come back to it later. The next day, he considers the list again and begins to see that all of the topics that he has checked are related. *Rebel Without a Cause* is a landmark American feature-length film; it is a film of social realism that is an indictment of certain social values. Its star, James Dean, is considered by some to be one of the most charismatic actors of the twentieth century, and, what is more, he became a cult figure. Michael takes a clean sheet of paper and writes the following questions:

How does a film like *Rebel* come to be made?
How can we account for its success?
What influence did it have?
Was James Dean's charisma responsible for its impact?

LISA LEE

Delighted when her English teacher approves her proposal to write a research paper on some aspect of life in tropical forests, Lisa heads for the library and checks out five general books on the subject. She spends several hours a day reading about topics that particularly interest her, developing a general understanding of tropical forests and of the complex economic and political forces that affect their future. She decides to focus on the scientific aspects of her subject. Using her word processor, she adds the following possible topics to the list she began earlier:

```
Chemical defenses in insects and frogs
Defense mechanisms in plants
Gap ecology
```

```
Life in the canopy
Medicinal use of plants
Nutrient cycling
Reproduction systems of tropical frogs
Seed dispersal
Soil nutrients
Treefalls
```

Lisa is also taking a course in botany, and so she makes an appointment with her biology teacher to discuss which of these topics seem most appropriate. Together they brainstorm, and it soon becomes clear that she is particularly interested in the ways that animals and plants interact. She first considers defense mechanisms, the ways that plants defend themselves from being eaten by insects and other creatures, a subject which is studied by scientists interested in the chemical composition of the poisons that plants produce.

More interesting to Lisa, however, is the way seeds are dispersed throughout the forest and what conditions make it possible for a seed to germinate and grow. Consulting her library books again, she learns that seeds of most tropical trees are in fact dispersed by animals. At last she arrives at a tentative title for her research paper: How Animals Disperse Seeds in a Tropical Forest. Lisa's topic will become much more focused and structured as she discovers what scientists already know about the topic and what they are attempting to find out.

Like Michael Gold, Lisa has identified a subject that really interests her. Like Michael, she has much to learn. Both will do research that leads to unexpected discoveries.

Adapting the Assigned Topic

College teachers frequently ask their students to research some aspect of a general subject. A psychology teacher, for example, may assign a term paper on some aspect of developmental psychology, an economics teacher on deficit spending, a physics teacher on applied technology, and an English teacher on twentieth-century fiction. Students who are assigned such general topics face the challenge of narrowing the broad subject area to a manageable topic.

DAVID HARRIS

When David was a college student in the mid-eighties, many people feared that war might break out between the Soviet Union and the United States and that any war between the then superpowers would inevitably lead to the use of nuclear weapons. In those days, psychologists and educators in both countries worked together to devise ways to help children and young adults deal with their fears. This general concern influenced David's choice of topic in a course on developmental psychology.

David's instructor required all students to research some aspect of child psychology and to write a paper based on the research. David studied the table of contents and the index to his textbook and considered various possibilities, but a visit home one weekend focused his thoughts. His eight-year-old brother, whom David was fond of but whom he didn't normally give much thought to, woke up screaming from a nightmare. Shaken, David learned from his mother that John had been suffering on and off from nightmares for months; they all involved a nuclear explosion and the end of the world. David returned to college determined to learn more about the effects on children of growing up in a nuclear age.

Since the breakup of the Soviet Union, there is still concern that nuclear weapons will fall into the hands of reckless leaders who might use them to hold the world hostage; but at least today there are fewer children plagued by the nuclear nightmares that were common less than a decade ago.

CARLA MEDINA

Carla is taking an English course in which she is required to write two research papers, each focusing on a controversial literary work. The first assignment is to combine research findings with her own analysis of a work. The second is to conduct extensive research on an actual controversy, to take a position about the source and significance of the controversy, and finally to write a paper using her research findings to support her position. The professor provides the class with the following list:

Baldwin, James, _Another Country_ (1962)

Baudelaire, Charles, _The Flowers of Evil_ (1857)

Beckett, Samuel, _Waiting for Godot_ (1955)

Brontë, Emily, _Wuthering Heights_ (1848)

Chopin, Kate, _The Awakening_ (1899)

Clemens, Samuel (Mark Twain), _Adventures of Huckleberry Finn_ (1885)

Eliot, T. S., _The Waste Land_ (1922)

Flaubert, Gustave, _Madame Bovary_ (1856)

Hemingway, Ernest, _The Sun Also Rises_ (1926); _A Farewell to Arms_ (1929)

Ginsberg, Allen, _Howl_ (1956)

Golding, William, _Lord of the Flies_ (1954)

Hall, Radclyffe, _The Well of Loneliness_ (1928)

Hurston, Zora Neale, _Their Eyes Were Watching God_ (1937)

Jackson, Shirley Anne, "The Lottery" (1948)

Joyce, James, _Dubliners_ (1914)

Lawrence, D. H., _Lady Chatterley's Lover_ (1928)

Nabokov, Vladimir, _Lolita_ (1955)

Salinger, J. D., _Catcher in the Rye_ (1951)

Stowe, Harriet Beecher, _Uncle Tom's Cabin_ (1853)

Styron, William, _The Confessions of Nat Turner_ (1967)

Walker, Alice, _The Color Purple_ (1982)

Zola, Émile, _Nana_ (1880)

Carla chooses to write her first paper on the work from this list that most interests her: Alice Walker's novel _The Color Purple_. Her second paper will be on Mark Twain's _Adventures of Huckleberry Finn_.

Activities

A. The items in the list below each include a general subject followed by a specific topic. Identify other topics related to each subject:

1. "All-Time Best Sellers" → "Public Response to _Gone with the Wind_ and _Scarlett_"

2. "Interpretations of Dreams" → "Dream Lore among the Xhosa People"

3. "African-American Religion" → "Malcolm X and the Rise of the Nation of Islam"

4. "Twentieth-Century Painting" → "Frieda Kahlo's Depiction of Women's Experience"
5. "American Literature of the 1920s" → "Fitzgerald's Use of Popular Culture in *The Great Gatsby*"
6. "Innovations in Business Technology" → "Uses of the Computer in Restaurants"
7. "Baseball Greats" → "Choosing a League's Most Valuable Player"
8. "History of Jazz" → "John Coltrane and the Be-bop Era"
9. "Neotropical Rain Forest Mammals" → "Feeding Habits of Howler Monkeys"
10. "Marketing Strategies" → "The Use of Color in Selling Food"
11. "Ethical Problems in Medicine" → "The Right of Physicians to Assist in Suicides"
12. "The AIDS Crisis" → "The Responsibility of the Federal Government for Funding AIDS Research"
13. "Environmental Policy" → "Keeping Forests a Renewable Resource"
14. "Wildlife Management" → "The Role of the Hunter in Wildlife Management"
15. "Photography as an Art" → "The Photographic Achievement of Mary Ellen Mark"
16. "Racism in America" → "The Internment of Japanese-Americans during World War II"
17. "The Struggle for a Sustainable World" → "Protecting the Ozone Layer"
18. "The Early Space Race" → "Sputnik: The Aftermath in American Education"
19. "Chinese Traditional Medicine" → "Acupuncture in the Operating Room"
20. "Hispanic-American Literature" → "Going Home: The Poetry of Gary Soto"

B. Study the list of reference works in appendix B. Then go to the library and find one of the specialized encyclopedias or dictionaries such as the *Encyclopedia of American History,* the *McGraw-Hill Encyclopedia of Science and Technology, Grzimek's Animal Life Encyclopedia,* or the *International Encyclopedia of Social Sciences.* Browse through it looking for material that interests you. Then make a list of general subject areas and another of specific topics that would be appropriate for student research.

C. For each of the following subjects, make a list of questions to which the answers are not readily available: space exploration, health risks of plastic surgery, venomous animals, the great apes, secret societies, assassinations of public figures, unsolved murders, the activities of the Central Intelligence Agency, crack use in small towns, and high-risk sports.

D. Make a list of questions you have about subjects that interest you.

E. Select a book from your own collection—perhaps a textbook—or one from the library on a subject that interests you. Study the index, and make a list of the topics that would be appropriate for student research.

IDENTIFYING

LIBRARY SOURCES

3

An academic library has many resources for informal learning as well as for formal research. A knowledge of the material and services available in your own college library is essential to your success as a student. When you can easily use your library, you will be able to supplement required reading, pass an hour of leisure browsing among books and periodicals, or pursue independent research. This chapter will introduce you to the main resources of an academic library, and it will indicate the kinds of material available in different sections of the library. There are more resources described in this chapter than you will use for a given research project, but you should know that there is library material to help you answer most research questions. The next chapter gives instructions for using the various library resources, including specific information about collecting and recording references for a research project as well as advice on evaluating the reliability of your sources (pp. 87–90). You may want to read these chapters in your academic library so that you can find the parts of the library as you read about them.

Libraries and Librarians

Some large universities may have several libraries: one library for general use, plus more specialized ones for the schools of law, medicine, or agriculture, for example, or a central library with several branches. But most universities have one main library for the general collection. Al-

31

though most of your library work will take place in the main library, you will probably be allowed to use other campus libraries as well.

Libraries may have sections of rooms, individual rooms, or even separate floors designated for material on specific subjects and for different kinds of material. If you are not familiar with the layout of your library, you may want to take an informal tour to locate and become familiar with each department. (See the activities at the end of this chapter.) Some libraries will provide you with a map or a formal tour. In any case, you will probably be more at ease in a library after you explore it on your own.

The people who work in libraries have various kinds of skills. Some are part-time student workers who only check out or reshelve books. Others are highly trained, sometimes specialized, librarians whose re-

Getting to Know Your Library: A Checklist

If your library provides organized orientation sessions to familiarize students with library resources, by all means attend one of these and ask questions about library procedures you do not understand. Before you actually begin a research project, however, you may want to know the following:

1. Where the circulation and reference desks are located.
2. Where reference books and circulating books are shelved.
3. Where periodicals are shelved and how they are indexed.
4. Where to find the card catalog and/or the computer catalog and when to use each.
5. Whether all your library's material is cataloged on-line.
6. Whether only recently acquired materials are cataloged on-line.
7. What information is available on CD-ROMs.
8. What you need to do to use your library's CD-ROMs.
9. What is available through computer terminals and how to use them.
10. Whether your library houses government documents.
11. How to make an appointment with a reference librarian for assistance in planning a search.
12. How to make an appointment for a computer search and how to get help using government documents, CD-ROMs, or other computerized indexes.

sponsibilities may include selecting and ordering new books, cataloging books, or managing the circulation department. Librarians who are mainly responsible for providing personal services to the patrons of the library are usually called reference librarians. It is important that you learn to identify the different members of the library staff. The person who checks out your books is probably a student worker; someone in an office behind the circulation desk may manage the circulation of books as well as the reserve room; a reference librarian will have a desk or office near the reference section.

The Reference Section

Any member of the library staff can answer general questions—where the card or computer catalog is, whether there are CD-ROMs available, or where the recent issues of newspapers are stored—but when you have questions about a specific research topic, you should ask a reference librarian. Some reference librarians are specialists in reference materials on particular subjects—science, social science, or literature, for example—and in a large library, there will probably be several reference librarians, along with other staff people whose job is to help you find what you need. Once you have located someone who is willing to help you, you should be as specific and clear as possible about what you want to know. Perhaps you are looking for some recent articles on word processors for the general reader. You find a reference librarian and ask where the *Readers' Guide to Periodical Literature* is located. The librarian may point to the appropriate shelf or suggest that you use one of the CD-ROM indexes of InfoTrac (a computerized collection of databases on current topics). If, however, you had explained from the beginning that you wanted to find information on the technology of word processors, the librarian could have led you to *Applied Science and Technology Index,* which cites articles in specialized journals of technology rather than in popular magazines. You should always tell a reference librarian exactly what you are looking for rather than ask for reference works that you think may have the information.

Remember that reference librarians can help you do your work, but they do not do it for you. Think of them as consultants, people with whom you can discuss your research and who will then make suggestions. It is usually best to have a short conversation with a librarian to explain your research project, what you have already found, and what you hope to find.

Michael goes to the reference desk, notes the librarian's name on a sign at the front of the desk, and explains that he is doing a research project on the movie *Rebel Without a Cause* and that he has found information in a few books and several magazines. He then asks for help finding articles in film journals. The librarian suggests that Michael consult the *International Index to Film Periodicals* and that he look under the name of the director as well as the title of the film. Within a few minutes of doing so, Michael has made a long list of articles, some of which he finds in his library and two of which are extremely useful for his project.

A SAMPLE REFERENCE IN THE *International Index to Film Periodicals,* 1979 EDITION

```
REBEL WITHOUT A CAUSE (US, Nicholas Ray,
    1955)

    Thomson,D.: Rebel without a cause.
    Take One VII/4,Mar 79,p. 15-16,illus.
    (Review).
    A reappraisal of the movie and its
    director, Nicholas Ray.
```

Before you ask a reference librarian for help, make sure that you have done what you can to find material. Read this chapter carefully, study the annotated list of references at the end of this book, and find out if there is a guide to your library. Once you have done these things, feel free to ask questions. When you find someone who is willing to help you, it is a good idea to come back to the same person for any further questions. Since librarians usually work shifts, you may want to ask when a particular person will be available.

The reference area of the library contains books that cannot be checked out, books such as dictionaries, bibliographies (lists of books and articles), encyclopedias, indexes, and other catalogs of information. Many reference books are intended to provide small pieces of information as quickly as possible—the spelling of a word, the publication date of a book, the birthplace of a famous person. Others, such as encyclopedias, give an overview of large topics; and still others, such as indexes and bibliographies, help you find information in periodicals and other books. For a description of specific reference works, see appendix B.

In the reference section of many libraries you will also find computers that are linked to databases and/or others that read CD-ROMs (see pp. 47–51).

GENERAL ENCYCLOPEDIAS

Encyclopedias are familiar to most students, but you may need to be reminded that the major encyclopedias in English differ from one another in significant ways.

Academic American Encyclopedia is the newest multivolume encyclopedia intended for students. The articles are brief and most entries are current. A good source for accurate facts, but not for in-depth coverage, this encyclopedia is particularly strong in scientific and technical subjects. There is a general index for the twenty-one bound volumes, and the entire work is available in electronic versions.

Collier's Encyclopedia has an accessible style and balanced coverage emphasizing the kinds of things taught in American colleges. It is factually reliable and up-to-date. A general, comprehensive index makes it easy for you to find what you are looking for, and an annotated bibliography suggests further reading. Both index and bibliography are in the final volume.

The *Encyclopedia Americana,* aimed at a similar readership (age fifteen and up), is approximately 30 percent longer and features twice as many articles. The *Americana* is particularly strong in the history, culture, and geography of the United States and Canada; 40 percent of its entries are biographies, and it includes brief articles on particular works of literature,

LISA LEE

An article under the heading "jungle and rain forest" in the *Academic American Encyclopedia* is of great help to Lisa as she focuses and refines her topic. Not only does it provide a clear, brief overview of the subject, but it also includes useful bibliographic information. The entire article is reprinted on the following pages.

tients are made aware of both the personal and collective (archetypal) meanings inherent in their symptoms and difficulties. Under favorable conditions they may enter into the individuation process: a lengthy series of psychological transformations culminating in the integration of opposite tendencies and functions and the achievement of personal wholeness.

GEORGE ATWOOD

Bibliography: Bennet, E. A., *What Jung Really Said* (1971; repr. 1983); Brome, Vincent, *Jung* (1978); Jacobi, Jolande, *The Psychology of C. G. Jung*, 7th ed. (1968); Jung, Carl G., *The Collected Works of Carl G. Jung*, 20 vols. (1953–75), and *The Essential Jung*, ed. by A. Storr (1983); Moreno, Antonio, *Jung, Gods and Modern Man* (1970); Nagy, Marilyn, *Philosophical Issues in the Psychology of C. G. Jung* (1991); Stern, Paul, *C. G. Jung: The Haunted Prophet* (1976); Wehr, Gerhard, *Jung: A Biography* (1987; repr. 1989).

Jungfrau   [yung'-frow]

The Jungfrau is a famous peak in the Bernese Alps, on the border of the Bern and Valais cantons of Switzerland. Noted for its graceful contours and the dazzling whiteness of its snow cover (Jungfrau in German means "virgin"), it rises to a height of 4,158 m (13,642 ft). ALETSCH GLACIER lies on its south side, which was first ascended in 1927. The eastern side was climbed in 1811. Tourists and winter sports enthusiasts can ascend by rail to the Jungfraujoch, a mountain saddle at 3,454 m (11,332 ft), which is also the site of a scientific research observatory.

Jungle, The

The Jungle (1906), a novel by Upton SINCLAIR, is a particularly graphic example of "muckraking" fiction (see MUCKRAKERS). The book centers on the life of a Lithuanian immigrant, Jurgis Rudkus, who finds work in the Chicago stockyards. As the story proceeds, the unsanitary, exploitative conditions of the stockyards are fully documented. Working in such a barbaric environment, Rudkus becomes completely demoralized and,

seeking a remedy, turns to socialism. The novel caused a public outcry when published and is believed to have been instrumental in the passage of the Pure Food and Drug Act of 1906. Corrective labor regulation, however, did not come for another 30 years.

CHARLOTTE D. SOLOMON

Jungle Book, The

The Jungle Book (1894) is a group of stories by the English writer Rudyard KIPLING. They relate the history of an Indian boy, Mowgli, who strays from his village and is reared by a family of wolves. Mowgli's intelligence and manual dexterity make him valuable to the animals, who defend him from the perils of the wilderness. Mowgli learns the complex "Law of the Jungle" and in turn imparts human qualities to the animals. Although ostensibly a work for children, *The Jungle Book* has found many appreciative adult readers, some of whom have regarded it as an allegory of colonial government. Kipling repeated his success with *The Second Jungle Book* (1895).

jungle and rain forest

Jungle and *rain forest* are terms that are often used synonymously but with little precision. The more meaningful and restrictive of these terms is *rain forest*, which refers to the climax or primary forest in regions with high rainfall (greater than 1.8 m/70 in per year), chiefly but not exclusively found in the tropics. Rain forests are significant for their valuable timber resources, and in the tropics they afford sites for commercial crops such as rubber, tea, coffee, bananas, and sugarcane. They also include some of the last remaining areas of the Earth that are both unexploited economically and inadequately known scientifically.

The term *jungle* originally referred to the tangled, brushy vegetation of lowlands in India, but it has come to be used for any type of tropical forest or woodland. The word is more

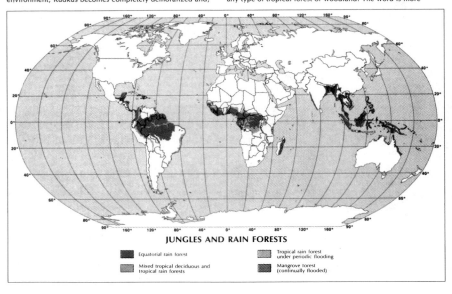

JUNGLES AND RAIN FORESTS

■	Equatorial rain forest	■	Tropical rain forest under periodic flooding
■	Mixed tropical deciduous and tropical rain forests	■	Mangrove forest (continually flooded)

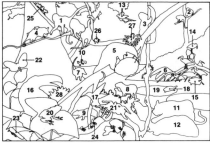

Animals of a South American rain forest include: black-capped capuchins (1), Cebus appella, and howler monkeys (2), Alovatta seniculus; the three-toed sloth (3), Bradypus tricactylus; and the opossum (4), Didelphis marsupialis. The tamandua (5), Tamandua tetradactyla, is related to the great anteater (6), Myrmelophaga tridactyla. Other inhabitants are the brown coatimundi (7), Nasua narica; the capybara (8), Hydrochoerus hydrochaeris, and the paca (9), Cuniculus paca; and the red brocket deer (10), Mazama americana. A jaguar (11), Panthera onca, strikes its prey, a tapir (12), Tapirus terrestris. Birds include: the scarlet macaw (13), Ara macao; the scarlet ibis (14), Eudocimus ruber, and the roseate spoonbill (15), A. ajaia; the keel-billed toucan (16), Ramphastos sulfuratus; and the ruby-topaz hummingbird (17), Chrysolampis mosquitus. Other animals are: a South American river turtle, the Arrau (18), Podocnemis expansa, shown on a giant lily pad (19), Victoria amazonica; the arrow poison frog (20), genus Dendrobates; the bird-eating spider (21), family Avicularidae; a rare butterfly (22), Heliconius ethillus; a leaf hopper (23), family Cicadellica; and leaf-cutter ants (24), genus Atta. Three epiphytic plants are two orchid genera, Oncidium (25) and Cattleya (26), and a bromeliad (27). Cephaelis (28) carpets the floor.

meaningful if limited to the dense, scrubby vegetation that develops when primary rain forest has been degraded by destructive forms of logging or by cultivation followed by abandonment.

Types of Rain Forest. Rain forests may be grouped into two major types: tropical and temperate. Tropical rain forest is characterized by broadleaf evergreen trees that form a closed canopy, below which is found a zone of vines and epiphytes (plants growing on the trees), a relatively open forest floor, and a very large number of species of both plant and animal life. The largest trees have buttressed trunks and emerge above the continuous canopy, while smaller trees commonly form a layer of more shade-tolerant species beneath the upper canopy. The maximum height of the upper canopy of tropical rain forests is generally about 30 to 50 m (100 to 165 ft), with some individual trees rising as high as 60 m (200 ft) above the forest floor.

The largest areas of tropical rain forest are in the Amazon basin of South America, in the Congo basin and other lowland equatorial regions of Africa, and on both the mainland and the islands off Southeast Asia, where they are especially abundant on Sumatra and New Guinea. Small areas are found in Central America and along the Queensland coast of Australia.

Temperate rain forests, growing in higher-latitude regions having wet, maritime climates, are less extensive than those of the tropics but include some of the most valuable timber in the world. Notable forests in this category are those on the northwest coast of North America, in southern Chile, in Tasmania, and in parts of southeastern Australia and New Zealand. These forests contain trees that may exceed in height those of tropical rain forests, but there is less diversity of species. Conifers such as REDWOOD and Sitka spruce tend to predominate in North America, while their counterparts in the southern hemisphere include various species of EUCALYPTUS, *Araucaria,* and *Nothofagus* (Antarctic beech).

Ecology. Rain forests cover less than six percent of the Earth's total land surface, but they are the home for up to three-fourths of all known species of plants and animals; undoubtedly they also contain many more species as yet undiscovered. Recent studies suggest that this great diversity of species is related to the apparently dynamic and unstable nature of rain forests over geological time. The fact is that despite their appearance of fertile abundance, rain forests are fragile ecosystems. Their soils can quickly lose the ability to support most forms of vegetation once the forest cover is removed, and some soils even turn into hard LATERITE clay. The effect of forest removal on local climates is also often profound, although the role of rain forests in world climatic changes is not yet clear.

Humans and Rain Forests. Throughout history, human beings have encroached on rain forests for living space, timber, and agricultural purposes. In vast portions of upland tropical forests, for example, the practice of "shifting cultivation" has caused deterioration of the primary forest. In this primitive system of agriculture, trees are killed in small plots that are cropped for two or three seasons and then abandoned; if the plots are again cultivated before primary vegetation has reestablished itself, the result is a progressive deterioration of the forest, leading to coarse grass or jungle. Lowland forests are similarly being reduced in many areas; on the island of Java, the lowland primary forest has been almost totally removed and replaced with rice fields or plantation crops such as rubber. In the 20th century these incursions on rain forests have grown rapidly, and numerous organizations are now attempting to reduce the rate of the loss.   WILLIAM C. ROBISON

Bibliography: Caufield, Catherine, *In the Rainforest* (1985); Forsyth, Adrian, and Miyata, Ken, *Tropical Nature: Life and Death in the Rain Forests of Central and South America* (1984); Sutton, S. L., et al., *Tropical Rain Forest: Ecology and Management* (1984); Whitmore, T. C., *Tropical Rain Forests of the Far East*, 2d ed. (1984).

junior colleges: see COMMUNITY AND JUNIOR COLLEGES.

junior high school: see MIDDLE SCHOOLS AND JUNIOR HIGH SCHOOLS.

juniper [joon'-ih-pur]

Junipers, *Juniperus*, are evergreen trees or SHRUBS belonging to the cypress family, Cupressceae. They include approximately 35 species found throughout the Northern Hemisphere from the Arctic Circle to Mexico and the West Indies, Azores, Canary Islands, North Africa, Abyssinia, the mountains of tropical East Africa, the Himalayas, China, and Formosa.

Juniper bark is usually thin and scales off in longitudinal strips. Leaves are awl-shaped, closely pressed, and scalelike. The wood is fragrant, usually highly colored, reddish brown, and very durable. An essential oil is distilled from the wood and used for perfume and, sometimes, in medicine. Juniper leaves have powerful diuretic properties, and the characteristic taste of gin is derived from juniper berries. The common juniper, *J. communis*, is a small tree that is found in the colder northern areas of the Northern Hemisphere, and many are grown as landscape plants. Red "cedar," *J. virginiana*, is the most important juniper native to the United States. Its wood is the main source of "cedar" lining used to mothproof closets.

Junius [joon'-ee-uhs]

Junius was the pseudonym of the author of a series of political lampoons published in the *London Public Advertiser* between Jan. 21, 1769, and Jan. 21, 1772. With eloquent wit and sarcasm, the essays—commonly called the "Letters of the Junius"—denounced the government of King George III and many of its major officials, including the prime minister, Lord NORTH. Since that time dozens of writers have been tentatively identified as Junius, among them such eminent figures as Edward Gibbon, John Wilkes, Edmund Burke, and Thomas Paine. But Sir Philip Francis, then a clerk in the war office, is currently considered the likeliest candidate.

Bibliography: Cannon, John, ed., *The Letters of Junius* (1978); Cordasco, Francesco, *A Junius Bibliography* (1973).

junk

By the late Middle Ages the ancient Chinese sailing ship had evolved into the junk, one of the world's strongest and most seaworthy ships. (The term probably is derived from the Chinese *Ch'uan*, "boat," via Malay *djong*.) The junk is notable for two innovations in shipbuilding, the construction of the hull and the rigging of the sails. Lacking three components—the keel as well as the stemposts and sternposts (upright beams at the bow and the stern)—that are basic to other types of ships, the junk has a hull that is partitioned off by solid plank walls, or bulkheads, running both lengthwise and crosswise, dividing the junk into watertight compartments and giving it structural rigidity. (Crosswise bulkheads were not adopted in the West until the 19th century.) The lack of a keel is compensated for by using a deep, heavy rudder mounted so that it can be raised and lowered. The sails, made of narrow, horizontal sheets of linen or of matting panels, are carried on masts numbering from one to five. Each panel has its own

The juniper is a small, coniferous tree that has scaly leaves and berrylike cones, each of which contains one to six seeds. The western juniper (left), *J. occidentalis, is found in the Sierra Nevada mountains of California. The common juniper (right), J. communis, is found throughout temperate and cold northern climates.*

music, and art. It is generally up-to-date on urgent topics such as political upheavals, but because the revision is spread out over a period of years, some articles are not current. An effective general index is easy to use, and bibliographies of recommended reading are included at the end of all major articles and many shorter ones.

The *New Encyclopaedia Britannica* is the least accessible of the three both because of its sophisticated style and because of its elaborate three-part structure: the Propaedia, which outlines the world of knowledge; the Micropaedia, which provides short articles on many subjects and serves as both a ready reference and an index; and the Macropaedia, which contains in-depth, signed articles. The *Britannica* emphasizes international subjects and historical data. Leisure and previous knowledge of a subject are sometimes necessary to appreciate the abstract discussion, and it is often difficult to find all the material on a given subject because of a complicated and sometimes inadequate system of cross-references. But at times the effort required to use the *Britannica* is worthwhile. Its depth and complexity make it more informative and authoritative in the long run.

The *New Columbia Encyclopedia* is an excellent single-volume reference work that provides reliable information on a wide range of subjects in condensed form. It is particularly useful for quick reference—getting an overview of a person's life or work, discovering the exact location and size of a state or country (there are maps), learning the average size of a particular breed of dog. The articles are cross-referenced, and many of them include lists of books for additional reading.

These are all good encyclopedias. The best one for you will depend on what you want to find out, how much time you are willing to spend, and how much you already know about a subject.

ENCYCLOPEDIA INDEXES AND BIBLIOGRAPHIES

The general index of a standard encyclopedia may refer you to a number of articles that treat your subject, but you will find that consulting the encyclopedia index will be more productive for some topics than for others. For example, the *Encyclopedia Americana* lists seven subheadings under "Conscientious Objector," while "Woodstock Festival" is included only under "Rock Music." At the end of some encyclopedia articles, you will also find a list of books used or recommended by the author of the article. One encyclopedia may provide a useful bibliography on a subject for which no references are cited in another standard encyclopedia. A case in point is the *New Columbia Encyclopedia,* which lists five books on the subject of conscientious objection, while the *Encyclopedia Americana* lists none. You may therefore want to consult all the standard encyclopedias before going to more specialized reference works. Note the following excerpt from a general encyclopedia index:

Motion, Newton's laws of: *see* Newton's laws of motion
Motion, Perpetual: *see* **Perpetual Motion**
MOTION PICTURE 19–505 ————————————————— main entry: volume 19, page 505
  Academy Award 1–71a
  Acting 1–123
  Argentina 2–268; 17–30
  art and technique 19–506
  Audiovisual Education 2–671 fol.   list of other articles with infor-
  Australia 2–751   mation about motion pictures
  Brazil 17–31
  California 5–205
  Camera 5–272
  Canada 5–443
  Cartoon, Animated 5–740
  Censorship 6–161, 163, 165, 167; 7–429
  China 6–589
  Cinemascope 6–728
  Cinerama 6–729 ————————————————— volume
  Civil Rights 6–771
  Comics 7–374
  Communication 7–427 ———————————————— page
  Copyright 7–772
  Czechoslovakia 8–411
  De Mille, Cecil B. 8–683
  Disney, W. 9–180
  documentary 19–537
  Education 9–729
  Electronic Video Recording 10–176
  exposure meter 17–458
  France 11–832
  Friese-Greene, W. 12–95
  Gaumont, L. 12–348
  Germany 12–650
  Great Britain 13–296
  Griffith, D. W. 13–492
  history 19–516
  Hollywood 14–298; 17–754
  India 14–928
  Journalism 16–219
  Latin America 17–30
  Library 17–386
  Lighting, Theatrical 17–471
  Lumière, L. J. 17–849
  Mexico 17–30
  Mime 19–143
  Montage 19–387
  music 27–615
  Negatives 20–61
  Negro in America 20–76
  Novel 20–510r
  Pathé, Charles 21–392
  Peep Show 21–468
  Poland 22–310
  Puppet 23–13
  Rome 23–687, 694
  Science Fiction 24–392
  sound track 25–248
  Stereoscopy 25–693
  Sweden 26–104
  technology 19–540
  Television 26–437
  USSR 27–421
  United States 27–561, 565, 603
  Westerns 28–662
  See also biographies of important actors, directors, and pro- —— suggestions for further
    ducers   information

SPECIALIZED REFERENCE WORKS

General encyclopedias are the most widely known of the books in the reference section, but their usefulness will be very limited for serious student researchers looking for material on a particular subject. There are many other reference works that you should know about—indexes and bibliographies; yearbooks and almanacs; and numerous specialized reference works, including directories, dictionaries, histories, and specialized encyclopedias. These specialized works will usually offer a more thorough treatment of a subject than that given by a general encyclopedia. For example, you are more likely to find an in-depth treatment of behavioral psychologist B. F. Skinner in the *International Encyclopedia of the Social Sciences* than in the most recent edition of *Collier's*.

The annotated list of reference works in appendix B will help you identify specialized reference works appropriate to particular research projects.

The Periodical Section

The most relaxed spot in a library is usually the current periodical section, where students can be found sitting in comfortable chairs, reading magazines, or consulting movie schedules. In this area there are two kinds of periodicals: popular magazines and newspapers—such as those you can buy on newsstands—and scholarly or professional journals, which contain articles for specialists and most of which are available only by subscription. Back issues of periodicals are stored in bound volumes or on microform—sometimes in the periodical room and sometimes in the stacks.

Indexes to periodicals are usually shelved in the reference section of the library. To locate material in magazines, newspapers, and journals, you will have to use a variety of indexes. For popular magazines, you can consult one of the following:

The *Readers' Guide to Periodical Literature* (New York: Wilson, 1900 to date) is useful for finding articles (by subject or author) in 150 popular magazines. Supplements are published every two weeks, so it can be used for very recent publications. Bound volumes consolidate all the entries with a single alphabetical listing. The following is an excerpt from *Readers' Guide:*

MOVING of machinery
  Huge generator moves on planks. il Pop Mech
    103:109 Mr '55
MOVING of structures, etc.
  Cash-and-carry houses. D. X. Manners. il Read Di-
    gest 68:145-7 Ap '56
  Hotel takes a ride. il Pop Mech 103:139 Je '55
  Houses that move around. D. Isaak. Am Mercury
    82:89-91 Mr '56
MOVING of trees. See Tree planting
MOVING picture acting
  Strange doings of actress at practice. il Life
    42:96-8 + Ja 28 '57
  That wonderful, deep silence; difference be-
    tween stage and screen. S. Winters. il Theatre
    Arts 40:30-1 + Je '56
  When you take a screen test. M. Arnow. Good H
    142:38 + Ja '56
MOVING picture actors and actresses
  American women pick: our favorite stars. P. T.
    Hartung. pors Womans Home C 82:12 Je '55
  Amour and the man. pors Sat R 39:29 O 13 '56;
    Reply. D. Beams. 39:23 N 10 '56
  Bells are ringing. L. Lerman. il Mlle 44:81-5 + N
    '56
  Bogart on Hollywood. il Look 20:96-8 + Ag 21 '56
  Bright young stars in fashions for off-stage
    hours. W. Cushman. il Ladies Home J 72:68-9
    My '55
  By any other name. Mr Harper. Harper 210:80-1
    Mr '55
  Discovery: British women are beautiful. il Look
    20:26-30 + Ag 21 '56
  Fans choose; Photoplay magazine winners. News-
    week 45:90 F 14 '55
  Film pioneers' roll of their living immortals. il
    pors Life 40:116-23 Ja 23 '56
  Foreign accent in starlets. M. Nichols. pors Coro-
    net 40:44-55 Ag '56
  Glamor gallery; Italian screen stars; photo-
    graphs. Theatre Arts 39:72-3 My '55
  Greatest stars; Timeless stars; Glamour in our
    time; Star system in 1956; Newcomers. il Cos-
    mop 141:28-37 O '56
  Hollywood actors win $80 day for now. Bsns W p
    170 Mr 24 '56

Hollywood and its people. R. Gehman. il Cosmop
141:46-51 O '56 ——————————— date of periodical
Hollywood fathers. il Look 19:38-41 Jl 12 '55
Hollywood hobbies. il pors McCalls 83:16 + O '55
Hollywood revisited. L. Rosten. il pors Look
20:17-28 Ja 10 '56 ——————————— pages
Hollywood tragedies. E. Honor. il Cosmop
141:38-9 O '56 ——————————— author
Hollywood, unhitching post. I. C. Kuhn. Am Mer-
cury 80:7-11 Ja '55
Hollywood's search for new faces. S. Peck. il pors
N Y Times Mag p28-9 O 7 '56 ——————————— title of article
Hollywood's search for stars. T. M. Pryor. il pors
N Y Times Mag p 14-15 + Je 12 '55
I make up Hollywood; ed. by P. Martin. W. West-
more. il Sat Eve Post 229:17-19 + Ag 4; 30 + ——————————— name of periodical
Ag 11 '56
Idols of Italy. il Look 19:100 + N 15 '55 ——————————— illustrated
Look annual movie awards. il Look 17:26-31 Mr
10 '53; 18:122-4 + Mr 23 '54; 19:100-4 + Mr 23
'55 ——————————— volume

Remember that *Readers' Guide* is limited. It indexes only popular magazines, the kind that depend primarily on advertising for most of their
income. If your research is at least in part concerned with popular reaction
to a movie, a book, or even a major political event, then of course you will
use this work or electronic indexes that cover the same material. If you are
investigating the contributions of Betty Friedan and Gloria Steinem to the
women's movement, you will read the books they have written as well as
any articles in scholarly journals, but you are likely to find most of your
material in magazines. On the other hand, if you want to find out the latest
information about the treatment of AIDS, you would want to search the
medical journals, using the index *Medline*. For most research projects, in
fact, you will want to consult specialized indexes that will lead you to
periodicals that contain articles written by experts in particular fields.
Many of these indexes are described in the annotated bibliography beginning on page 357.

Magazine Index covers considerably more titles than *Readers' Guide*.
Available in microfilm, on-line, and on CD-ROM *(Magazine Index Plus)*,
this index is primarily useful for current topics treated in popular magazines published in the last few years. Some libraries may have only the last
four years, others will have back files to 1980, and a few may have
microfilm files to 1976. Other periodical indexes available on CD-ROM
and on-line are the *Business Index* (seven hundred titles) and the *Academic
Index* (four hundred titles) sometimes combined as the *General Periodicals
Index*. There are now many electronic indexes that access specialized
journals and periodicals. Some are discussed on pages 53–54.

The *New York Times Index* lists all major articles that have appeared in that paper from 1913 to the present; it also indirectly indexes many other national and even local newspapers by revealing the date on which a news item most likely appeared there. It is kept up-to-date with supplements published every two weeks. There is also an index for selected articles for the years 1851–1912. Articles are listed by subject. Entries in recent volumes give the exact location of each article, an indication of length, and usually a brief summary of content. Note the following excerpt from the *New York Times Index:*

MOTION Picture Arts and Sciences, Academy of. See also
Head, Edith, D 7. Motion Pictures—Awards, F 18,19,24,
Mr 12,23,29,31, Ap 1,2,3,12, O 22, D 26
MOTION Picture Assn of America (MPAA). See also
Motion Pictures, Ja 16. Motion Pictures—US, My 24,
O 8. Television—Cable TV, My 15 ——————————— main heading
MOTION Picture Daily. See also Television—Programs,
Catch a Falling Star (TV Program), My 10 ————— explanation of how articles are
MOTION Pictures. Note: US and gen material are under—— organized
subject subheads. Foreign material is under geog subheads.
Specific films are under subhead Revs
    See also Pornography (for inclusion). Theater and ——— other suggested headings
performer names
    Vincent Canby movie quiz; illustrations, Ja 4,II,15:1
    Edwin Bigley, asst to Jack Valenti, pres of Motion Picture
Assn of Amer, reports that Pres Carter viewed some 500
films during his tenure in office, more than double that of any — (S) indicates a short article
previous Pres (S), Ja 16,III,6:6
    Kirk Honeycutt article on Lillian Michelson Research
Library, which provides meticulous background information
for writers, designers, dirs, and art dirs to recreate authentic — (L) indicates a long article
stories, sets, props and costumes (L), Mr 1,II,18:1; comment
on Acme-Dunn optical printer, used to enhance certain
special effects in films; noted developers of printer, Linwood
G Dunn, Cecil D Love and Edward Furer, were recognized —— (M) indicates an article of
with Oscar for technical merit; illustration (M), Ap 3,IV,5:1   medium length
    Comment on problem of old movie film that fades; Henry
Kaska, spokesman for Eastman Kodak, Larry Carr of Amer
Film Inst and filmmaker Martin Scorsese note preservation
steps that are being taken to improve situation (M), Ap 5,
III,19:1
    Natl Center for Jewish Film is established by Jewish ——— brief summary of article
Historical Soc; will be located on campus of Brandeis Univ
(S), My 3,70:6
    Gregory Peck comments on acting opposite Sophia Loren
(S), Jl 20,II,8:3 ———— author of article
    Bob Harelson, head of Berry Auction Co which specializes
in movie memorabilia, comments on trends (S), Ag 7,III,8:5
    Universal, Paramount, M-G-M, and United Artists have — date
joined together to form 1 orgn, United Internatl Pictures, to
distribute films abroad (S), O 6,IV,28:6
    Vincent Canby article on effect that society's repression —— section
has on filmmakers' styles; notes works of Frank Ripploh,
Andrzej Wajda, Dusan Makavejev and George Cukor (M),
N 15,II,23:1 ———— page
    Russell Baker humorous article on how old movies would
change if they were to be produced today; drawing (M), D
20,VI,p17 ———— column

There are subject indexes for other newspapers. *National Newspaper Index,* available on CD-ROM, on-line, and on microform, lists articles from the *Christian Science Monitor* the *Los Angeles Times,* the *New York Times,* the *Wall Street Journal,* and the *Washington Post.* Although some libraries do not carry microform files for all of these newspapers, they can usually be obtained through interlibrary loan. The *Times* [of London] *Official Index* is often helpful for international and especially British topics. The *Wall Street Journal Index* is helpful for locating up-to-date information on business and economics.

GENERAL INDEXES TO SCHOLARLY ARTICLES

The following indexes—actually one work with several title changes over the years—covers scholarly articles in the humanities and social sciences from 1907 to the present:
Readers' Guide Supplement and International Index covers articles from 1907 to 1919.
International Index to Periodicals, 1920 to 1965.
Social Sciences and Humanities Index, 1965 to 1974.
Since 1974, this index has been published in the following two parts:
Humanities Index lists articles published from 1974 to date.
Social Sciences Index lists by subject (anthropology, economics, psychology, etc.) articles published from 1974 to date.

INDEXES TO SPECIFIC DISCIPLINES

There are many indexes to specific disciplines, some highly specialized. Some are limited to periodicals, such as the *Art Index;* others combine an index to periodicals with lists of books on particular subjects, such as the *MLA International Bibliography.* A list of specialized indexes appears in appendix B, along with an explanation of how each might be useful. You may want to explore the shelves of the reference room of your own academic library to discover what specialized indexes your library carries.

CATALOG OF A LIBRARY'S PERIODICALS

After you have located articles you want to consult in periodicals, you need to find out if they are in your library. Libraries catalog periodicals in several ways: in a separate serial catalog, in the main card catalog, on computer or microform catalogs. You can easily find out which system a library uses by consulting a reference librarian or a printed guide to the library's resources. All systems, however, will give you the same basic information: which issues the library has; their location in the library, indicated by a call number; and whether they are bound, unbound, or on microform.

If articles that seem particularly important to your research are not in your library, you may want to try to get them from another library. To identify libraries that have a particular periodical, use the *Union List of Serials,* which catalogs periodicals in the United States and Canada through 1965. For articles after that date, consult *New Serial Titles,* which is kept up-to-date by periodic publication. Most academic libraries have a service for obtaining from other libraries copies of articles from periodicals that they do not have. Usually students pay a small fee to cover the cost of copying and mailing the article.

Computerized or Electronic Information Retrieval

Libraries store information in many different forms, including books, magazines and journals (serials), newspapers, computer disks, audio tapes and videotapes, and films. No library's collection is like another's. Libraries also vary in the tools they use to help you find these materials, but most libraries have computers and some of the new electronic tools that make finding library sources easy. Some have the catalogs of their entire collections "on-line," that is, stored in computers, but constantly updated. Others have only the books cataloged on-line, while still others have some forms of information cataloged on cards (the card catalog) and others on-line. Some may have books cataloged in one way, magazines in another, and non-print material in still another.

Most academic libraries have the ability to search databases that index materials, and the majority have CD-ROMs for the most frequently used indexes. It is important to understand how your library organizes and catalogs its materials and what tools it has for finding those materials. There is literally a revolution going on in the ways we retrieve information, and as a student, you will do well to learn what your library has available and to keep up with changes in the libraries you use.

The four different non-print media that you can use to find library materials are:

1. Microform (microfiche or microfilm)
2. CD-ROMs
3. On-line databases accessed through a computer search
4. Magnetic tape in a computer mainframe accessed by terminals

To use an index on microfiche or microfilm, you would use a microform reader, a machine designed for the particular product you are using. CD-ROMs are accessed by a specialized computer program (search software) along with a CD-ROM player attached to a computer. To find information in an electronic database, you may need to conduct an on-line search (see pp. 76–80), or if your library has databases stored in its mainframe computer, students can access them directly through a computer terminal in the library or elsewhere on campus. Most of the information stored in microforms, CD-ROMs, or databases is also available in print form.

PHOTOCOPYING FROM MICROFORM READERS

Some microform readers have the ability to photocopy material stored on film or tape. Once you have found an article or passage from an article that seems important, you may want to make a copy to use later. If you only need a small bit of information or a very short passage, then you may choose to record it on a note card; but sometimes you will want the whole article. As soon as you make a copy, take care to identify the source, including the date, page number, and any other information you need for your list of works cited.

CD-ROM INFORMATION DATA SOURCES

CD-ROM stands for "Compact Disc Read Only Memory," which means that information is permanently encoded onto the disc so that it can be "read" by a computer with a CD-ROM drive, but cannot be altered in any way. A floppy disk that allows you to add, erase, or change information is usually spelled with a "k," while a read-only-memory compact disc is usually, but not always, spelled with a "c." To find out about this revolutionary new information technology, all you need to remember is "CD-ROM." Almost identical to the small round disc produced by the music industry to be played in compact disc players, each CD-ROM contains an enormous amount of information—up to six hundred megabytes (hundreds of thousands of pages).

A reference librarian can tell you where CD-ROMs are kept and what you need to do to use them. These discs are very valuable and should be handled carefully. Usually you will be required to leave a deposit, your student ID card, or your driver's license as security.

Not all CD-ROMs are used in libraries. In fact, the majority furnish information to businesses, store government documents, provide training and education, or simply entertain. Most CD-ROMs intended as library tools are simply electronic alternatives to the printed indexes.

PRINTING INFORMATION FROM CD-ROMS

CD-ROMs are usually connected to printers. In most cases you can print out information from the CD-ROM simply by striking a key on the keyboard. Take the time to learn how to use all the features of a CD-ROM reader and printer. You may want to print everything on the screen, a whole list of items in a bibliography, or a few selected items. Librarians will help you if you do not understand the written instructions or if the equipment malfunctions.

ADVANTAGES AND DISADVANTAGES OF USING CD-ROMS

The most obvious advantages of using a CD-ROM index compared to its printed version are speed and the ability to focus a search. It allows you find information much faster than would be possible using books and to search several headings at once. It is of course much more efficient to print out information from a CD-ROM than to copy it by hand from a book. There is no fee for using the CD-ROM once the library has purchased it. It can be used continually and searched again and again, whereas an on-line computer search can be quite expensive.

There are, however, disadvantages in using a CD-ROM index over its printed version. Most compact disc versions cover only a few years (the MLA currently covers 1981 to the present, but plans to make the index available back to 1963; *Biological Abstracts* covers only 1989 to the present), whereas a printed index is complete. Since there is no standard CD-ROM format or program, it sometimes takes time to learn to use an electronic index, and you may find the written instructions and the program inadequate to get you started. Before you decide to use a CD-ROM, consider whether or not it is likely to be useful. Lisa Lee, for example, decided to use two CD-ROMs: *Biological Abstracts* and *General Sciences Index,* and she did in fact find a few useful articles that way. But the most important articles she found by combing through the bound volumes of *Biological Abstracts,* which provides abstracts (brief summaries) of each article.

Another disadvantage of CD-ROMs is that they can only be used by one person at a time, so that those that are frequently used may not be available when you want them. Some libraries allow you to schedule a particular time to use a disc. Finally, a CD-ROM disc may not be as up-to-date as its on-line version, and many databases that students can access with an on-line search are not available on CD-ROMs.

Indexes on CD-ROM that are commonly available in libraries include the following:

Books in Print Plus
Disclosure
ERIC
General Science Index
Government Printing Office Index
Humanities Index
MLA Index
Medline
PsycLit
Sociofile

InfoTrac is a delivery system that permits a student to choose among several databases located at the same computer or work station. Primarily intended for research in very current topics, the *InfoTrac* CDs are up-to-date, but most go back only a few years. A general academic library might subscribe to *National Newspaper Index* and *General Periodicals Index,* which includes the *Academic Index, Business Index,* and 70 percent of *Magazine Index/Plus.*

For a description of these and other indexes available on CD-ROMs, see appendix B. Whenever you use a CD-ROM, you should note what years are covered since they are frequently updated.

CARLA MEDINA

Carla has chosen to write her first paper on Alice Walker's novel *The Color Purple.* She has never used any of the computerized indexes in the library, and so she also makes an appointment with a reference librarian. The librarian asks her a few questions and finds out that Carla wants both critical articles as well as those published in popular magazines. She explains that Carla will be able to conduct her search in two indexes, the *MLA International Bibliography,* which indexes scholarly journals, and *InfoTrac,* which indexes current periodicals and newspapers. Carla's college library has both of these indexes on electronic discs (CD-ROM) that cover the years since the publication of *The Color Purple* in 1982. By carefully reading the instructions near the computer terminal, Carla is able to conduct her search electronically and in less than an hour to print out listings for more than twenty articles and essays that seem relevant to her topic.

Here is the first stage of Carla's search—*the MLA International Bibliography* as it appeared on-screen:

```
MLA International Bibliography              Data Coverage: 1/81 thru 12/26/91
                                                                    READY
───────────────────────────────────────────────────────────────────────────
 SEARCH  |              WILSEARCH                          | NUMBER of
   SET   |               COMMAND                           |  ENTRIES
───────────────────────────────────────────────────────────────────────────
    1    | FIND WALKER, ALICE:(AU) OR WALKER, ALICE:(PS)   |   145
         |              (AU) WALKER, ALICE:.....   6 Entries
         |              (PS) WALKER, ALICE:..... 139 Entries
    2    | FIND COLOR(TI) AND PURPLE(TI)                   |    38
         |              (TI) COLOR.....  207 Entries
         |              (TI) PURPLE.....   56 Entries
    3    | FIND 1 AND 2                                    |    37
         |              (ss # 1) .....  145 Entries

         ┌─────────────────────────────────────────────┐
         │        37 ENTRIES FOUND                      │
         │   HIT ┘ ENTER                                │
         └─────────────────────────────────────────────┘


                                       Mon Jan 27 15:02:36 1992

   F1 - HELP   F2 - END
```

And the beginning of Carla's *InfoTrac* printout:

```
InfoTrac - General Periodicals Index-A


  Heading:    THE COLOR PURPLE.
              -(book reviews)

    1.      The Color Purple. (book reviews) by Alice Walker
        rev by James Lovelace
      B v79 English Journal Oct '90 p83(1)

    2.      The color purple. (book reviews) by Alice Walker
        rev by Darryl Pinckney il
      C v34 The New York Review of Books Jan 29 '87 p17(2)

    3.      The color purple. (book reviews) by Alice Walker,
        Anne Carr and   rev by Anne Carr and
      A v111 Commonweal Feb 24 '84 p119(2)
        25F1574

    4.      The color purple. (book reviews) by Alice Walker
        rev by Dolores Leckey
      A v111 Commonweal Feb 24 '84 p125(1)
        25F1579

    5.      The color purple. (book reviews) by Alice Walker
      A- v133 Forbes Feb 13 '84 p25(1)
        21B1317                                        03R1943
```

Carla shows her printout to the librarian, who suggests that she also check *Book Review Index* and the *New York Times Index;* in these Carla finds a few references that she has missed in the electronic search. Her teacher has suggested that she read the chapter dealing with *The Color Purple* in Henry Louis Gates's *The Signifying Monkey,* and so she uses the computerized catalog to locate this book in the library's collection.

Before proceeding further, Carla takes the time to make sure she has all the bibliographic information for each source. She cuts out each individual citation from her printout sheet, tapes it to a large note card, leaving room for call numbers and notes about the source. For sources found in printed volumes, she carefully records all the information necessary for a full bibliographic reference.

To identify which articles are in her library, she goes to the serials catalog and records the call numbers for the available materials. Some are in bound periodicals, others on microfilm. She decides that she has plenty of material and will not need to order anything through interlibrary loan.

Carla's next task is to begin reading the material she has located, to decide how to focus her study, and either to make copies of the essays or to take notes. She sets aside an afternoon in the library and goes to work. After reading through several articles, she decides to focus her study on the voices of the novel and to show how reviewers and early critics of *The Color Purple* were especially attracted to Celie's voice. At the end of the day, Carla has made photocopies of three articles and taken notes from several others. She plans to come back to the library the next day to finish reading and taking notes.

Note: Students using libraries that do not have computer terminals and CD-ROM indexes can conduct the same search using the bound volumes of the *MLA International Bibliography* and *Readers' Guide to Periodical Literature* along with *Book Review Index, Book Review Digest,* and the *New York Times Index.*

On-line and Magnetic Tape Databases

Some of this chapter may seem repetitious since many reference works are available in more than one form. By the time this book goes to press some works currently available in print form will become accessible on-line, in a CD-ROM format, or both. Similarly, a database now available only on CD-ROM may be published on magnetic tape. The following list includes databases commonly available through a computer search, that is, on-line or through magnetic tape loaded into a computer mainframe.

GENERAL REFERENCE WORKS

Academic American Encyclopedia
   An up-to-date general encyclopedia; the on-line version is updated quarterly. See page 35.

Biography and Genealogy Master Index
   Serves as an index to more than 600 biographical dictionaries, directories, and handbooks of authors, providing access to information about historical and contemporary figures in all fields. See page 362.

Book Review Index
   Cites the sources of book reviews appearing in more than 380 journals. See page 362.

Books in Print
   Provides instant access to the most recent editions of this multivolume work and its supplements. See page 358.

Facts on File
   Provides weekly news summaries of contemporary events ranging from politics to sports. See page 363.

Magazine Index
   Offers broad coverage of general-interest magazines on a wide range of topics. See page 362.

Marquis Who's Who
   Updated quarterly, this on-line database contains detailed biographies on nearly 90,000 individuals. Corresponds to the printed publications *Who's Who in America* (see page 359) and *Who's Who in Frontier Science and Technology.*

ON-LINE INFORMATION SERVICES IN THE HUMANITIES

America: History and Life
   A comprehensive guide to finding information on historical topics. See page 365.

Historical Abstracts
Provides citations and abstracts of periodical literature in history. See page 365.

MLA International Bibliography
Indexes books and journal articles published on the modern languages, literature, and linguistics. See page 367.

Philosopher's Index
A comprehensive index to books and periodicals in philosophy. See page 370.

Religion Index
Provides indexing and abstracts to articles on various aspects of religion. See page 370.

ON-LINE INFORMATION SERVICES IN THE SOCIAL SCIENCES

ERIC
The complete database on educational materials from the Educational Resources Information Center. Contains *Resources in Education* and *Current Index to Journals in Education.* See page 374.

Moody's Corporate Profiles
For information on U.S. business. See *Moody's Manuals,* page 373.

PAIS International
Contains information from the PAIS bulletin as well as a foreign language index. Covers all fields of social science. See page 371.

PsycINFO
Covers the world's literature in psychology. Corresponds to *Psychological Abstracts.* See page 372.

Standard and Poor's News
Provides general news and financial information on more than ten thousand U.S. companies. See page 373.

ON-LINE INFORMATION SERVICES IN THE NATURAL AND APPLIED SCIENCES

American Men and Women of Science
Provides biographical information on scientists actively working in all scientific fields. See page 376.

Compendex
>The on-line version of *Engineering Index*. See page 379.

Medline
>One of the major sources for biomedical literature. Corresponds to three printed indexes: *Index Medicus, Index to Dental Literature,* and *International Nursing Index.* See page 378.

Scisearch
>Contains all the records published in *Science Citation Index.* See page 377.

The Main Library Catalog

A library's main, or central, card catalog may be in the form of cards, an on-line computer database, or a computer-generated catalog called a COM catalog or COMCAT (Computer Output Microfilm—or Microfiche—Catalog). If there is more than one library on your campus, there is probably a *union catalog,* that is, a single catalog (card, computer, or microform) that contains records for all the libraries—perhaps medical, law, business, and so on. Regardless of a catalog's form, you will need to understand how your library classifies its materials.

THE CARD CATALOG

If your library uses a card catalog and on-line catalog, you will also need to know what information is in which form. Some libraries will have only recent materials cataloged on-line, others will have books, but not periodicals, or circulating books but not reference books. Others will have the entire collection on-line. A card catalog consists of individual three-by-five-inch cards stored in small drawers in a series of cabinets. For most books in the collection there will be at least three cards: an author card, a title card, and a subject card. Individual poems, short stories, and longer works of imaginative literature—fiction, poetry, and drama—usually will not have a subject card, though any type of work may be cited on additional cards for editors, illustrators, or translators. Each item in the catalog is assigned a unique identifying number called the call number, which is in the upper left corner of each card. Whether your library uses the Dewey decimal system or the Library of Congress system for classifying books, you will need to record the complete call number before you try to find a book in the stacks or before someone can retrieve it for you.

Many academic libraries have an on-line computer catalog, which researchers access through a computer terminal in the main or branch library, a dormitory, and even off-campus. Before you use an on-line catalog, follow the directions placed near the terminals. You will request information by typing key words (such as author, title, or subject). If you have difficulties, reference librarians are available to help you.

LISA LEE

When Lisa goes to the library to find books about rain forests, she searches the on-line computer catalog by subject. The first subject she tries is "forest." Under that heading she finds various subject subheadings that include the singular word "forest"—so many in fact that it would take her a long time to find the one that includes rain forests. Trying the plural "forests," she finds both rain forests and also two subheadings, "rain forests, Africa" and "rain forests, Amazon basin." Since she is interested in finding general information about rain forests, she looks at the general heading for "rain forests," which yields another general heading as well as many subheadings leading her to materials about rain forests all over the world.

The general heading includes seventeen books listed chronologically in the order they were received by the library. Lisa copies down call numbers for the books that are not checked out. She locates Collins's *The Last Rain Forests* and *Lessons of the Rainforests,* edited by Head and Heinszman.

Lisa then goes back to the on-line catalog and tries a more specific subheading: "rain forests, ecology." Under that heading she locates other sources, including *The Tropical Forest and Its Environment,* by Longman and Jenik.

Lisa learns that it is best to begin her search with the most specific heading she can think of and then move to more general ones.

One advantage of an on-line catalog is that it can be accessed through computer terminals in various locations. Another benefit is that a researcher can gain access to information many different ways. For example, if you know only an author's last name or part of a title, you can probably find a book you are looking for. An on-line catalog also offers many different ways (called the **access points**) to find a particular source. By combining subjects, authors, and parts of titles, you may locate materials. If you are looking for material on a particular subject, there will be various ways for you to search an on-line catalog.

Libraries that have a computer-generated catalog stored on microfilm or microfiche provide microform readers conveniently placed around the library. Usually called a COM catalog (or COMCAT) for Computer Output Microform Catalog, this system is easy to use, but not as flexible as the on-line catalog. Some libraries that have on-line catalogs also have a COM catalog that is used as a backup system at times when the main computer is down. Typically, a COM catalog is updated quarterly.

Whether your library has a card, an on-line, or a COM catalog—or a combination—you will want to be familiar with how they work before you are under the pressure of a deadline.

CLASSIFICATION SYSTEMS FOR BOOKS

To locate a specific book, you need to understand the classification system used by your library. Most libraries use either the Dewey decimal or the Library of Congress system of classification. Although it is not necessary to memorize the classification systems, you will find it easier to use a library if you know which system it uses and what kinds of books are in the general categories.

The **Dewey decimal system** uses a number system to classify books into these ten major categories:

000–099	General Works
100–199	Philosophy
200–299	Religion
300–399	Social Sciences
400–499	Language
500–599	Pure Science
600–699	Technology (Applied Science)
700–799	The Arts
800–899	Literature and Rhetoric
900–999	Geography and History

These major divisions are then subdivided by tens:

000 General Works

010 Bibliography
020 Library and information sciences
030 General encyclopedic works
040
050 General serials & their indexes
060 General organizations & museology
070 News media, journalism, publishing
080 General collections
090 Manuscripts and rare books

100 Philosophy

110 Metaphysics
120 Epistemology, causation, humankind
130 Paranormal phenomena
140 Specific philosophical schools
150 Psychology
160 Logic
170 Ethics (Moral philosophy)
180 Ancient, medieval, Oriental philosophy
190 Modern Western philosophy

200 Religion

210 Natural theology
220 Bible
230 Christian theology
240 Christian moral and devotional theology
250 Christian orders and local church
260 Christian social theology
270 Christian church history
280 Christian denominations & sects
290 Other and comparative religions

300 Social Sciences

310 General statistics
320 Political science
330 Economics
340 Law
350 Public administration
360 Social services; association
370 Education
380 Commerce, communications, transport
390 Customs, etiquette, folklore

400 Language

410 Linguistics
420 English and Old English
430 Germanic languages   German
440 Romance languages   French
450 Italian, Romanian, Rhaeto-Romanic
460 Spanish and Portuguese languages
470 Italic languages   Latin
480 Hellenic languages   Classical Greek
490 Other languages

500 Pure Science

510 Mathematics
520 Astronomy and allied sciences
530 Physics
540 Chemistry and allied sciences
550 Earth sciences
560 Paleontology   Paleozoology
570 Life sciences
580 Botanical sciences
590 Zoological sciences

600 Technology (Applied Science)

610 Medical sciences   Medicine
620 Engineering and allied operations
630 Agriculture
640 Home economics and family living
650 Management and auxiliary services
660 Chemical engineering
670 Manufacturing
680 Manufacture for specific uses
690 Buildings

700 The Arts

710 Civic and landscape art
720 Architecture
730 Plastic arts   Sculpture
740 Drawing and decorative arts
750 Painting and paintings
760 Graphic arts   Printmaking and prints
770 Photography and photographs
780 Music
790 Recreational and performing arts

(continued on following page)

800	**Literature and Rhetoric**	900	**Geography and History**
810	American literature in English	910	Geography and travel
820	English and Old English literatures	920	Biography, genealogy, insignia
830	Literatures of Germanic languages	930	History of ancient world
840	Literatures of Romance languages	940	General history of Europe
850	Italian, Romanian, Rhaeto-Romanic	950	General history of Asia Far East
860	Spanish and Portuguese literatures	960	General history of Africa
870	Italic literatures Latin	970	General history of North America
880	Hellenic literatures Classical Greek	980	General history of South America
890	Literatures of other languages	990	General history of other areas

For example, the numbers 810 to 819 designate American literature, with 813 indicating American fiction. Additional numbers indicate the content of a book. Under the Dewey decimal number is an author number made up of the first initial of the author's last name, a code number assigned to the author's name, and the first letter or letters of the book's title. The combination of the Dewey decimal number and the author number is unique. It applies to one book only. In a library where you have access to the stacks, you can locate a book easily with a complete call number. Note this example for Cleanth Brooks's *William Faulkner: The Yoknapatawpha Country:*

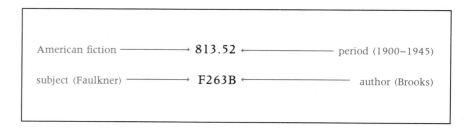

American fiction ⟶ 813.52 ⟵ period (1900–1945)

subject (Faulkner) ⟶ F263B ⟵ author (Brooks)

The **Library of Congress system** uses twenty-one major divisions, each indicated by a letter of the alphabet:

- A   General Works
- B   Philosophy, Psychology, and Religion
- C   History and Auxiliary Sciences
- D   History: General and Old World
- E-F History: North and South America
- G   Geography, Anthropology, and Recreation
- H   Social Science
- J   Political Science
- K   Law

Deciphering the Code

Volumes are arranged on the shelves:

1. **Alphabetically** by the letter(s) at the start of the call number. The letters come from the Library of Congress classification scheme.

    Example: A (before) AE (before) B (before) BD (before) DA, etc.

2. Then **numerically** by the numbers that follow.

    Example: A6 A23 B299 BF3 BF35

3. Then in **alphabetical and decimal order** by the **second** letter/number combination. On a catalog card or on the book this letter/number combination would be the second line of the call number. The second combination of a Library of Congress call number is arranged as if the number following the letter were a decimal. The call numbers below are arranged in correct order because .28 is smaller than .6 and .68 is smaller than .8.

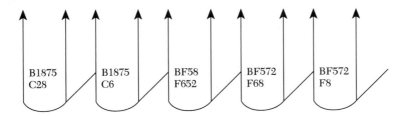

4. Then by **date of publication**. Not all call numbers end in a year. Dates are added to the call number only when a new edition is published or an earlier work is reprinted.

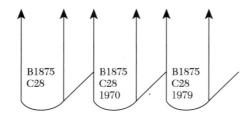

L	Education
M	Music
N	Fine Arts
P	Language and Literature
Q	Science
R	Medicine
S	Agriculture
T	Technology
U	Military Science
V	Naval Science
Z	Bibliography and Library Science

Additional letters and numbers indicate more specific categories, and, as with the Dewey decimal system, an author number designates a particular book within a category. The following call number is for Erik Erikson's *Identity: Youth and Crisis:*

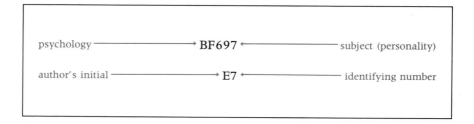

Although it is not necessary to memorize categories and subcategories in the Library of Congress system, you will find it easier to use an open-stack library if you know in a general way where the books in different categories are found.

AUTHOR, SUBJECT, AND TITLE CARDS

The difference between author, subject, and title cards is simple. An author card contains all the information of the other two, but the first item is the last name of the author. And the subject card is identical to the author card, except that the subject heading is typed at the top. Cards on different books vary according to the content of the individual book.

If you know both the author and the title of a book—as you would if you located it in a bibliography—then look for it under the author. That way you may find other books on your subject by the same author. When you are ready to look for sources under subject cards, you will want to try to identify all the appropriate headings.

You will also find heading cards in the card catalog, which will list other subjects that may lead you to related material. For example, you may find a card with the heading SOLAR POWER that directs you to "see SOLAR ENERGY" or another headed SOUL MUSIC that directs you to "see MUSIC, POPULAR."

LINDA ORTON

After looking through the *Encyclopedia Americana* article, Linda consults the card catalog under "Roosevelt, Eleanor" and finds three books that contain considerable material about her concern for women's issues. The subject card for one of these books follows:

SUBJECT CARD

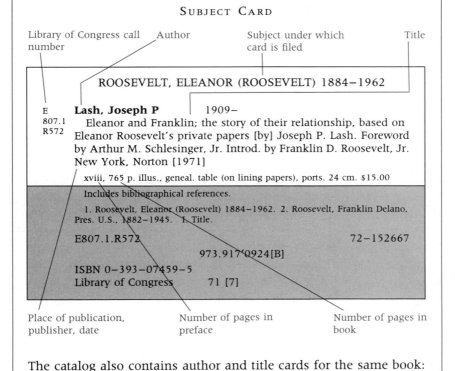

Library of Congress call number   Author   Subject under which card is filed   Title

ROOSEVELT, ELEANOR (ROOSEVELT) 1884–1962

E 807.1 R572   **Lash, Joseph P**   1909–
Eleanor and Franklin; the story of their relationship, based on Eleanor Roosevelt's private papers [by] Joseph P. Lash. Foreword by Arthur M. Schlesinger, Jr. Introd. by Franklin D. Roosevelt, Jr. New York, Norton [1971]

xviii, 765 p. illus., geneal. table (on lining papers), ports. 24 cm. $15.00

Includes bibliographical references.

1. Roosevelt, Eleanor (Roosevelt) 1884–1962. 2. Roosevelt, Franklin Delano, Pres. U.S., 1882–1945. I. Title.

E807.1.R572   72–152667
973.917′0924[B]

ISBN 0–393–07459–5
Library of Congress   71 [7]

Place of publication, publisher, date   Number of pages in preface   Number of pages in book

The catalog also contains author and title cards for the same book:

Author Card

Other headings under which cards on this book are filed

Contains illustrations, a genealogical table, and portraits

Book size and original price

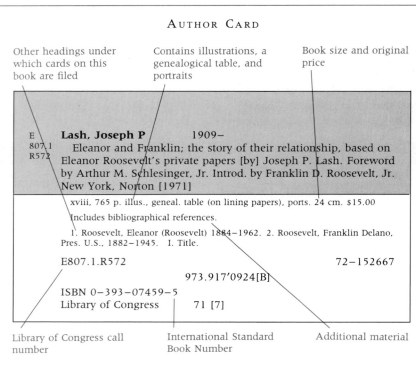

E 807.1 R572 **Lash, Joseph P** 1909–
Eleanor and Franklin; the story of their relationship, based on Eleanor Roosevelt's private papers [by] Joseph P. Lash. Foreword by Arthur M. Schlesinger, Jr. Introd. by Franklin D. Roosevelt, Jr. New York, Norton [1971]

xviii, 765 p. illus., geneal. table (on lining papers), ports. 24 cm. $15.00

Includes bibliographical references.

1. Roosevelt, Eleanor (Roosevelt) 1884–1962. 2. Roosevelt, Franklin Delano, Pres. U.S., 1882–1945. I. Title.

E807.1.R572   72–152667

973.917'0924[B]

ISBN 0–393–07459–5
Library of Congress   71 [7]

Library of Congress call number

International Standard Book Number

Additional material

Title Card

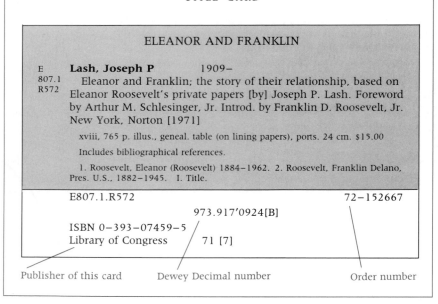

ELEANOR AND FRANKLIN

E 807.1 R572 **Lash, Joseph P** 1909–
Eleanor and Franklin; the story of their relationship, based on Eleanor Roosevelt's private papers [by] Joseph P. Lash. Foreword by Arthur M. Schlesinger, Jr. Introd. by Franklin D. Roosevelt, Jr. New York, Norton [1971]

xviii, 765 p. illus., geneal. table (on lining papers), ports. 24 cm. $15.00

Includes bibliographical references.

1. Roosevelt, Eleanor (Roosevelt) 1884–1962. 2. Roosevelt, Franklin Delano, Pres. U.S., 1882–1945. I. Title.

E807.1.R572   72–152667

973.917'0924[B]

ISBN 0–393–07459–5
Library of Congress   71 [7]

Publisher of this card

Dewey Decimal number

Order number

Linda checks out two of these books, and with the help of the *New York Times Index* she finds several articles about Roosevelt's work for women. Linda decides to concentrate on Roosevelt's efforts to help women: her work for charities, her attitude toward suffrage, and her involvement in women's political groups.

Other Book Catalogs

You may want to compile a list of all the books on your topic that you think you would like to consult, even if they are not in your library. Some of them may be available from interlibrary loan, or you may be able to borrow directly from other libraries or friends. There are bibliographies—lists of sources—on many subjects. Many of them are complete books themselves. To find out if there is a published bibliography on your topic or the general subject you are studying, you may consult the *Bibliographic Index,* which is published in cumulative volumes every year; it lists both single-volume bibliographies and those incorporated into books and journals, many of which will not be available in small libraries (see p. 358). Easier to use than the *Bibliographic Index* is Eugene P. Sheehy's *Guide to Reference Books,* which includes an annotated appendix indicating which reference works have bibliographies.

Books in Print is a multivolume work that lists all books in English currently available for purchase by bookstores and libraries. There are volumes that list books alphabetically by author and others that alphabetize by title. Both volumes include complete publication information for each listing. In addition, the *Subject Guide to Books in Print* classifies books by subject and the *Paperbound Books in Print* lists those books published only in paper, as well as those in both paper and hardcover. Any of the volumes of *Books in Print* may be helpful for identifying very recent books that may be ordered but not yet cataloged in your library.

OCLC (Online Computer Library Center) and *RLIN* (Research Libraries Information Network) are massive on-line catalogs that provide a listing of the books found in libraries throughout the United States and Canada. *RLIN* allows searching by subject, while *OCLC* requires that you know the title or author. See page 80.

The Circulation Desk

The circulation desk is not only the place where you check out books; it is also the place where records are kept on all books that are not on the shelves: those that are checked out, on reserve, or being repaired. Staff people behind the circulation desk can usually tell you where books are and when you can expect to use them. If you have reason to think that a book has been stolen or misplaced, you should report it to the circulation desk.

The Stacks

Libraries shelve books that can be checked out in an area usually referred to as the stacks. In some libraries, the stacks are open, which means that you have free access to the circulating books. You can browse among the shelves, take a book down to skim it, carry it to a library carrel, or check it out. In open stacks, it is easy to find books on a particular topic and to select individual books directly from the shelves. In a library with closed stacks, you must make your selections from the card catalog, fill out a request form, and wait to have a book brought to the circulation desk.

The Microform and Non-print Collection

Microform is the general term for all information stored as very small images called microimages, which are actually reproductions of printed material—books, newspapers, periodicals, and documents. To use microforms, you must have a machine called a reader, which enlarges the print to a readable size. The most common microforms are microfilm, microfiche, and microprint. Since most libraries have some material on more than one type of microform, you should use the general term when inquiring about these materials. Non-print material is the term used to refer to audio tapes, videotapes, records, and films. Some libraries store these materials in a separate room near the equipment necessary to use them. You may want to learn to use the machinery before you need to use it under the pressure of an assignment.

The Reserve Book Section

Academic libraries have a section for books that have been set aside for use by students in a particular class. You will, however, usually be allowed to use reserve books in the library, and in some cases, you may be able to check them out overnight. When a book that you want is not on the shelf, you should ask at the circulation desk whether the book is on reserve. In some libraries, reserve books are kept behind the circulation desk; in others, they are in a separate section or even a special reserve reading room.

Special Collections

Library materials that require unusual care are kept in a separate room, often behind locked doors, or in a separate building. Old or particularly valuable books, fragile materials, letters, manuscripts, and all rare publications are usually kept together in the special collections room. There may be times when you will consult material in the special collections or when you will design a research project based on the collections of letters, manuscripts, or other rare or unique materials to which you have access. Once you have discovered what particularly valuable material your library has, you should ask whether it is available to students and what procedures you should follow to use it.

Library Services

ASSISTANCE IN FINDING INFORMATION

The circulation department will provide you with information about the whereabouts and availability of circulating books. The reference department will help you answer more specific questions on a wide range of topics. Even after you have studied the annotated list of reference works in appendix B, you will probably need some guidance about the best reference work to consult for a particular question.

David wants to find out something about Robert Coles, the author of one of the books he is using for his research on the effects of the nuclear threat on children. He goes to the reference room and looks for information in several encyclopedias. When he does not find what he wants, he asks the reference librarian, who suggests that he consult *Biography and Genealogy Master Index.* There he finds Coles listed in several reference works, including *American Men and Women of Science,* 1979, where he finds the information he needs.

INSTRUCTION IN LIBRARY USE

Many libraries provide pamphlets, maps, and other materials that explain how to use a particular library's services and resources. Some provide tours, workshops, or formal classes in library skills. It is a good idea to look for notices about these services or to inquire at the circulation or reference desk. Your college catalog may explain which of these services are available to you.

ASSISTANCE USING MICROFORM, CD-ROM, OR ON-LINE MATERIAL

While all reference librarians can help you use general reference works, the serial catalog, or the main catalog, most libraries will have particular people trained to do computer searches or even to use the CD-ROM indexes. It is a good idea to spend some time locating the computer terminals and finding out what you can access through each one. Terminals may be used only to search the library's main catalog on-line, others to read CD-ROM discs, and still others to access catalogs of other libraries. Terminals are often connected to printers that will provide you with a printout of the information you want. Some may provide full texts of journals, magazines, or articles in reference works. People trained to help you with electronic or machine-read materials are often available at particular times, so it is a good idea to learn their names and schedules.

STUDY AREAS AND STORAGE SPACE

Certain sections of a library are designated for quiet study, and some libraries have carrels that can be reserved for use by individual students. Most libraries have space set aside for typing. Many also provide lockers where students can leave their books and papers overnight. You will need to take the initiative to find out if any of these services are available.

COPYING SERVICES

Using a library's copying service can save you time. Most libraries have coin-operated machines that students can use to copy single pages, whole articles, or even chapters in books. Some have staff people who will make copies for you, usually for a small fee. At all times, of course, you will want to respect the copyright laws that make it illegal for you to copy large portions of a book rather than purchasing the book. The law allows you to copy for educational purposes up to a chapter in a book, three articles in an annual volume of a periodical, and a story or a poem from an anthology.

INTERLIBRARY SERVICES

Libraries exchange various services, ranging from reference assistance to copying services. If your library does not receive certain periodicals, you may be able to get copies of articles from them from another library. This service is usually arranged through the reference section, where you will need to fill out request forms and pay a small fee for copying.

You may be able to borrow books from other libraries through a loan system arranged by your college library. To do this you will usually need to consult with the reference librarian, fill out a form, and sometimes pay a small fee. In some cases, you will be able to obtain a book very quickly; in others, there may be a considerable wait. In any case, ask how long it will take to get the book and respect what restrictions, if any, the lending library places on its use and on the length of time it is lent. Many libraries limit the interlibrary loan service to graduate students and faculty; others provide the service in a limited way to undergraduates. Before you try to find books in other libraries, find out if it is possible for you to borrow them.

Activities

A. On your own take an informal tour of your college library. If a map or other guide is available, use it. Otherwise, you may need to ask a few questions of the library staff before you locate everything. The following activities should lead you to all the sections of the library:

1. Visit the section where the current periodicals are shelved. Select a popular magazine that attracts your attention and skim it, stopping to read articles that interest you.
2. Locate the bound periodicals and skim through a single volume, such as a few months of *Life* or *National Geographic*.
3. Browse through a scholarly journal that interests you.
4. Find the reference section of the library, identify the reference desk, and find out which staff people are the reference librarians.
5. Find out how the books in the library are cataloged. Are they on cards, microform, or on-line.
6. If the stacks are open, browse among the circulating books and note whether the library uses the Dewey decimal system or the Library of Congress system.
7. Select a book that interests you, or, if the stacks are closed, select one from the catalog and fill out a request form. Take the book to the circulation desk and follow the procedure for checking it out.

B. Locate the computer terminals and read any material explaining what they do. Find out if there is a computerized on-line catalog. Locate any computer terminals with indexes to magazines and newspapers. Find out if there are computers for reading CD-ROMs.

C. Go to the section of the library where encyclopedias are shelved.

1. Select a noncontroversial topic in which most people have some interest, such as "Dogs." Look the topic up in the three major encyclopedias. What differences and what similarities do you note? Are there cross-references within the article? If you wanted to buy a dog, which article would provide you with the most practical information for choosing the right breed?
2. Choose a subject you feel you know rather well—classic cars, nuclear energy, Nigeria, the Civil War, football, piano composers—and see how much you can learn from reading articles in two encyclopedias. Read carefully to see if you can spot any errors, out-of-date material, or opinions stated as fact.
3. Choose a controversial topic such as abortion and look it up in three encyclopedias, using the index to find all the articles that treat the topic. Note the varied treatments and whether the material in each

encyclopedia is current; then make a list of the suggested further reading on the topic in each encyclopedia and compare the sources, noting particularly the dates of each. Do some sources appear in more than one encyclopedia? in all three? Which article gives you the most thorough, up-to-date treatment of the topic?

D. Visit the reference room again.

1. Look up B. F. Skinner in the following reference works: the *American Heritage Dictionary,* the *New Columbia Encyclopedia, Collier's Encyclopedia,* and the *International Encyclopedia of the Social Sciences.* You will find that each is more detailed than the last; as you proceed through each of the last three sources, jot down three facts not found in the previous source or sources. Jot down publication dates of Skinner's major books. Look to see if his work is discussed in more than one entry in the last source, and look up the titles of his works *Walden Two* and *Beyond Freedom and Dignity* to see if they are treated separately. Notice that the *International Encyclopedia of the Social Sciences* also has a *Biographical Supplement* that is indexed separately. You may find so much material in the final source that you will only have time to skim it.

2. Locate the *Readers' Guide to Periodical Literature* and select a volume for a year in which Skinner published a major book (1961 for *Walden Two* and 1971 for *Beyond Freedom and Dignity*). Look up Skinner and note how frequently articles were published about him in periodicals for those years.

3. Find the *Book Review Digest* and skim the reviews of one of these books. Would you be interested in reading the book?

E. Go to the library at a busy time and observe the activities of the people there. Write a paragraph or more describing how people are actually using the library.

F. Evaluate your own library. Make a list of the library materials and services mentioned in this chapter, and then find out which are available in your library. Write a paper in which you describe the resources in your library.

Project Activity

Write a paragraph or more about the library resources that you expect to use for your topic.

USING LIBRARY
SOURCES

4

When you go to the library to research a topic that truly interests you, you may find that your greatest difficulty is limiting the amount of time you spend finding and reading articles and books. It is a good idea to plan the steps of your research and to estimate in advance how much time you can spend looking for library sources. You will probably be more efficient if you allow several hours for each session in the library.

Preparing to Work in the Library

Before you begin collecting library material for a particular project, you will want to do the following:

Preparing to Work in the Library: A Checklist

1. Locate the forms you will need for checking out books, making an appointment with a reference librarian, ordering books or articles by interlibrary loan, and scheduling a computer search or assistance with CD-ROM readers.
2. Obtain materials such as cards, paper slips, writing pads, scissors, etc.
3. Study suggestions for making source cards (see pp. 82–85).

4. Examine examples of note cards in chapter 6.

5. Decide which style is best for documenting your paper (see pp. 185–87).

USING A COMPUTER IN THE LIBRARY

If you have a small battery-powered portable computer, you may want to take it to the library and record your sources and notes directly on a computer disk from the beginning. Before deciding whether you want to do this, read the list of recommendations on pages 115–16 of chapter 6.

SELECTING WRITING MATERIALS

You will save time if you always have enough writing material with you: three-by-five-inch cards for recording sources; five-by-eight-inch cards for note taking; a legal pad for your first draft; pens and pencils; and a large manila envelope, folder, or some other container that you use strictly for your research. To some extent, the kinds of materials you use will be a matter of personal preference. Some students enjoy using different-colored cards so that they can coordinate colors with types of notes or use one color for direct quotations and white cards for all other notes. (This also would help you avoid accidental plagiarism.) You may prefer more flexible slips of quality paper to the stiff index cards. Some students like to use single sides of the pages of a notebook. Regardless of color or size, individual note cards have the advantage of being easy to organize when you are ready to write your first draft, and individual source cards can be quickly put in order to form your list of sources. Whether you use long or short writing pads or small or large note cards should be determined by the scale of your handwriting and the directions of your instructor.

USING THE APPROPRIATE DOCUMENTATION STYLE

Decide which documentation style you will use for the final bibliography and notes of your paper before you make your source cards. The

Modern Language Association (MLA) style of documenting with parenthetical references is illustrated by the short paper in chapter 8, by the papers in chapters 11 and 14, and with complete instructions and sample references in chapter 9. Appendix A provides sample pages from a paper, model references, and detailed instruction for documenting a paper with endnotes or footnotes, a method that is also approved by the Modern Language Association. Chapter 12 provides a sample paper and instruction for using the American Psychological Association (APA) documentation style, used for papers on topics in the social sciences. The sample paper in chapter 13 provides all you need to know to document a research paper using the citation-sequence, or number, system endorsed by the Council of Biology editors, a documentation style suitable for papers in the natural sciences. (A list of style manuals sometimes used for other disciplines is included on p. 187.)

Your instructor may recommend a particular style or request that you study these options and choose the one that is most appropriate. In any event, now is the time to review the possibilities and to understand that your subject matter will determine the most appropriate style. To save time later, record bibliographic information as it will appear in your list of sources.

REVIEWING AVAILABLE SOURCES

To narrow your topic as you explore your sources, begin with general sources and move to more specific ones in approximately this order:

1. General reference works such as encyclopedias, bibliographies, dictionaries, and handbooks
2. The card, on-line, or COM catalog
3. Other book catalogs and specialized bibliographies
4. General periodical indexes
5. Specialized periodical indexes

Keep in mind, however, that there are no fixed rules for ordering a search. For his paper on *Rebel Without a Cause,* Michael Gold did follow approximately this order. Lisa Lee, however, began by searching the on-line catalog for books on tropical forests, and then, after deciding to focus on seed dispersal, she turned to specific periodical indexes: *General Science Index* and *Biological Abstracts.* Lisa also found valuable sources in the bibliographies of scientific articles.

Finding the sources that you expect to use involves a number of activities that have already been suggested in this book, but it is helpful to review these activities before you begin to take extensive notes. Although you have been advised to move from general to specific sources, you will probably backtrack, and even after you have found most of your material, you may go back to the card catalog or consult an index under a different heading. Always keep a record of your progress, noting specific volumes of indexes as you consult them. Before you conclude this stage of your research, you will want to do the following:

Collecting Sources: A Checklist

1. Locate and read articles in general encyclopedias and specialized reference works.
2. Consult the list of subjects in *Library of Congress Subject Headings*.
3. Consult the library's main catalog (either card or on-line) and record titles and call numbers of promising books.
4. Check out appropriate books.
5. Consult other book catalogs and bibliographies.
6. Study general periodical indexes for magazines and newspapers.
7. Explore specialized periodical indexes for scholarly journals.
8. Discover which periodicals are in your library and locate the ones you want.
9. Photocopy articles that you feel will be especially pertinent to your topic.
10. Discuss with a librarian the possibility of doing a computer search.
11. Request copies of books or articles in periodicals (using interlibrary loan forms) from other libraries.
12. Locate non-print material—records, tapes, microform—on your topic.
13. Make a card for each source, using appropriate bibliographic style.

Some of these steps will not be appropriate for all topics. For example, your library may not provide a service for borrowing books from other libraries; there may not be any non-print material available on your topic; and abstracts (brief summaries) may not be available for journals in the particular discipline you are researching.

DEFINING AND EXPLAINING WHAT YOU WANT TO KNOW

Before you plan your search strategy—the steps you expect to follow in locating material—try to define what you want to know. If you can condense your research questions to a single sentence, you will be able to explain quickly what you want to find out to the reference librarians and others who may guide you to appropriate material. A simple statement of what you want to know can also serve as a guide to keep you on the subject and to help you decide quickly which sources should be profitable and which, though interesting, are in fact irrelevant to *your* project. You might write a summary statement similar to one below.
I want to know:

1. how seeds are dispersed by animals in tropical forests
2. how the nuclear threat affects children and adolescents
3. about the people who created the film *Rebel Without a Cause*
4. why *Huckleberry Finn* has been so controversial
5. about Eleanor Roosevelt's work to help women

Librarians and others can be much more helpful if you explain as precisely as possible what you want to know rather than ask general questions. If you want to learn about Eleanor Roosevelt's public activities in the 1920s, say so instead of asking for general information about her life.

Planning the Steps of Your Search: The Search Strategy

Try to identify the steps on the checklist above that will be helpful for your topic. Some topics will not be treated in general encyclopedias. For example, a subject like the psychological effects of the nuclear threat does not even appear in the *Encyclopedia Americana*. When David Harris fails to find books on his subject, he decides to do a computer search, which yields a number of valuable sources. For help in devising a search strategy—a plan for locating material—consult the annotated list of reference works in appendix B and make a list of those that you think will be helpful.

MICHAEL GOLD

Before he makes a plan, Michael makes a list of the steps that led him to his topic:

1. Studied the "Motion Picture" article in the Encyclopedia Americana.
2. Read the chapter on movies in the 1950s in David Cook's History of Narrative Film.
3. Watched a videotape of Rebel Without a Cause.

He then devises the following plan:

1. Consult the World Encyclopedia of Film and the Biographical Dictionary of Film.
2. Check the card catalog under Rebel Without a Cause, James Dean, and Nicholas Ray.
3. Check out books that look promising.
4. Consult the Readers' Guide to Periodical Literature for 1955 and 1956 for reviews of Rebel and articles about James Dean.
5. Ask the reference librarian for guidance.

After Michael completes these steps, he identifies other areas that he wants to explore and expands his plan to include the following:

6. Consult the International Index to Film Periodicals.
7. Read Robert Lindner's 1944 book, Rebel Without a Cause.
8. Consult Book Review Digest for reviews of Lindner's book.
9. Check Readers' Guide to Periodical Literature for more recent articles about Dean, Ray, or Rebel.
10. Check Essay and General Literature Index for chapters in books.
11. Locate and photocopy promising articles.
12. Begin reading.

A computer search of an appropriate topic using carefully chosen subject headings or key words (called descriptors) to access a database can yield many useful sources in a very short time. Before beginning a computer search, you may want to consult the *Library of Congress Subject Headings* since many databases follow it. Some databases have their own subject dictionaries (thesaurae). A skilled searcher can combine more than one descriptor at a time and in this way find narrowly focused sources that would take hours to find in more traditional indexes. Topics such as business, medicine, or chemistry are best searched with a computer since databases in these fields are up-to-date. For example, the update for *Standard and Poor's News* is daily, for *Chemsearch* biweekly, and for *Medline* monthly. Some databases provide abstracts—short summaries—of the articles as well as all the information you need to locate them.

A computer search, however, can be expensive, so inquire about cost before you begin. Not all topics are suited for a computer search since some databases cover only a limited time period. Databases are constantly being updated and extended back in time, so inquire about the time period covered by each database you plan to search.

In order to help the searcher find material for you, you must explain your topic in some detail and answer any questions that arise. For this reason, you should not begin a computer search until you have limited your topic adequately. Once this is accomplished, a searcher can combine terms in several different ways, using one of three connectors: *and, or,* and *not.* For example, a student looking for material on solar energy might instruct the computer to locate sources that contain the words "solar" *and* "energy." Someone researching energy sources other than nuclear energy might ask for "energy" *not* "nuclear." (The *not* connector must be used with caution since it would exclude articles that discuss nuclear energy along with other forms of energy.)

Not all topics are suited for a computer searches. To decide if a search is appropriate for your topic consider the following:

1. *Is the data you are looking for also available (at no cost) on CD-ROM?* There would be no advantage for Carla Medina to conduct a computer search for her research on *The Color Purple* since the novel was published in 1982 and both the *MLA Index* on CD-ROM and the indexes in *InfoTrac* cover all the years since the book was published.

2. *Will the search be worth the cost, which is determined by the number of citations found?* An unrestricted computer search on a major public figure—John F. Kennedy or Eleanor Roosevelt—would be expensive since it would yield many citations.

3. *Is there a suitable database for your topic?* Many on-line databases cover only recent years. For example, the volumes on *Biological Abstracts* that yield the most material for Lisa Lee's research on seed dispersal are not yet—and may never be—included in the on-line or CD-ROM versions

---

DAVID HARRIS

Some topics are particularly suited for a computer search. David Harris finds that searching the card catalog and the indexes in book form is very tedious and nonproductive. "Nuclear war" in the *Library of Congress Subject Headings* eventually leads him to "atomic warfare—psychological aspects," but he finds nothing in his library's card catalog. Next he turns to *Psychological Abstracts*, but searching one subject at a time proves to be so tedious that David feels overwhelmed and gives up. He then consults a reference librarian, who explains that with the help of a computer, he can search several subject headings at once. He makes an appointment with the librarian who specializes in computer searches and together they plan the search.

Considering the material covered in the various available databases, the librarian recommends a search in *ERIC* and *PsycINFO*. After listening to David explain his topic and consulting the thesaurus of *ERIC* descriptors, beginning with "nuclear warfare," the librarian then identifies four other descriptors she can use to limit the topic: "young children," "childhood attitudes," "children," and "adolescents." Using the *and* as well as the *or* connector, she instructs the computer to look for sources that contain "nuclear war" *and* "childhood attitudes" *or* "children," or "young children," *or* "adolescents." She then searches for articles on the subject of nuclear warfare and finds 347 items. When she checks for material on any of the other four, she finds there are 33,803. By directing the computer to identify those sources about nuclear warfare that contain information about children, childhood attitudes, children or adolescents, she finds a manageable 25 articles. Following a similar procedure, she searches *PsycINFO* and finds 50 sources, some of which overlap with those from the *ERIC* database. Here is a small portion of the printout of the sources David locates in his computer search:

HARRIS — NUCLEAR WAR
DIALOG File 11: PSYCINFO - 67-85/NOV (Copr. Am. Psych. Assn.)

72-23763
 A **decisionmaking approach to nuclear education. Special
Issue: Education and the threat of nuclear war.**
 Snow, Roberta; Goodman, Lisa
 Harvard Medical School, Boston
 Harvard Educational Review, 1984 Aug Vol 54(3) 321-328
CODEN: HVERAP ISSN: 00178055
 Journal Announcement: 7209
 Language: ENGLISH Document Type: JOURNAL ARTICLE
 Describes a US senior high school curriculum that addresses
4 areas: personal values as a basis for political views,
technological aspects of the nuclear arms race, the history of
the nuclear arms race, and action for social change. The
program's content, focus, and structure are detailed, and its
effects on student attitudes are discussed. Excerpts from
student essays are presented, and examples of appropriate
class projects are suggested.
 Descriptors: NUCLEAR WAR .(34567); STUDENT ATTITUDES
.(50300); EDUCATION .(16000); CURRICULUM .(12810); HIGH SCHOOL
STUDENTS .(22930); ADOLESCENCE .(00920)
 Identifiers: high school curriculum, decisionmaking approach
to nuclear education, high school students
 Section Headings: 3530 .(CURRICULUM PROGRAMS & TEACHING
METHODS)

72-23746
 **Resistances to knowing in the nuclear age. Special Issue:
Education and the threat of nuclear war.**
 Mack, John E.
 Harvard Medical School, Boston
 Harvard Educational Review, 1984 Aug Vol 54(3) 260-270
CODEN: HVERAP ISSN: 00178055
 Journal Announcement: 7209
 Language: ENGLISH Document Type: JOURNAL ARTICLE
 Explores psychological reasons why educators and parents
resist dealing with the nuclear issue, arguing that the
controversy surrounding nuclear education reflects the
conflicts of society as a whole with regard to nuclear weapons
and nuclear arms policy. Individual resistance, the avoidance
of the emotional pain associated with nuclear war, and
collective resistance, the result of a nation's political and
economic assumptions to which citizens feel committed and
which they support through corporate structures, are examined.
The psychological attachment and personal emotional security
associated with alignment with these structures are described.
A collectively based fear among those involved in this
hierarchy of imparting a balanced view of Soviet ideology and
intentions to adolescents also hinders efforts to provide
nuclear education. It is concluded that, if these collective
assumptions are not questioned, advocacy for nuclear
education, no matter how well-intended or impassioned, will
not succeed. (22 ref)

Author's affiliation   Source (journal, date, volume,
                         number, and pages)   A short description of the
                                                     article

Descriptors: NUCLEAR WAR .(34567); EDUCATION .(16000);·
PARENTS .(36680); TEACHERS .(51690); ADULTHOOD .(01150)
 Identifiers: psychological reasons for resistance to dealing
with nuclear issue, educators & parents
 Section Headings: 3530 .(CURRICULUM PROGRAMS & TEACHING
METHODS); 2900 .(SOCIAL PROCESSES AND SOCIAL ISSUES)

72-23687
**The role of education in preventing nuclear war. Special
Issue: Education and the threat of nuclear war.**
 Markusen, Eric; Harris, John B.
 Southwest State U
 Harvard Educational Review, 1984 Aug Vol 54(3) 282-303
CODEN: HVERAP ISSN: 00178055
 Journal Announcement: 7209
 Language: ENGLISH Document Type: JOURNAL ARTICLE
 Argues that education should play a crucial role in reducing
the threat of nuclear war and examines the role of education
in formulating and implementing policies and attitudes that
caused the Holocaust of World War II Nazi Germany. A parallel
is drawn to the role of American education in maintaining the
nuclear arms race between the US and USSR. Aspects of US
nuclear weapons policymaking and factors of psychological
resistance (e.g., psychic numbing, apathy, ignorance,
parochialism, distractions of daily life) that have limited
citizen participation in nuclear decision making are examined.
The propagation of nuclearism, in which organizations and
individuals develop incentives to maintain the status quo of
searching for nuclear superiority and of the readiness to wage
nuclear war, as an institutional phenomenon is described. The
concentration of power in these policymaking structures has
eroded the democratic process as it relates to nuclear
planning and policy. The potential of education to help
prevent nuclear war and ways that educators are attempting to
accomplish this task are discussed.
 Descriptors: NUCLEAR WAR .(34567); EDUCATION .(16000);
PREVENTION .(40290)
 Identifiers: role of education in preventing of nuclear war
 Section Headings: 3500 .(EDUCATIONAL PSYCHOLOGY)

72-22365
**Between feeling and fact: Listening to children. Special
Issue: Education and the threat of nuclear war.**
 Engel, Brenda S.
 Lesley Coll, Program Evaluation & Research Group
 Harvard Educational Review, 1984 Aug Vol 54(3) 304-314
CODEN: HVERAP ISSN: 00178055
 Journal Announcement: 7209
 Language: ENGLISH Document Type: JOURNAL ARTICLE

The computer search is very helpful and productive for David.
Not all of the sources he finds are appropriate or available, but he
very easily locates several sources on the list, which lead him to still
others. In a short time, David feels he has more information than he
actually needs. A computer search, he discovers, is the perfect way
to obtain the sort of information he is looking for.

of the index. Even though *Medline,* the on-line version of the *Index Medicus,* covers the years beginning in 1966, certain topics would not be suitable for a *Medline* search. For example, the early reports on smoking and cancer were published in the early 1960s and would not be accessible through current databases.

4. *Can you efficiently search the topic in print form?* After Linda Orton reads about her subject in biographies of Eleanor Roosevelt, she is able to search the *New York Times Index* quickly since she knows she wants articles from the 1920s, and she therefore consults only volumes for those years.

To do a computer search in most libraries you will need to follow these steps:

Doing a Computer Search: A Checklist

1. Fill out a form for a search request.
2. Make an appointment and meet with a computer librarian (a professional searcher).
3. With the librarian's assistance, choose the databases to search, determine the cost of the search, and decide whether you want the information in an on-line printout available immediately or in an off-line printout that you will receive normally within five days.
4. Consult a thesaurus if available to find the appropriate descriptors (subject headings) to use for the search.
5. Devise a search strategy that will combine descriptors in the most effective way.
6. Begin the search, adjusting descriptors as needed. You may have to make another appointment to meet with the librarian to actually conduct the search.

USING A LIBRARY NETWORK

There are three major national bibliographic networks: *OCLC* (Online Computer Library Center), *RLIN* (Research Libraries Information Network), and *WLN* (Washington Library Network). These systems link libraries by providing computerized lists of books in the collections of libraries throughout the United States and Canada. A network is useful for a variety of purposes. You may, for example, use it to locate a book that is not available in your library or to verify publication information about a book that you do not have in hand.

IDENTIFYING SUBJECT HEADINGS

Certain indexes have their own guides to subject headings (sometimes called a thesaurus). Some include the guide in each cumulative volume; and some—the *ERIC* publications and *Psychological Abstracts*—provide a

---

Uncovering Secrets

Most people did not know about many of the events surrounding the Watergate affair until more than two years after they had occurred. If you were researching the role that presidential aides played in the Watergate scandal, you would not find much in periodical indexes for the year 1972; rather, you would need to consult indexes for 1973 and 1974, the years during which the story was gradually told in the press. In order to research news accounts of such events, you would need to find out when they were announced or when media coverage began, as well as when they occurred. To find the dates of the reporting of the events of the Watergate affair, check an encyclopedia article. The *New Columbia Encyclopedia* gives a good summary with dates. Once you find the dates of coverage in the *New York Times,* you can usually refer to approximately the same dates for coverage of the same events in other papers. An article in a newspaper, magazine, or professional journal will be listed only in the index for the year it was published. If that same article is reprinted, it will be listed again in the index for the year in which it was reprinted.

If you are investigating the allegations that the release of the Iranian hostages in 1980 was delayed to discredit President Jimmy Carter, you would probably begin by searching periodical indexes of 1991 since the allegations were not widely publicized until then. If your library has a CD-ROM periodical database such as those pro- vided by *InfoTrac,* that would be a good place to begin.

Students who want to look into the banking crisis involving the Bank of Commerce and Credit International (BCCI) would search indexes at the time the news broke in 1990 and 1991, perhaps a computerized database like *National Newspaper Index* available through *InfoTrac* or, if that is not available, the *New York Times Index.*

---

separate volume for subject headings. Still other indexes use the Library of Congress headings. Before you use an index, study the introductory material to find out how subjects are classified. When you are looking for books on a particular subject or articles listed in indexes that use the Library of Congress system, you should consult the *Library of Congress Subject Headings*. This and other guides may suggest headings that you would otherwise not think to consult.

FINDING THE RIGHT DATE

If you are studying the public response to a movie or a book, you will consult indexes to periodicals published at the same time or shortly after. Most films are reviewed immediately after they are released, and popular books are reviewed within a few months. If you have trouble finding reviews of a book, you should check at least three years after publication dates since publication of reviews of certain books, especially scholarly ones, may be delayed that long.

To find information on historical subjects, keep in mind that events are sometimes not written about for some time after they occur; some events are of course kept from the public by people who do not want them to be known.

PRINTING SOURCE CITATIONS DIRECTLY FROM THE COMPUTER

It is usually possible to print directly from the computer terminal the citations for sources that you find in a computer search or on a CD-ROM disc. You may later want to cut these citations and paste them to a card so that you can more easily alphabetize them; organize them according to subject categories; or, if you are using the number system for a scientific paper, arrange them according to the sequence in which you use them in the final paper. Citations taken directly from a database do not always have all the information you will need for your final citation, so when you find the original source, make sure you add any missing details to each reference.

Making Source Cards

Plan to make two kinds of cards from the beginning: *source cards,* for all the information you will need to prepare your bibliography, and *note cards,* for material that you plan to use in writing the paper. Before you begin to make source cards, study the forms for reference citations in chapter 9 for MLA style. If you plan to use the APA style, consult pages 253–59. For the CBE style, see pages 282–86.

As soon as you find the titles of books or articles on your topic, you should make a card for each reference that seems promising. You may be tempted to jot down all the references you find on a single sheet of paper, but it is better from the beginning to use a single card or sheet for each source. Why? Quite simply because it is easier and more efficient in the long run to have a single slip or card for each. There is room on a card to add call numbers and other information. You may later want room to jot down a note about what someone has told you about a source or a comment to indicate how you have actually used a source. This can be helpful later, since your instructor may ask you to annotate your bibliography, that is, to indicate after each item in your list of sources how you have actually used it. In addition, individual source cards are easy to alphabetize or otherwise organize for the final list of sources.

When you first find a reference to a book that you want to consult, note the author, title, and—if you have found it in the card catalog—the call number. Leave room for publication information of the edition that you actually use. (Note the first example on the next page.) Later, when you have the source in hand, you can double-check the spelling of the author and title and then add the place and date of publication and the publisher. Keep in mind that there may be more than one edition of a book in your

A SAMPLE SOURCE CARD

Lash, Joseph. *Eleanor and Franklin*.
New York: Norton, 1971.

library, and you may use a different edition from the one you first found cited in a catalog or bibliography. In any case, before you make your first source card, find out from your instructor which documentation style you should use, and record the information as it will appear on your list of sources.

When you make a source card for an article in a periodical—newspaper, magazine, or journal—record all the information needed for the cita-

A SOURCE CARD NOTING CONTENT

Woolf, S. J. "A Woman Speaks Her Political Mind."
New York Times 8 April 1928: 3.

Good quotes from a speech by E. Roosevelt.

tion in your list of sources. Include date, volume number, and page number, as well as author, title of article, and complete title of the periodical. Consider the following example:

Roosevelt, Eleanor. "Why Democrats Favor Smith." *North American Review* 224 (1927-1928): 472-475.

MAKING A COMPUTER FILE OF SOURCES

In addition to your source cards, you may want to start a computer file in which you record your sources alphabetically using the appropriate documentation style exactly as you want it to appear in your final paper. Some word-processing programs have the capability to alphabetize entries and even to arrange the data according to the format required by a specific style such as the MLA or APA. But even the simplest programs allow you to build a list of sources easily, by recording them alphabetically and adding new sources by inserting them in the appropriate place.

If you have a portable, battery-operated computer with you whenever you are collecting material, you may choose to record all the necessary information about sources directly into the computer, eliminating the need for source cards. If you do this, you should print a hard copy of your list of sources and/or make a backup copy on another disk. Most students, however, prefer the convenience of source cards, which they can easily carry about the library. Source cards also serve as insurance against losing your data if disks are lost or damaged.

Taking Preliminary Notes and Classifying Sources

Although most of your note taking will take place later, there will be times even in the earliest stages of your research when you will want to record dates, facts, statistics, or ideas as you read general reference works or skim periodicals or books. You probably will not quote from an encyclopedia or cite it later, since you will seek far more specialized sources dealing with your topic, but writing out a summary of an encyclopedia overview can contribute to your understanding of a topic. When you take notes, identify the source of the note with the first item from the source card—either the

---

CARLA MEDINA

In the early stages of her research on *The Color Purple,* Carla decides to focus on the voices of the novel (p. 116), with emphasis on Celie's special way of speaking. As she reads through articles about the novel, she chooses to make source cards for those that include a discussion of Celie's voice. Note how on the following card Carla has included all the necessary bibliographic information as well as a brief note about its content:

> Harris, Trudier. "On *The Color Purple,* Stereotypes, and Silence." *Black American Literature Forum* 18 (1984): 155–61.
>
> Critical of the novel's moral vision and lack of realism, but praises Celie's voice as "powerful, engaging, subtly humorous..." (156).

author or, when there is no author, the title—followed by the page number (see chapter 6). If you should jot down a complete sentence or even a phrase written by someone other than yourself, make sure that you put quotation marks around it (see p. 120). Make separate cards for notes you expect to use for writing your paper, and put only one note on a card.

It will be easy to measure your progress by classifying your source cards as you go along. Put them in three stacks or mark them with Roman numerals indicating which of three categories they belong in:

I. Sources that you have found and hope to use
II. Those that you hope to find, either by recalling them from users of your own library or by borrowing them from other libraries
III. Those that you do not expect to be able to find

Adding a note now to each reference about its availability and possible usefulness can be helpful later.

It is best to use only one note for each card so that when you are ready to organize your notes you can shuffle and sort them easily into categories. If you take notes directly on a computer file from the beginning, you can easily rearrange them as needed.

Evaluating Sources

In general, specialized journals in which the articles are signed and written by experts are more reliable than those published in popular magazines that depend on advertising to make a profit. This is not always the case, but remember that articles published in weekly newsmagazines are often written under the pressure of a deadline and vary considerably in accuracy, objectivity, and reliability of sources used.

Some magazines are known to publish dependable articles and excerpts from books. Among these are the *Atlantic,* the *New Yorker,* and the *New York Times Magazine.* You may decide to trust an article if it is signed and includes a brief summary of the author's credentials.

Some special-interest magazines are published by private and/or publically funded institutes and societies that are committed to particular goals. *World Watch* is published by the Worldwatch Institute, which has a staff of people committed to disseminating information about recent trends and activities that threaten the environment and the welfare of people everywhere. An article in this publication would probably give you more reliable information on the cholera epidemic in South America than a travel magazine that depends on revenue from airlines that fly there.

Judging the value of a book is not easy. In general a book published by a university press is likely but not necessarily more trustworthy than mass-market books that are written in a hurry to make a quick profit. For example, a book on the Persian Gulf War that was in bookstores in the spring of 1991, weeks after the war ended, could not have been very thoughtfully produced. On the other hand, a book written by a Middle East specialist and published two years later would probably be more reliable. But not necessarily. People have many motives for writing books. Some write to reinforce a particular point of view or political position. Others write to persuade readers to think a certain way on issues. Still others report the findings of investigations and research.

The more you learn about a subject, the more you will be able to judge the value of your sources. You will learn to check the book's bibliography, documentary notes, and index; based on what you are learning about a topic, you will be able to discount some books and rely on others. You will certainly want your work to be based on the most authoritative sources available to you.

If you doubt the reliability of a source, you might consider the following questions:

1. *Is it up-to-date?* An article on drug use among teenagers written in 1960 will not tell you much about the drug culture that developed a few years later, though it could be quite illuminating in contrast. An encyclopedia article on computers that lists a bibliography from 1965 and earlier will be worthless to someone studying current computer technology. Keep in mind that current editions of standard encyclopedias often include out-of-date material. The dates on the sources at the end of an article will usually let you know if the article is current, but not all articles include a list of sources. The difficulty of knowing if some encyclopedia articles are up-to-date is one reason for their limited usefulness.

2. *What are the author's credentials?* You may be able to learn about an author's background and other publications from *Contemporary Authors*. You can often find information about authors with an academic background—usually established scholars who have published with a university press—in the *Directory of American Scholars* or *American Men and Women of Science*. An author's academic or institutional affiliation is often listed on the title page or the jacket of a book. You should be wary, however, of

accepting the evaluation of a book found on its jacket or sometimes on pages inserted before the title page. These comments, often called blurbs, may have been solicited from the author's friends; and those quoted from published reviews are of course selected because they are the most favorable.

3. Is a journal or newspaper known to be generally fair, or is it biased in some definite way? You might try looking it up in Katz and Katz's *Magazines for Libraries,* which evaluates periodicals and indicates those that have a particular bias.

4. Does the author have a special interest in the topic that might affect the reliability of the source? Completely unbiased sources don't exist; individuals filter information through their experience in subtly different ways. Yet you should try to be aware of inherent or obvious biases. The CEO of an oil company would interpret "factual" information about the damage done by oil spills in a very different way than members of a radical environmental organization. You should also learn to recognize *your own* biases and keep them in mind when researching controversial subjects.

5. Does the source seem adequately documented? You may be surprised to learn that some books and articles have less documentation than you will be required to have in your paper. Most reliable books, however, will have at the very least a comprehensive list of sources, either after each chapter or at the end of the book. Others will include notes as well. Articles in popular magazines are less likely to indicate their sources than are those in scholarly journals, which will almost always include precise information about sources. You need not necessarily discard a source simply because it lacks a bibliography. A personal memoir, for example, is often based on notes and diaries recorded by the author. Eleanor Roosevelt's account of her career as a social activist would of course be a valuable source, but one that should be treated for what it is: a personal account that is based on memory and private records and that presents the author in the way that she wants to be remembered.

6. In the case of controversial topics, does a source give a balanced or a one-sided view? If you know that a topic is controversial, you can usually determine whether a source acknowledges both sides of an issue. For example, an article on the future of nuclear power that fails to mention that many people see nuclear power as a serious threat to the environment would clearly be biased. You may, however, be unaware of the controversial aspects of a topic. For example, if you were doing research on the conviction of Alger Hiss and you consulted only sources that assumed his guilt, you might never know that there are people who insist on Hiss's innocence. Similarly if you were interested in theories about the origins of homosexuality, you might find considerable material about psychological causes. To understand the extent of the controversy about this subject, however, you would also need to consult studies concerned with the possible biological and neurological factors involved. By beginning with objective sources—encyclopedia articles or other reference works—at the beginning of a project, you can usually discover the controversial aspects of a topic and judge your sources accordingly. Comparing the material in two or more encyclopedia articles can be helpful.

7. *Does the source's language reveal a bias or call the author's reliability into question?* In addition to the other suggestions given here, you should also determine if a source uses confusing language or misleading statistics. Beware of the following:

• *Vague, nonspecific use of language,* such as the word "average." A statement that the average annual income for a group of first-year college graduates is twelve thousand dollars is meaningless unless we know whether that figure refers to the arithmetic average of all the salaries added together (the mean average); whether it means that half the group makes more than that and half makes less (the median average); or whether more people make twelve thousand dollars than any other amount (the modal average).

• *Discriminatory language.* Review the accuracy of general or blanket statements about a particular group: "old people," "African Americans," "women." Beware of sources that make definitive statements about the sexes yet use sexist or gender-specific language: "man" for "humanity"; "he" when "he or she" (or a plural pronoun) is more appropriate.

• *Percentages that are misleading.* A label that claims a product contains "30% less fat" does not indicate less than what, while the phrase "95% fat free" leaves you to wonder how much fat that product contains.

8. *Is a book published by a respected publishing house?* This is sometimes difficult for the beginning student to discover. If you have never heard of the publishing house, you might ask your instructor about it, find other books by the same publisher and see if you can judge their quality, or look the publishing house up in a book like *Writer's Market* for the current year. This reference work will tell you what a particular house usually publishes, who its target audience is, and what its standards for accepting new work might be.

9. *How was the book reviewed?* (See *Book Review Digest* and other book review sources mentioned in appendix B.) Checking reviews can also give you some idea of what the book contains and how it might be useful in your research.

Reading Effectively

Reading an article or a book for research is rarely a matter of reading steadily from beginning to end, word for word. There are times when you will read that way, but even then you will probably first skim through the text, noting its length, chapter or paragraph headings, and sometimes its conclusion. Let us consider various ways of learning from a text, beginning with a short article and ending with a substantial book.

Many articles found in popular periodicals can be skimmed quickly with attention to facts or ideas relevant to your topic. One technique is to read the introduction and the conclusion; a second is to read first sentences of paragraphs; a third is to look for headings, graphs, illustrations, or a summary. Depending on the content of an article, one or more of these approaches may be adequate for you to decide if you want to read more carefully.

PQRST

A helpful device for a thorough reading of a paragraph, an article, a chapter, or a complete book is known as the PQRST method.* When you decide that you really want to master the facts and ideas of a particular text, you may want to follow these steps:

P: Preview
Q: Question
R: Read
S: Summarize
T: Test

To *preview* a text you can follow the appropriate steps described for skimming: looking at the table of contents, the introduction, conclusion, beginning sentences, illustrations, and index. You may then want to make a list of *questions* that you expect or hope the text

*The PQRST method has been used for years to teach study skills (I learned it from my high school English teacher). Recent versions can be found in these texts: Ellen Lamar Thomas and H. Alan Robinson, *Improving Reading in Every Class*, 3rd ed. (Boston: Allyn and Bacon, 1982); George Spache and Paul Berg, *The Art of Efficient Reading*, 4th ed. (New York: Macmillan, 1984).

---

will answer. You then *read* the text with those questions in mind. When you finish reading, try to *summarize* what you have read, either by telling someone about it or by writing it down. The final step is to give yourself a *test:* Try to answer the questions that you posed in the beginning. Good readers often apply this method unconsciously. You may be one of them. Perhaps you examine a book, looking for clues to its content; you think of questions you hope it will answer; you read carefully, summarize what you have read, and finally test yourself—and the book—for answers. Even so, if you would like to be a better reader, you might want to apply the PQRST method consciously.

There will be times when the process stops during the third step. You may approach a text you have examined with an open mind, looking for answers to questions, only to discover that it does not really treat the topics you are researching or answer the questions you are asking. On the other hand, that text may introduce you to an intriguing aspect of your topic (or to another topic altogether) of which you may not have been aware. At this point you'll have to decide whether this new aspect or topic is intriguing *enough* to make you want to change the course of your research. If it isn't—or if you come upon it late in the research process—make a note of it as something to explore in the future and lay it aside for now.

Similar techniques apply to skimming a book. A detailed table of contents can tell you a lot, as can a good index. You may also want to look at the introduction and the conclusion of a book. Sometimes books are organized in such a way that you can learn much about their content by reading the beginning and concluding paragraphs of each chapter.

Keeping an open mind is an important part of effective reading. Good researchers may expect or look for certain answers, but they must be open to other possibilities. If you approach a book expecting to find particular answers, you run the risk of misinterpreting it, of finding only what you want to find, of ignoring qualifications and alternative points of view. Just as we can put words in the mouth of another person, so we can misread a text, taking statements out of context and even seeing words that are not there. The best way to avoid misreading is to be aware of the possibility of its happening and to keep an open mind as to what the author is actually saying.

Returning to the Library

Most students will use library resources throughout the stages of reading, note taking, and drafting a paper. By scheduling work time in the library, you can easily look up the new people, places, words, and events that you encounter in your reading. To identify reference works that you may want to consult once your research is underway, study the descriptions of reference materials in appendix B.

The actual business of conducting research is never quite as systematic as might be inferred from the guidelines of this book. A step-by-step procedure suggests a formula that, if followed carefully, will result in a polished, finished product; but the reality of asking questions and seeking answers—the essence of meaningful research—is often messy and erratic. You may find yourself wandering down a dead-end road or digressing to a subject that leads away from your topic. The steps suggested here can help you stick to a manageable number of questions and to reach realistic, if qualified or tentative, conclusions.

Activity

Visit your library at a time when it is not crowded (college libraries are usually least crowded during the first hours of the morning early in the term) and do any of the activities below that interest you:

1. If there is a computerized catalog, locate a terminal and use it to locate a book first by author and then by title.
2. Using either a computerized catalog or a card catalog, find out how many books your library has by Rachel Carson, Angela Davis, Norman Mailer, Toni Morrison, Ralph Nader, and D. H. Janzen.
3. Consulting the subject catalog, find out how many books there are about Sigmund Freud, Mikhail Gorbachev, Doris Lessing, Martin Luther King, Jr., and Margaret Mead.
4. Look up some of the following medical topics in two general encyclopedias, such as *Academic American Encyclopedia* and *Encyclopaedia Britannica,* and notice which is the most up-to-date and thorough: AIDS, birth control, cholera, cholesterol, cocaine, depression, migraine, radiology, and schizophrenia.
5. Using either indexes on *InfoTrac* or the *New York Times Index* for the last ten years, look up the following names and note how widely

these people have been treated in the press: Saddam Hussein, Catharine MacKinnon, Ann Richards, Pat Schroeder, Bishop Desmond Tutu, Terry Waite, and Boris Yeltsin.

Project Activities

A. Make a list of the questions you hope to answer through your research.

B. Try to reduce those questions to a single statement beginning with "I want to know."

C. Study the annotated list of reference works in appendix B and mark those that you think may be useful to your project. Make a list of those you have marked, putting them in the order in which you expect to consult them.

D. Design your own search strategy by listing the steps you expect to follow to find library material on your topic and those that will take you beyond the library. (See the next chapter.)

E. After consulting bibliographies, periodical indexes, and the main library catalog, record on index cards the sources that you expect to consult, including all the information that you will need to document your final paper.

F. Choose at least one book on your list and consult *Book Review Digest* to find out how it was reviewed. Write a paragraph summarizing the reviews you find there.

SEARCHING BEYOND THE LIBRARY

5

You may prefer using books and periodicals to find out what you want to know about a topic, but some questions simply cannot be answered by reading. Sometimes first-hand information is more current than anything you can find in print. Certain types of information change constantly. Consider the following questions: What is the current interest rate? How are property taxes computed in a community? What services are available at a public health facility? How many members are there in a political organization? To answer such questions, you would probably want to ask an expert—a banker, a tax assessor, an administrator of a public health organization. An expert, unlike a book, can talk back to you, correcting misperceptions, making connections between things you have learned, and suggesting further avenues for you to explore. Often public interest groups and charitable organizations provide topical and up-to-date information that is not available elsewhere. The League of Women Voters, for example, usually has current information about political candidates, and the Better Business Bureau offers basic information about companies—how long they have been in the community and how well they deal with consumer complaints. Even if people with special knowledge do not have time to talk to you, they may be able to provide or recommend reading material or suggest other people who can talk to you.

Some research requires that you question people directly; other research will depend largely on exploring printed material. All research, however, will be more meaningful if you can talk about it with someone else. Even if you expect that your research will be conducted mainly in the library, it is a good idea to try to find someone else who has an interest in your topic—a teacher, a family member, or a friend.

Deciding When to Ask Questions

Many topics are suited to extensive oral research. The following list will give you an idea of the kind of topics that would be enriched by talking to people and asking them questions:

1. The value of services provided by public facilities—a public health department, a drug rehabilitation center, a public school, the food stamp program, an AIDS information service
2. Job opportunities in particular fields—nursing, computers, the military
3. The function and impact of a business or industrial organization in a community
4. The problems of elderly people confined to nursing homes
5. Public responses to a historical event—the day John Kennedy was killed, the end of World War II, the release of the Iranian hostages, the beginning of the Persian Gulf War

Students researching topics like these might spend much of their time asking questions, but others researching topics that depend mainly on written materials can also learn in this way. Michael Gold, for example, has read about the James Dean cult, but it becomes real to him when he talks to people who were teenagers during the time it flourished. Lisa Lee has read about some of the ways that plants and animals in tropical forests interact, but only after interviewing Professor Vitousek, an expert in tropical forests, does she begin to understand that the very survival of some trees depends on the presence of particular animals.

Just as you should not write a research paper using a single book, you should not base your conclusions on what you learn from one person. If you were researching careers in the military, for example, you would want to talk not only to recruitment officers but to people who have been recruited as well.

Contacting People

There are many different ways to ask questions: writing letters of inquiry, making phone calls, or posting notices; arranging an appointment in someone's office, dropping by an office unannounced, or stopping people on the street; arranging a formal interview or asking one or more people to fill out a prepared questionnaire. There are no set rules to tell you which approach is best. Every time you want to learn from other people you will have to consider their personalities, their situations—how busy they are or how free to talk—as well as your relationship with them. Your history teacher, for example, may have encouraged you to stop by during office hours whenever you have a question; the academic dean of the college may be willing to answer your questions if you write a letter explaining what you want to know; and the admissions officer may make an appointment to see you, but may not be specific about what is actually required for admission.

The suggestions and examples in this chapter will serve as a guide to your own research. Some suggestions may be helpful, and others may seem irrelevant to the kind of research you are conducting. In seeking information from people, however, you should observe these rules in every case:

Contacting People: A Checklist

1. Be respectful of the time and needs of anyone that you question. Never be late for an appointment.
2. Remember that no one is obligated to answer your questions, and that even though many people may be happy to talk to you, they do so as a courtesy.
3. Be courteous in return, even if you are angered by a response.

POSTING NOTICES

In a college community, it is often easy to find people who know about a subject that you are researching. A proven way to make such contacts is to post notices on bulletin boards in the student center, dormitories, or other appropriate places. The notice may include your telephone number and a request that interested people call you, or it may include a space for them to write their names and telephone numbers. The following list suggests the kinds of notices that may yield results:

1. Wanted: people who are willing to talk about their experiences in the Persian Gulf War.
2. I am interested in talking to students who have feminist mothers. Do you, or do you know anyone who does?
3. I am collecting campus folklore. Please telephone me if you know any stories about strange or funny happenings on this campus.
4. I am trying to construct a profile of the typical college student's eating habits. Will you help?

FINDING ORGANIZATIONS TO CONTACT

If you live in a city, you have many places to visit where you will find people with special interests, but even small towns have organizations that exist to inform the public. Students researching some aspect of business may want to visit the chamber of commerce. Those studying a foreign country may want to contact a consulate, cultural organization, language school, airline, or even a restaurant connected with or run by people from that country. For almost any topic that you research, someone in your community probably would like to talk about it. If you are exploring the role of unions in a factory town, consider calling the local chapter of the AFL-CIO. If you are studying some aspect of early childhood development, you may be able to visit a Montessori school. For students of medical topics, there are public service organizations—Alcoholics Anonymous, the American Diabetes Association, the American Heart Association, an AIDS information service—that provide information to the public. Other organizations, such as mental health associations or councils that deal with drug abuse or children's issues, exist primarily to educate the public. In many communities public service agencies can help you identify specific organizations that may be helpful. If you are looking for a nursing home to visit, contact the local community council on aging. The yellow pages of the telephone book list a variety of such organizations under "Social Services." In some communities, the United Way has an information and referral service that directs people with specific questions to appropriate organizations.

REACHING THE RIGHT PEOPLE

Identifying appropriate people to question requires more thought for some topics than for others. If you are researching an event that has occurred in the last fifty years, you may want to talk to people who remember the event; but to choose the right ones, you will want to consider how old they were at the time of the event. For example, a man who was in college when the Depression hit will remember it much differently than will someone who was a child at the time. People who were in their teens in the 1960s will respond differently to questions about hippies or the antiwar movement than will people who were in their late thirties. A woman who was sixteen when the Beatles first came to America will probably remember them more vividly than someone who was ten years older.

Age is only one consideration in determining a person's ability to answer a question. A person of appropriate age with little interest in public events might talk about Martin Luther King, Jr., but probably would not remember Angela Davis. A person who actually fought in the Vietnam War probably will not be a good source for information about the antiwar movement; some people who survived Nazi concentration camps might feel reluctant to discuss the Holocaust, while others may want to share their experiences.

It is important to try to find out how people have learned what they know. Are they amateurs or professionals? Do they have a vested interest in a subject? Do they have personal experience or second-hand knowledge? While you might reject a rancher as a reliable source of information about the health risks of eating beef, you might seek out such a person for information about cattle breeding.

CHOOSING AN INTERVIEW METHOD

Once you have identified the people who are willing to talk to you, you still have to decide what approach to take. Should you ask them to fill out a questionnaire, to answer a series of prepared questions, or to answer questions as they come up in conversation? Sometimes a written questionnaire can help you to identify what a person is likely to know or be willing to talk about, but generally questionnaires have a limited use, and it is usually best to follow up a written questionnaire with a face-to-face conversation. Some people—particularly government officials and administrators who speak for an organization or bureau—will only answer prepared questions to which they have agreed in advance.

If you decide to use a questionnaire with a group of people, make sure the group is large enough to provide meaningful results. Also take care that the group you question is representative of the larger population to which you intend to apply your conclusions. For example, if you want to find out if people who live in middle-class neighborhoods are willing to recycle their newspapers, you would question a significant but manageable number of people currently living in a number of different such neighborhoods. Those you question would need to include people of different ages and both sexes. Five people would not be enough, five hundred would be unmanageable for most students, while fifty would probably help you reach significant conclusions.

Questionnaires that rely on short answers often lead to false or meaningless conclusions. In his study of *Rebel Without a Cause,* Michael Gold might ask a number of people who were teenagers when the movie first came out to fill out a questionnaire about their memories of the movie in which they would indicate whether or not they thought the movie influenced them. But people who said yes would not really tell Michael very much unless he knew what kind of influence they were referring to. Did they wear red nylon jackets? rebel against their parents? engage in delinquent behavior? To find out, Michael would have to ask people to explain their answers.

WRITING LETTERS

There will be times when you will want to ask questions by writing a letter. Many important people—government officials, politicians, writers, and even entertainers—employ people to help them handle their mail. While such people are not likely to grant you an interview, they may answer a letter. Remember that the mails are often slow; for that reason, you should write letters as soon as possible, always indicating the time restrictions of your research.

When you write an administrator of a charitable organization, an editor, a writer, or other individuals, you should always include a self-addressed stamped envelope. There are no fixed rules about when to include postage, but usually government offices have a budget for answering mail. In general, you should think about the convenience of the person from whom you are requesting information.

There may be times when you will write a letter to request an interview. In addition to your address, you may want to include your telephone number along with the times when you can be reached or a time when you will call the person. Often people who have received a letter informing them of the purpose of your research and suggesting a convenient time will be receptive to an interview.

Michael decides to write a letter to the president of a company that distributes *Rebel Without a Cause*. His questions are pointed and specific, and his letter is effective.

Box 5012
Brooklyn, NY 11210

February 21, 1992

Mr. Jack Lusk, President
Swank Motion Pictures, Inc.
201 S. Jefferson
St. Louis, MO 63103

Dear Mr. Lusk:

I am writing you at the suggestion of Beverly Cooper, who works in the media center at Brooklyn College. I am doing a research project about <u>Rebel Without a Cause</u>, directed by Nicholas Ray. I know your company distributes the film, and I would like to know how often the film is shown. Is it still popular? Do you send it all over the country?

Since the deadline for my paper is March 13, I would be very grateful if you could answer this letter in the next ten days. I have enclosed a stamped self-addressed envelope for your convenience.

Yours sincerely,

Michael Gold

Michael Gold

Within a week after sending the letter, Michael receives answers to his questions that he is able to incorporate into his paper (see pp. 237 and 239).

Lisa writes a letter to Professor Peter Vitousek, whose lecture first got her interested in the subject of rain forests.

333 Ocean Avenue
Santa Cruz, CA 95064
January 7, 1993

Professor Peter Vitousek
Department of Biological Sciences
Stanford University
Stanford, CA 94305

Dear Professor Vitousek:

I will be in the audience when you speak at my college on January 21, and I would very much appreciate an opportunity to ask you a few questions after the lecture. I am doing a research project about seed dispersal in tropical forests, and there is still much I do not understand about this very complex topic. I know that you are very busy, and I will not take very much of your time.

I will be wearing a black sweater and will sit near the front of the lecture hall.

Yours sincerely,

Lisa Lee

Lisa Lee

Lisa's request is also successful; Professor Vitousek answers her letter, suggesting that she introduce herself after the question-and-answer session.

Whenever you telephone someone to obtain information, remember to be considerate of that person's time and privacy. If you go through a secretary, identify yourself, explain briefly why you have called, and ask when it would be convenient for the person to talk with you.

There may be times when you will make phone calls to ask questions requiring short answers: Do you employ part-time help? How large is the book collection in your library? Do you offer training in computer programming? When is the next meeting of the National Organization for Women? How many organizations does the United Fund support in this community? In cases when you need a quick answer, it is best to ask the question, express your appreciation, and hang up.

CARLA MEDINA

When Carla is doing research about *The Color Purple,* her roommate, who is taking a course in African-American women's literature, suggests that she talk with the instructor for the course. Carla calls Professor Miller during her office hours and opens the conversation as follows: "My name is Carla Medina, and I'm writing a paper on *The Color Purple* for my English 110 class. I'd like to ask you a few questions about the novel. Is this a convenient time?" In just a few minutes on the telephone, Professor Miller answers Carla's questions, and though the answers do not appear in the final paper, this conversation helps Carla understand some of the ways that critics have approached and analyzed the novel.

MAKING APPOINTMENTS

Whenever you ask people for favors, it is best to do so at their convenience. That means making appointments. On a college campus, most faculty members who post office hours expect students to drop by or call during those hours. If you have more than a few brief questions, however, ask for an appointment. If you have trouble getting in touch with someone, leave a message with his or her secretary or a note on the office door. Simple courtesy and consideration of other people will lead you to the best way to arrange an interview. Most people in a college community will cooperate with an interview request if they have time and feel that they can be of help to you—and if your request is courteous and appropriate.

Conducting a Successful Interview

Before you begin an interview, whether on the telephone or in person, be prepared to record what you want to remember, either by writing it down or by tape recording it. At the very least, you should have a pencil and note pad with you to jot down brief notes. You do not want to borrow a pencil, of course, or keep someone waiting on the telephone while you look for a piece of paper. There are instructions at the end of this chapter for recording information you receive by talking to people. In addition, the different kinds of note cards described in chapter 6 can be adapted to oral research. There may be times when you want to quote a person directly, paraphrase a response, or summarize a whole interview.

ASKING THE FIRST QUESTION

A very specific question at the beginning of an interview can limit the whole process by locking the interviewer into a narrow focus. Usually when you are interviewing people, you want to ask initial questions that are general enough to allow them to reveal their attitudes and special interests. You also want to ask questions or make simple observations that invite a response.

Usually, however, if someone has agreed to talk to you about a topic, you should state in a straightforward way what you want to know. Explain your project, and then ask a general question to begin.

LEADING PEOPLE TO TALK

In most cases, you will learn more from people by leading them to talk than by rigidly sticking to a prepared list of questions. Keep in mind that people are individuals and that they have unique experiences as well as specific information they can give you. The following questions and responses are often productive:

What can you tell me about . . . ?
What do you remember about . . . ?
Can you explain that to me?
Tell me what you mean.
Can you help me understand?

This last response may be helpful if you encounter hostility or when people tell you that you cannot possibly understand what they mean. In

Tall Tales

Sometimes finding just the right opening is a matter of luck. That was the experience of a student in Wyoming who was investigating the legends of hardship that circulate among the rangers. He arranged to talk to an old man who was in his youth during one of the worst winters ever recorded. His opening question, "Could you tell me about how many cattle died in the winter of nineteen eleven to nineteen twelve?" led only to "Nope, no idea." The student was lucky enough to get a second chance, and the next time he came at the subject indirectly by observing, "Sure has been a hard winter." That was all that was needed to stimulate the old man's memory. "Bad? You don't know anything about bad. You should have been around in the the winter of nineteen twelve. . . ." An hour later the student had what he wanted: a first-hand account of the hardships of that year, including a tall tale or two.

It may be necessary for you to get into relationship with nonexperts, particularly people who are not accustomed to being interviewed. If you listen carefully to how people respond to your initial questions, you will learn to be an effective interviewer.

the long run, one way to ask questions will work for you, and others may seem strange. You want to find a way to say "talk to me" to the person you want to learn from, and you want to say it in a way that is natural to you and appropriate to the situation. Usually, if you can lead people to talk about a subject that interests them, you will be able to get them to tell you what you want to know.

DEVELOPING PATIENCE

Hearing what people have to say, rather than what we want to hear them say, is not always easy. Discovering the special interests of others and uncovering the significant experiences that have informed their lives call for care and sensitivity. Learning to recognize what people are willing or able to talk about takes practice, and you may have a few failures before you succeed. One of the most difficult tasks is to know when and how to respect people's privacy. If you are too cautious about asking personal questions, you may never learn anything from others; on the other hand, if you probe too deeply or too quickly into private matters, you may alienate some people. To find out if an issue is too personal for an individual, you may ask, "Do you object to talking about . . . ?" And indeed some people do. Here are some final suggestions that may help you in speaking with people:

Developing Patience: A Checklist

1. Listen carefully for details and ask the person to elaborate on those that seem important.
2. Avoid interrupting with your own suggestions.
3. Use requests like "tell me more about that" when you want the person to focus on a detail.
4. Try to ask questions in a neutral way that does not indicate what you think.
5. Assume the attitude of a willing student. Do not be afraid to show your ignorance.
6. Do not push when someone seems reluctant to answer a question. You can always come back to subjects later if the person becomes more open with you.
7. Keep an open mind.

Recording Oral Responses

There are three common ways of recording and storing information from oral sources. One, appropriate to brief interviews, is to listen carefully and then to write down what you want to remember immediately afterward. The second is to take notes during the interview; the most accurate is, of course, to make a tape recording. You will have to decide which method is most appropriate for each situation.

TAKING NOTES

For very short interviews and for times when people object to the use of a tape recorder, you may choose to jot down notes as you listen. Notes are particularly useful for proper names that you want to remember and for questions that you want to come back to. For more extensive note taking, you may plan in advance how to organize what you hear. One way is to divide a sheet of paper in half—one side for generalities, the other for details. If you think you will quote what someone says, make sure you have an accurate record. If possible, have the person read and verify what you want to quote.

An audio tape recording is easy to make. You simply ask permission to make the tape, set up the recorder in a convenient place, and turn it on at the beginning of an interview. The only disadvantage of using a recorder is that some people may not speak as frankly in the presence of a recorder as they would otherwise. Most people, however, are not troubled by a recorder and soon forget that it is there. When you want to make a recording, you should consider the following:

Recording: A Checklist

1. It is best to ask permission for the taping in a positive way. You might simply say, "I would like to record our conversation. Is that all right with you?" When asked this way, most people will agree.
2. Plan ahead: Make sure that you have enough tape and either an extension cord to assure easy access to an electrical outlet or a battery-powered recorder.
3. Label your tapes carefully.

A video recorder is much more difficult to use, and many people are considerably inhibited when they are being videotaped. If you have access to a video recorder, however, there may be times when you will want to use it. For example, your media department may provide videotaping services of lectures by visiting speakers, including the question-and-answer session afterward. It is a good idea to get written permission from a lecturer before making a recording.

TRANSCRIBING A RECORDING

If you decide to write out a recorded interview, you may be surprised at how long it will take. If your side of an interview has consisted of short questions and responses, an hour of tape may turn out to be as many as twenty typewritten pages. Often when we talk, we repeat ourselves, sometimes three or four times, so you may want to listen to the tape once, and then go back to select what you want to copy down.

A Sample Interview

Lisa is well prepared for her interview with Professor Vitousek. During her preliminary reading about tropical rain forests, she keeps a list of questions about topics she does not understand. From these questions—a long list—she carefully chooses fewer than twenty that are relevant to the subject of seed dispersal and animals. Before the interview, she makes a list using a word processor, beginning with general questions and progressing to more specific ones. When she prints the list, Lisa leaves space between the questions to jot down notes, and with the questions secured to a clipboard, she goes up to Professor Vitousek after his lecture, introduces herself, and begins the interview. Immediately afterward, she goes back to her word processor and reconstructs Professor Vitousek's answers. The following is Lisa's reconstructed version of the interview:

LISA LEE: I have done some general reading about tropical nature, but for the last two weeks, I have focused on the interrelation of animals and plants in Central and South American forests near the equator. I'd like to ask you some questions, but first, please tell me how much time you have.

PROFESSOR PETER VITOUSEK: Let's see how much we can accomplish in twenty minutes.

LEE: I understand that many tropical plants could not survive without the help of animals. I'd like to know which animals are most essential to the propagation of seeds.

VITOUSEK: You need to understand that animals serve plants in three important ways: They pollinate plants so that they can produce seeds, they transport seeds away from the parent tree, and they change seeds in ways that allow them to germinate. As for dispersing seeds, some animals are more important than others. In general, birds are the most effective, mammals next, and then bats.

LEE: I have just read *Tropical Nature* by Adrian Forsyth and Ken Miyata. I learned about strategies that plants use to attract pollinators. For example, some attract nocturnal animals by producing large white flowers. Do trees employ similar strategies for the dispersal of seeds?

VITOUSEK: Yes. Bird-dispersed plants might produce small red fruit with seeds encased in fruit pulp. Birds swallow the fruit whole, their stomachs remove the fruit, and the seeds are eventually defecated. Trees that attract large mammals produce large fruit that falls to the ground, where large animals can find it.

LEE: Do particular trees have strategies to attract particular animals?

VITOUSEK: As much as you can say that a plant can have a strategy, yes. In attracting pollinators, the size and depth of flowers are factors. Darwin argued, based on the depth of a flower in Madagascar, that there must exist a moth with a tongue more than a foot long that pollinates it, which few believed until that moth was found.

LEE: Clearly trees do not have brains, but sometimes they act as if they do. I've learned that some will ripen when certain dispersers are abundant. How do they ''know'' that the animals are present?

VITOUSEK: They probably ''know'' only if the animals are consistently present at a particular time of year. It's really a matter of evolution by natural selection. Those trees in the population that fruit when particular animals are abundant have more offspring and ultimately win out over trees that fruit at other times.

LEE: I have been reading about treefall gaps. Could you explain exactly what scientists mean when they refer to gaps and tell me why gaps are important?

VITOUSEK: Gaps form when a tree that is up in the canopy of the forest falls, often knocking down other trees in the process. That allows sunlight to penetrate to the normally shady soil surface, which in turn allows rapid plant growth.

LEE: I think that it is important for some seeds of large trees to end up in treefall gaps. Do trees have a way of attracting animals that are likely to visit the site of a treefall?

VITOUSEK: That question is harder to answer. Many animals frequent treefalls, but I don't know any specific examples of large trees that grow away from gaps and produce fruit that is selected by gap-dwelling animals in particular.

LEE: Other than carrying seeds from one place to another, how do animals facilitate the germination of seeds?

VITOUSEK: Mainly by removing the fruit pulp from the seed and by scarifying the seed, either mechanically as they chew, or chemically through the action of stomach acid on the seed coating.

LEE: Tell me a little more about scarification. Is it always necessary?

VITOUSEK: To scarify simply means to break down the seed coat partially. This is required for germination by seeds of a few species and it hastens germination in many more. However, there are many species for which it doesn't matter at all.

LEE: Help me understand something about the digestive process. I've learned that some vegetarian animals (the red howler monkeys, for example) require more time for seeds to pass through the digestive system than for omnivores. Do we know how this lengthy digestive process affects seeds?

VITOUSEK: I don't really know anything about that.

LEE: How much is actually known about how the digestive process of particular animals affects the viability of seeds?

VITOUSEK: There is still much we do not know about this. Relatively few specific pairs have been studied. We know about a few pairs, such as the jicaro tree and the horse; seeds of this tree were originally eaten by now-extinct animals that lived in Central America more than ten thousand years ago, but they are now eaten by horses. We know that these seeds are still viable after passing through the digestive system of the horse. We also know that some of these seeds are further dispersed by the spiney pocket mouse that takes them from the horse dung. Many are destroyed when the mouse eats them, but a few survive. You may want to read the articles published by D. H. Janzen about this.

LEE: I wonder about birds that regurgitate seeds. Is the seed made more or less viable by that process?

VITOUSEK: I don't really know about this either. We could extrapolate from other studies and guess that it is likely that a seed would be affected by stomach acid in ways that in some cases make the seed more viable.

LEE: I am also interested in what happens to seeds that are neither defecated nor regurgitated, but hoarded. I know that agoutis hoard seeds. What chance do these seeds have of germinating and growing to sizable trees?

VITOUSEK: Animals hoard seeds because they plan to eat them later, but hoarded seeds are not always eaten. Agoutis might forget where seeds are hoarded, or they might have the misfortune of being eaten themselves, by an ocelot, for example.

LEE: Are animals that are strictly carnivorous ever involved indirectly in dispersing seeds? Do they, for example, kill and eat other animals that have seeds in their guts, and then later defecate viable seeds?

VITOUSEK: I don't know. That's an interesting question. Perhaps someone will find out by examinating the feces of jaguars, for example.

LEE: What are the greatest threats to the future of effective seed dispersal?

VITOUSEK: Extinction of animals and loss of forest that seeds could disperse to. There have been some very good studies done in Mexico that found how the forest changes when particular mammals and birds are largely destroyed by hunting. In many areas the guan, a large bird, has been hunted to the point that it no longer disperses large-seeded trees effectively. We don't yet know how this will affect populations of these trees, but the effect is not likely to be good.

LEE: What effect would widespread loss of animal life have on a forest that is otherwise unchanged?

VITOUSEK: Specific plant species would be unable to disperse and would ultimately be lost, and others would become more abundant due to decreased grazing by animals.

LEE: The impression I have from my reading is that scientists know very little about this complex subject. Is that true?

VITOUSEK: That's a little strong, but only a little. We would like to learn a lot more about particular trees and animals. We need more examples and detail. With more specific examples of how animals interact with plants, we hope to generalize more effectively.

LEE: What are the most urgent questions?

VITOUSEK: What will be the effect of losing animals on the way the whole forest functions? Can we find ways to keep animals in the forest in the face of rapidly growing human populations?

LEE: Our time is up. Professor Vitousek, this has been very helpful. Thank you very much.

VITOUSEK: It was my pleasure to help you. This is a very important subject you are studying. Don't stop here.

Activities

A. Explore the resources of your community by looking through the yellow pages of the telephone book. Consult the following headings and make a list of places you would like to visit:
    Art galleries
    Athletic organizations
    Bookstores
    Libraries
    Political organizations
    Restaurants
    Special schools for children
    Social service organizations
    Theaters
    Colleges and universities

B. Talking to the appropriate people in your community would help you learn about each of the following topics. Choose one or more of these to investigate by making contacts and asking questions.
    1. Shelters and soup kitchens for the homeless
    2. Drug rehabilitation programs
    3. Birth control clinics
    4. AIDS testing and prevention services
    5. Waste disposal
    6. Recycling facilities
    7. Animal shelters
    8. Dog trainers
    9. Abortion clinics
    10. Anti-abortion organizations
    11. Handicap access in buildings open to the public
    12. Public transportation for the handicapped
    13. Scholarships for students with special needs
    14. Scholarships for minority students
    15. Language-training programs for recent immigrants
    16. Services for immigrants from the former Soviet Union
    17. Support for starting a small business
    18. Procedures for getting a business license
    19. Medical care for the uninsured
    20. Medical insurance for students

C. Choose one subject you would like to know more about, and make a list of questions to use for an interview. Conduct an interview, writing up the results from your notes or tape recording.

Project Activities

A. Think of someone who would be able to give you information about your topic that you cannot find in other sources. Write a letter to that person in which you explain the purpose of your research project and request information.

B. Think of some aspect of your topic that you might learn about through an interview and make a list of the questions that you would like to have answered. Then think of a person who could help you; try to arrange an interview.

RECORDING
INFORMATION

6

The early stages of research include three kinds of activities: **choosing and narrowing a topic, collecting and studying sources**, and **taking notes**. To explain how to go about accomplishing these tasks, it is helpful to present them as steps that follow one after another. But in reality these steps overlap. You may find when you are making notes that you need more sources; and as you evaluate your notes, you may discover that though you have narrowed your topic, you must focus it even more. You will be a more successful researcher if you allot sufficient time, after you have collected sources, to alternately skim and read material, take and classify notes, go back to your sources, and, when necessary, gather new material.

Taking Notes

Taking notes is an essential part of learning, studying, and researching; but it is not always easy to know when to take notes or how much to record. The way you take notes is to some extent a personal choice and depends on your study habits and how you learn. For example, some students are able to listen more attentively to a lecture if they take notes throughout, writing down most of what the speaker says; others prefer to jot down a few key words and phrases that they later use to reconstruct or summarize a lecture. In some cases, you may want to take down only what you do not know; in others, you may want a record of whatever a particular person says. The same is true for reading. Some students prefer to record main ideas as they read, others to make a few jottings and to summarize the whole at the end. At times, you may simply want to jot down only the facts that you do not already know about a specific topic. Taking notes for a research project can help you learn about a topic as well as provide a record of the facts and ideas to be used in a final report of that research.

USING A COMPUTER FOR TAKING NOTES

Before you decide whether to take notes directly onto a computer disk, consider whether doing so will save you time. If the only access you have to a computer is in a writing lab or computer room that is often crowded, then you would probably do better to make notes on paper or cards. If you have easy access to a computer where you live but cannot carry it with you to the library, then you may want to use it for taking notes from materials that you own or have borrowed. On the other hand, if you have a portable computer that you can easily carry with you about the library, then you may decide to use it for all your note taking.

If you think it is appropriate to take all or some of your notes into a computer file, make sure that you have a word-processing program that will allow you to move material easily from one file to another—from a note file, for example, to a draft of your paper. Since some word-processing programs have special features to help you organize your notes, you will want to study the program you use and decide how you should take your notes so that they can be easily organized and transferred into the draft of your paper.

Particularly useful are programs with a split-screen feature that allows you to divide your screen into two or more parts. Using the split-screen mode, you can call up your draft on one part of the screen and notes on another part. You can then edit both files and move material from one to the other. Other programs have a window feature that will allow you to have your main draft on the screen and to open up a window to display a note you want to consult and perhaps move into the draft.

If your program does not have a split-screen or window mode, it probably has a simple method for moving material from one file to another. In any case, know your program before you begin.

You may find that a printed copy of your notes is useful. Reading through a printout, you can edit, evaluate, and organize your notes before moving a particular note into the body of your paper.

TAKING NOTES ON PAPER OR CARDS

Before taking notes in your handwriting, you will do well to plan ahead and decide what materials to use and how to organize and store your notes. Some writers take notes directly into a notebook. If you make sure that you have only one note for each sheet, then you will later be able to tear out and sort the individual sheets as you organize your findings.

Many students prefer to take notes directly on index cards, which are easy to store, stack, and classify. Some students like to file such cards into categories, making it easy to see what is missing in their research findings.

CARLA MEDINA

When she was doing preliminary research for her paper on *The Color Purple,* Carla found that early critics focused on three main aspects of the novel: the voices of Celie and Nettie, its moral issues, and its upbeat vision. Carla took notes on these three categories, but when she sorted her cards she found she had considerably more material on the novel's voices than on the other two categories. Based on this evaluation of her sources, Carla decided to focus on the novel's voices.

Remember that you will have two kinds of cards for recording information. You will have a set of **source cards,** one for each source with all the information needed for documentation exactly as it will appear in your list of sources at the end of your paper. You will also have a set of **note cards**. Keep your source cards with you for easy reference, so that when you begin to take notes, you can identify the source of each with the first item of the source card—the author's name or the title when there is no author.

You may not take all of the kinds of notes described in this chapter, but you probably will find most of the suggestions helpful. There are, however, a few rules that should be followed by all student researchers:

Taking Notes: A Checklist

1. Document each note, clearly indicating the source on each card at the top. You will be taking too many notes to be able to remember where each came from.
2. Stop before making each note and ask yourself if it is really relevant to your topic.
3. Before you make a note from a passage, decide whether you need to quote it entirely, whether you can paraphrase it effectively, or whether it should be included in a summary.
4. Clarify with proper punctuation or abbreviations whether a note is a direct quotation, a paraphrase, an original observation, or a fact of general knowledge.
5. To save time and insure accuracy, you may want to photocopy passages of more than a few lines.
6. Pause from time to time and evaluate your progress: Sort your notes into categories, consult your bibliography cards to identify which sources you have not read, and make a list of what you still have to do.

Photocopying

Copying machines make it possible for you to have your own copies of articles or passages from books, and at times you will find it very convenient to have an exact copy of material that you expect to use. You can, however, waste time and money by copying material before you are sure that you will use it. After you have sufficiently narrowed your topic and identified most of your sources, you may want to consider what you would like to photocopy. Most libraries have machines that will copy directly from microform materials such as newspapers on microfilm. Since it can be particularly tedious to copy by hand from microform materials, you probably will want to have copies made for articles and passages that are crucial to your research. You may also find it helpful to photocopy magazine or journal articles that you would like to be able to study carefully or come back to when you are working outside the library. But before you do, take the time to evaluate each source. Read through an article carefully and decide if it's relevant to your topic; then ask yourself the following questions:

Photocopying: A Checklist

1. Is it important?
2. Will I be able to find it later?
3. Do I need all of it or just a small part?
4. Would it be better simply to take a few notes?
5. Would I learn more from taking notes?

Once you have made a copy, be especially careful to record *on the copy itself* all the details necessary to identify the source. For journal articles, note the author, title, date, page number, volume number, and issue number (if each issue is paginated separately).

Documenting Notes

To document your sources in a final paper is to cite—with a list of sources at the end of a paper, with parenthetical or numerical references within a paper, or with endnotes or footnotes—the books, articles, interviews, or other sources you have used to obtain information. It is important that you document each note as you make it by indicating both the **source** and the **page number**. Since your bibliography cards include complete documentary information—author, title, place of publication, date, etc.—you do not need to repeat it on your note cards. All you need is an identifying word or two and a page number. For many sources, you can simply use the last name of the author. When there are two works by the same author, you may choose to use both the author's last name and a key word from the title; if there is no author, a shortened version of the title is adequate.

Identify your own ideas as well as facts of general knowledge with an appropriate code. For example, if you use your initials for your own observations and GK for general knowledge, you will later know exactly what conclusions you have reached independently, what seems to be generally known, and what is the unique property of another author.

Other precautions will help you avoid confusion when you begin to write your paper. You will find it helpful to have only one reference per card. Each card should have a general subject heading as well as a reference to the source:

Use conventional quotation marks along with large marks in the margin of a card to avoid mistaking a direct quotation for a paraphrased passage.

In the beginning, you may be tempted to copy everything that interests you, but it is important that you select very carefully which material you want to record and what is the best form for each note. You will probably make cards for the following: **quotations** (p. 120), **paraphrases** (p. 121), **interpretations** (p. 127), **summaries** (p. 129), **lists** (p. 130), **statistics** (p. 130), **original ideas and conclusions** (p. 132), and **facts of general knowledge** (p. 133). In the early stages of research, you are more likely to quote directly; as you learn more about your subject, you will know how to assimilate and paraphrase material; and toward the end, you will probably interpret your sources and reach some conclusions on your own.

To quote is to reproduce exactly someone else's words. Always put quotation marks around quoted matter, including short phrases and key words. In addition, large quotation marks in the margin of a quotation card serve as a double precaution against accidental plagiarism—mistaking someone else's ideas, information, or manner of expression for your own thoughts or conclusions.

Personal   Roosevelt, E.

                                               My Story

                                               p. 308

"In all our contacts it is probably the sense of being really needed and wanted which gives us the greatest satisfaction and creates the most lasting bond."

It is very easy to misquote—to leave out a word or phrase or to write the wrong word—when you are copying a passage. Double-check each quotation after you have finished transcribing it. For particularly long passages, you may want to have photocopies on hand to verify the quotations as you prepare the final draft.

In a research paper, it is best to use only a few quotations, selecting those that are expressed in a highly imaginative way, that are particularly characteristic of the person you are quoting, or that for any other reason you want to preserve in the original. No one, for example, would want to paraphrase John Kennedy's famous words in his inaugural address: "And so, my fellow Americans, ask not what your country can do for you; ask what you can do for your country." No paraphrase could be so concise and memorable. Another example of words that should not be changed is this moving appeal in *You Learn by Living,* by Eleanor Roosevelt: "You gain strength, courage and confidence by every experience in which you really stop to look fear in the face. . . . You must do the thing you think you cannot do.''

A few direct quotations, carefully placed, can contribute authority to your paper and can make it more lively and interesting. You should certainly quote striking and memorable statements such as the two examples mentioned above. In other cases, however, when you are considering using a direct quotation, ask yourself what purpose the quotation will serve and whether it would be better to express the idea in your own words.

Some writers make the mistake of stringing together a series of quotations that they have not fully understood. If you find that most of your notes are direct quotations, you need to stop and decide how you are likely to use them. Try putting some of the quotations that you think you will use into your own words, explaining what they mean and what conclusions they have helped you reach. Before you write your first draft, sort your note cards and decide which direct quotations should be kept in their original form and which should be incorporated into your own prose. Make sure that you know exactly what each quotation means and how and why you are using it.

Paraphrasing

To paraphrase is to reproduce the exact sense of a written passage or oral statement in your own words—to convey accurately the ideas, facts, or attitudes of someone else in words that are natural to you. A paraphrase may be clearer or more concise than an original passage or statement. Paraphrasing is a necessary skill for reporting research findings, but it is more than that. You paraphrase in your own mind as soon as you finish reading a passage and try to review what you have read; and you paraphrase when you tell someone about an article you have read or a lecture you have heard or when you answer a question on a history test based on information your instructor has given you in class. In each case, you are restating someone else's ideas. The skill with which you paraphrase is a measure of what you know. If you read a paragraph and are easily able to put the ideas in your own words, then you have a good understanding of what you have read.

In the course of a research project, you will often want to restate in your own words the exact meaning of a passage. Paraphrasing helps to clarify ideas as well as identify the material you expect to use in your final research report. And by recording facts and ideas in your own words, you develop your own style: a form of expression that is natural to you.

In the beginning, you may find it difficult to paraphrase, but the more you know about a subject, the easier it is to assimilate and restate what you read. At first, you may have trouble putting unfamiliar words, names, and concepts in your own words. Rather than quoting long undigested passages, it is better simply to make a note indicating a passage you think you will want to paraphrase when you know more. Note the following example:

Lash, E + F 280-82

Discussion of Eleanor's involvement with the Women's Trade Union League.

Come back to this later.

You also may want to make a photocopy of material that seems important, but which you are not ready to paraphrase.

Once you are familiar with a subject, you will probably be able to write effective paraphrases of significant passages, but even then it is not always easy to know when to take the time to record a passage in your own words and when to make yourself a note about where certain information can be found. To avoid wasting time and effort trying to assimilate and paraphrase material that you will never use, when you come to a passage in your reading that seems important, ask yourself if it is really relevant to your topic. If so, you may want to take the time to record it clearly and fully in your own words while remaining absolutely faithful to the meaning of the original.

You may want to introduce a paraphrase with an identifying transition:

```
Eleanor Roosevelt believed that . . .
In his study of children, Robert Coles found that . . .
According to Lash, . . .
John Mack argues that . . .
```

Below are excerpts from books followed by accurate paraphrases. Note how each paraphrase avoids using even a phrase from the original source.

Original Passage from Robert Coles's
The Moral Life of Children

Children know and favor the concrete. An abstract moral issue is hard for them to comprehend as thoroughly real and pressing. Thus it was that Sue did her best to make some concreteness for herself, for me—that unforgettable painting.

Paraphrased Note

moral issues   Coles 275

According to Coles, children prefer to think in concrete images since moral abstractions seem unreal and irrelevant to them. Sue's memorable painting was the result of her effort to make her feelings concrete for him and for herself.

Original Passage from Joseph Lash's
Eleanor and Franklin

Among the organizations she turned to in the hope of being able to help improve the world was the League of Women Voters, the successor to the National Woman Suffrage Association. Its leaders had emerged from the long suffrage struggle as militant advocates of better working conditions for women, children's rights, reform of the political process, and peace.

> organizations   Look 353
>
> The League of Women Voters, one of the
> organizations Eleanor Roosevelt joined, evolved
> from the National Woman Suffrage Association.
> Its leaders, who had all been engaged in
> the fight for woman's suffrage, took on
> new causes: improved conditions for women
> in the workplace, political reform, rights
> of children, and peace.

ORIGINAL PASSAGE FROM ALICE WALKER'S
In Search of Our Mothers' Gardens

During the sixties, political assassinations, the Civil Rights Movement, and the Vietnam War turned many people away from concern about atomic weapons and toward problems they felt they could do something about.

PARAPHRASED NOTE

> nuclear threat   Walker 343
>
> Alice Walker argues that in the sixties,
> political upheavals, social injustice, and the
> war in Vietnam — problems they felt they
> could do something about — absorbed the
> attention of many people, distracting them
> from the problems posed by nuclear weapons.

Consider how this note card combines paraphrase with a quotation:

ORIGINAL PASSAGE FROM DOUGLAS T. MILLER
AND MARION NOWAK'S *The Fifties:*

Three classic youth-problem films of the fifties were released in 1954–55: *The Wild One* with Brando's moving portrayal of the tough but sensitive motorcycle gang leader; *Rebel Without a Cause,* the James Dean vehicle that took delinquency films out of the slums and into the suburbs, and *Blackboard Jungle,* which unequivocally associated delinquency with rock music. Although these films vaguely hint at larger social ills, they fail to explore them, and imply . . . that serious rebelliousness has no real cause but can be attributed to individuals.

PARAPHRASED NOTE

> *Rebel*   Douglas and Nowak 333
>
> Douglas and Nowak contend that like
> *The Wild One* and *Blackboard Jungle,* two
> other classic films of the mid-fifties, *Rebel
> without a Cause* only hints at real social
> problems, but unlike the others, it moved
> delinquency from the "slums and into the
> suburbs."

Effective paraphrasing requires concentration and practice. You may have to write more than one draft to capture the substance of a passage entirely in your own words. At some point, however, you may be surprised to discover that you can write a paraphrase that is actually clearer than the original.

MICHAEL GOLD

In his research on *Rebel Without a Cause,* Michael finds he has to understand a passage fully in order to put it in his own words. His own paraphrases sometimes make more sense to him than the original. In the following example, he decides that he has also improved on the source:

ORIGINAL PASSAGE

Dean's appeal   Astrachan 17

"But in each of the Dean roles, the distinguishing elements are the absence of his knowing who he is, and what is right and wrong. Dean is always mixed-up and it is this that has made him so susceptible to teenage adulation."

MICHAEL'S VERSION

Dean's appeal   Astrachan 17

James Dean always played a character who is unsure about his own identity and about moral issues. Teenagers are particularly attracted to this young man's portrayal of doubt and confusion.

Sometimes you may want to quote a word, phrase, or clause within a paraphrase as in the following note:

Public Life

Roosevelt, E.
My Story
297

Although she was slow to become a public person, and even slower to take up the cause of women's rights, she eventually referred to herself as an "ardent citizen and feminist."

Paraphrasing often overlaps other forms of note taking, such as interpreting—making sense out of a statement or passage—and summarizing—reducing a longer work to its main points. The more you know about a topic, the more you will be able to interpret what you read.

Interpreting

Interpretation begins as soon as you start to say what something means, to draw conclusions from facts, to explain why certain information is significant. For example, in Tamara Hareven's *Eleanor Roosevelt: An American Conscience,* Roosevelt is quoted as follows: "I don't have any more energy than anyone else. But I never waste any of it on regrets." This statement could be interpreted to mean that Roosevelt was driven to work and to do what she conceived of as her duty. It also might be used as evidence of her determination always to look forward to possible accomplishments rather than backward to failures.

Our appreciation of a book, a film, a political statement, or a psychological theory usually is increased if we are aware of its context. Michael Gold's understanding of *Rebel* grows as he learns something about the

The way we interpret a person's words often depends on what else we know about that person and about the time in which the statement was made. The following example is from the first chapter of Robert Lindner's *Rebel Without a Cause . . . The Hypnoanalysis of a Criminal Psychopath*. Michael first copies it word for word:

> History has assigned to this country and her allies the task of cleansing civilization of the predatory creature whose typical history is presented in this volume. Psychological science has provided us with an instrument to study him closely and at first hand; to examine him thoroughly as we would a virulent bacillus; to dissect him and obtain his measure; perhaps even—assisted by those great social forces which are beginning to clear the slime and muck of underprivilege and economic expediency—to make of him a good citizen in a new world.

Later, Michael interprets this quotation in the following note:

> Robert Lindner's <u>Rebel Without a Cause</u> was published in 1944, a year when the whole world was all too aware of the evil—in the form of Adolf Hitler—that the psychopathic mind could create. Lindner was an idealist; he thought of his work as a contribution to the fight against fascism, and he hoped that his study would help change the social conditions that create the psychopathic personality in the first place. He wanted to change society by changing its individual victim: "to make of him a good citizen in a new world. . . ."

To reach this interpretation of the original passage, Michael notes the copyright date, 1944, and infers that the book was written during World War II. He then associates "the predatory creature" with Hitler and fascism and concludes from the last sentence that Lindner was a social reformer. It is always a good idea to know the date of your sources, and sometimes that knowledge will be essential to interpretation.

time in which it was made; and by considering the historical context of the controversies about *Huckleberry Finn,* both at the time it was published and in the last few decades, Carla Medina can begin to understand what the fuss is all about.

Summarizing

Summarizing, like paraphrasing, is a process of putting someone else's material in your own words. Rather than the careful rewriting of an original passage, a summary may be jottings, sentence fragments, or a loose outline of the main ideas of anything from a short passage to an entire book. After reading a dense paragraph, the introduction or conclusion to a book, an essay, or a magazine or newspaper article, you may want to condense what you have read by writing down the main points.

The following note is a summary of a newspaper article that reported the main points of a speech that Eleanor Roosevelt gave in 1929:

Women   "Mrs. Roosevelt
                                            Prepares,"
                                               2

Eleanor Roosevelt advised women who want to enter politics that they must work up through the ranks, rigorously educate themselves, and be willing to work a little harder than men. Women should seek office only because they are competent to do the job, not because they are women.

The ability to summarize—to restate concisely the main facts, ideas, or episodes of a longer work—is a useful skill for all kinds of learning, and it is *essential* for writing research papers. Whenever you summarize, you must choose what is essential and what can be omitted. In most cases, you will delete illustrations, examples, and analogies; and you will discard passages intended to attract the reader's attention, to entertain, or to persuade. As with all note taking, you should stop and ask yourself if a passage is relevant to your topic before you take the time to summarize. To summarize, you may choose one of the following forms:

A list of words or numbers
A series of phrases or clauses
Several loosely connected sentences
An informal paragraph
A polished paragraph
A series of paragraphs

Summaries may require several note cards. To avoid confusion, number each card directly above the source in the upper right corner.

Collecting Data: Lists and Statistics

Making a list is a way of recording information in an abbreviated form. There will be times when you will want to make a list from a single source—the main points of a book or, from an encyclopedia article, the titles and dates of publication of a novelist's major works. But not all lists will come from a single source. The information in the note below was gathered from two sources:

Although you have been advised to put only one note on a card, there may be times when you want to consolidate facts from different sources on a single card (as in the previous note), indicating the sources in order in the upper right corner or in parentheses after each item. Students doing many kinds of research jot down lists: of organizations Eleanor Roosevelt belonged to and positions she held; of important films of the 1950s; of countries with nuclear weapons; of animals that disperse seeds; of controversial novels.

You may want to use a separate card for noting numerical data:

Bachman study   Beardsley and Mack
                                                    83

Male high school seniors who
say they often worry about the nuclear
threat :

1976 : 7.2%
1982 : 31.2%

You have been advised to beware of the misuse of statistics; used properly, however, statistics can help you make sense of what you learn. One of the most common kinds of statistical studies is the sampling of a group of people to determine their behavior, opinions, or income. The results of such studies are usually expressed in percentages. Assuming that they are based on reliable sampling, statistics are significant to certain studies and essential to others. The list below gives examples of research topics and statistical information that might be significant to them:

1. The Future of the Women's Movement: the percentage of women who actively support the movement
2. The Economics of the Popular Recording Industry: the percentage of recordings that are pirated
3. Interpreting the Gross National Product: the percentage that is related to true productivity and that which is generated by illness and catastrophe

4. The Popularity of Movies about Teenagers: the percentage of moviegoers who are under twenty-one
5. The Consequences of Deforestation: the percentage of the world's tropical forests that are destroyed each year

Recording Original Observations and Conclusions

Throughout the process of research, you will want to make cards on which you record your own thoughts and observations. The note below, for example, is an effort to explain contradictory statements in different sources. The student, Linda Orton, has used her own initials to indicate that the ideas are hers:

> E. Roosevelt's motives   L.O. 10/9/91
>
> The articles in Ency. Americana and Brittanica state that ER entered public life to help FDR. Both she and Lash say that she was urged to work to keep the Roosevelt name before the public while FDR recuperated. However, as a public person ER pursued her own interests and not necessarily those of her husband. Perhaps she used her husband's illness as an excuse or defense for doing what she really _wanted_ to do anyway.

If you date each card right under or beside your own initials, you will have a record of the evolution of your own thoughts about your topic. Some students find that their research leads them to conclusions different from what they had originally expected; others discover evidence that supports their original ideas about a topic. For example, Michael Gold expected to find that the success of *Rebel Without a Cause* was due to the personal charisma of James Dean and the attraction that he held for teenagers who grew up in the conservative 1950s. But in fact he discovers that the success of the film was much more complicated and depended on the contributions of a number of people. On the other hand, Lisa Lee expected to find that animals are important to the welfare of plants, and she finds that some animals are not only important, but essential to the survival of certain plant species.

Stating General Knowledge

You do not need to cite a source for notes recording information that most people already know or information that is found in a number of books and articles on a subject. That Eleanor Roosevelt was the wife of Franklin Roosevelt, the niece of Theodore Roosevelt, and the mother of five children are all facts of general knowledge. The following note gives another piece of general knowledge:

GK

Eleanor Roosevelt was First Lady for twelve years, from 1933 until 1945.

From time to time, you will make cards to remind you of facts that you have absorbed from a number of sources, which you assume that anyone with a basic understanding of your topic would know and which can readily be found in general reference books. Many students have difficulty deciding what is general knowledge and what must be documented with the appropriate source. Before making a note of general knowledge, ask yourself the following questions: *Is this information available in a variety of sources? Would most people familiar with the topic know this information?*

Knowing When to Document

The list below should help you distinguish between statements of general knowledge and paraphrased information that must be documented. The first item under each number is a statement of general knowledge; the second, a paraphrase with the source indicated in parentheses; and the third, a full citation for the source.

1. *General knowledge:* Rachel Carson wrote *Silent Spring.*
   Paraphrase: Forty states passed legislation restricting the use of pesticides within two years of the publication of Rachel Carson's *Silent Spring* in 1962 (Hodgson 402).
   Citation: Hodgson, Godfrey. *America in Our Time.* 1976; New York: Vintage, 1978.
2. *General knowledge:* The Amazonian rain forests are being destroyed at an alarming rate.
   Paraphrase: The part of the Brazilian Amazonia known as Acre, the remote region where Chico Mendez lived and was assassinated, has undergone severe destruction in the last decade (Maxwell 39).
   Citation: Maxwell, Kenneth. "The Mystery of Chico Mendes." *The New York Review of Books* 28 Mar. 1991: 39–48.
3. *General knowledge:* Betty Friedan, author of *The Feminine Mystique* and *The Second Stage,* is associated with the beginning of the women's movement.
   Paraphrase: Betty Friedan and other moderate feminists recommended working for change through the established political and legal channels (Hodgson 411).
   Citation: See 1 (*citation*).
4. *General knowledge:* Many people in the late sixties questioned the wisdom of American involvement in Vietnam.
   Paraphrase: Among the many young men who attempted to avoid the draft during the Vietnam War were some 172,000 conscientious objectors, most of whom worked for two years in an alternative public service (Baskir 41).
   Citation: Baskir, Lawrence M., and William A. Strauss. *Chance and Circumstance.* New York: Vintage, 1978.
5. *General knowledge:* Japan bombed Pearl Harbor on December 7, 1941.

Paraphrase: One of the consequences of the bombing of Pearl Harbor and the subsequent declaration of war by the United States was the detention of tens of thousands of Japanese Americans in relocation camps (Kelly 786).

Citation: Kelly, Alfred H., and Winfred H. Harbison. *The American Constitution.* 5th ed. New York: Norton, 1976.

6. *General knowledge:* High levels of serum cholesterol can contribute to heart disease.

Paraphrase: Cholesterol is carried through the blood by high-density lipoproteins (HDL), which appear to help remove excessive cholesterol from the body; low-density lipoproteins (LDL) and very-low-density lipoproteins (VLDL) keep cholesterol circulating in the blood (Brody 64).

Citation: Brody, Jane. *Jane Brody's Nutrition Book.* New York: Norton, 1981.

Avoiding Plagiarism

To plagiarize is to take the language, ideas, or conclusions of another person and to represent them as one's own. Plagiarizing, paraphrasing, and documenting need to be understood in relation to each other; most people never have to be concerned with plagiarism as long as they learn to paraphrase correctly, to distinguish general knowledge from information that must be documented, and to document with care.

Some students come to college confused about what plagiarism is. Perhaps in grammar school they dutifully copied an article from an encyclopedia, turned it in to the teacher as a report, and received an A. Even in high school, they may have written papers that included phrases, sentences, or even paragraphs that were copied from books or articles without using quotations marks and citing the sources. At the college level, this is absolutely unacceptable. You must always make perfectly clear which of the words and ideas that you are using were taken from someone else.

You should also avoid plagiarizing accidentally. Some students think that they are paraphrasing correctly when in fact they have retained the

Consider the following passage from Norman Myers's book about tropical rain forests, *The Primary Source,* a work that Lisa consults when she is doing background reading for her project:

> Even more to the point, I feel, as an individual—not as a scientist or a conservationist, but as a human being—that this is a splendid time to be alive, when, at long, glorious last, we can penetrate to the furthest reaches of tropical forests, not only their remote heartlands but also the zone that, paradoxically, has remained more concealed from us than have the depths of Amazonia or Borneo and that forms the forest canopy scores of meters above the ground: the last, great unexplored frontier of life on Earth.

This passage does not contain facts so much as the author's expression of his strong feelings of excitement about the upper level (canopy) of tropical forests. Lisa wants to use the phrase "the last, great unexplored frontier of life on Earth" for her final paragraph and so she correctly quotes it exactly and gives the author full credit (see p. 300).

The following use of the same passage, however, would be plagiarism. Imagine that a student, who is concluding a paper on rain forests, has read this passage and adapts it as follows:

```
Rain forests are truly amazing territory for those who want to
explore what may be the only unexplored frontier left on the
Earth.
```

Even though the passage is used in a new context with different sentence structure, the student has still plagiarized. The phrase "unexplored frontier," and the idea that rain forests or their canopies may be the last, belongs to Norman Myers and he must be given credit.

sentence structure of the original source or even a phrase or an unusual use of a word. At times, people plagiarize accidentally when they sincerely forget what was their own idea and what they learned from other people.

You will never plagiarize accidentally if you observe these rules:

Avoiding Plagiarism: A Checklist

1. Document all material from other sources, including direct quotations, paraphrases, summaries of facts, statistics, lists, charts, and illustrations.
2. Exempt from documentation only material of general knowledge and your own thoughts and conclusions.
3. Review your note cards and sources after you have finished your paper to make sure that you have not unconsciously confused someone else's ideas with your own.
4. Put a pair of large quotation marks on either side of a quotation note so that there will be no confusion in your mind about which notes are quotations.
5. In your final paper, carefully observe the conventions for quoting (enclose short quotations in quotation marks and set off longer ones) so that there will be no question about where a quotation begins and ends.
6. Paraphrase and summarize by completely casting information and ideas in your own words and style, inserting quotation marks within your paraphrase or summary whenever a unique word or phrase is retained from the original source.
7. Observe all the rules of the particular documentary style that you use.

Activities

A. Turn back to the *Academic American Encyclopedia* article on "jungle and rain forests" (pp. 36–38).
   1. Choose a paragraph from the article and paraphrase it.
   2. Reword part of the same paragraph, but retain the author's wording in a phrase or clause. Be sure to indicate this wording with quotation marks. Remember that whenever you use an author's words without giving credit, you are plagiarizing.
   3. Make a list of the main points of the article.
   4. Summarize the article in a single paragraph.

5. Note any statements in the article that are general knowledge. Remember that statements of general knowledge do not have to be documented in a research paper.
6. Note a phrase, clause, or sentence that you would quote in a research paper.

B. Read the short paper on Eleanor Roosevelt that begins on page 178. Using a light pencil, put a "q" beside each quotation, "gk" beside statements of general knowledge, and "c" by any original conclusions of the author. Indicate in the margin how many sources are used in each paragraph.

C. Study the five sample papers in chapters 11, 12, 13, and 14.
1. Note how each uses quotations. Which uses the most? Which the least?
2. Select a quotation from one of the papers and paraphrase it, trying to retain the sense of the original.
3. Write a brief summary—approximately one hundred fifty words—of Carla Medina's paper on *Huck Finn* (see p. 323).

Project Activities

A. Choose one of your notes that is a direct quotation.
1. Paraphrase it by objectively restating it in your own words and retaining the tone of the original, carefully avoiding any expression of your own opinion.
2. Using the same quotation, or selecting another, write a paragraph in which you combine paraphrase with interpretation.

B. After you have finished taking notes from all the sources that you have collected, stop, take stock, and evaluate your progress. The process of reading, taking notes, questioning people, and perhaps reading again may have led you to rethink your original intentions. Follow the steps on the next page to determine whether you need to redefine your topic:
1. Check each note card and make sure you have recorded all the information you need to identify the source in your paper.
2. Look over your note cards and make a list of the possible approaches to your topic.
3. Sort your cards to determine which aspect of your topic you have learned the most about.
4. Make a list of questions that you still need to answer.
5. List your next steps.

ORGANIZING MATERIAL

7

There are so many different ways to organize knowledge, and studying a topic always involves a struggle to make connections and to discover relationships. When you first try to order facts and ideas, you will probably discover for yourself what you actually know about a topic. You then have the task of trying to organize what you have found to make it clear to others. Working carefully in the preliminary stages of organization will help you to write a final paper that is clear and logical.

Sorting Note Cards

Ideally you have been assessing your progress all along, but when you have finished collecting materials, talking to people, reading, and taking notes, you will want to stop and systematically evaluate what you have done.

Sometimes students sort their notes only to discover that they have a miscellaneous collection of facts; if this happens to you, you should select the category that most interests you and return to your sources for more information or, if necessary, collect more sources. One student spent several days reading and taking notes on the subject of running. When he stopped to sort his note cards, he found that they fell into these categories:

Sprinting
Recreational jogging
Competitive running

The benefits of jogging
The Boston Marathon
Famous runners

After examining the categories, he discovered that he really had a little information on several different aspects of a large subject and that none of the categories related to each other in a meaningful way.

This student could have strung his notes together haphazardly, beginning with recreational jogging and ending for no particular reason with the Boston Marathon or famous runners. But the result would have been little more than a mishmash of facts. So, instead, he looked at his sorted

---

Getting It All Together: A Checklist

To begin organizing your thoughts, consider doing the following:

1. Clear out enough space—a table, desk, your bed, or even the floor—to spread out notes, computer printouts, books and photocopies of articles. Arrange them in categories.
2. Eliminate materials that are not relevant.
3. Consider making two categories: "yes" and "maybe."
4. Set aside the "maybe" stack and evaluate and further categorize the material you know you want to use.
5. Using your computer or a note pad, make a list of the main points you want to make about your topic.
6. Write an introductory paragraph in which you open the discussion of the main points and present a thesis you intend to explore.
7. Consider whether the sample papers are appropriate models for your topic. Will you write an argumentative paper like David Harris's paper on children's fears of nuclear catastrophe or Carla Medina's paper on *Huck Finn?* present your findings in a scientific format like that followed by Lisa Lee? analyze a literary text as Carla does in her paper on *The Color Purple?* or narrate a process using both topic categories and a rough chronological order as Michael Gold does in his paper about *Rebel Without a Cause?*
8. Go back through your own notes and sources, record the points you want to make, and experiment with different ways of organizing them.

Michael began his study of *Rebel Without a Cause* intending to learn about the success of the film and the contribution that James Dean made to it. When he categorizes his note cards, he discovers that in addition to material about Dean and the film's success, he has learned about the people who made the film—the director, the writers, the actors. He has learned about the James Dean cult; and he has also discovered that although many people associate the film with Dean, he was actually only one of many people who brought *Rebel* to fruition.

cards and chose the category that interested him the most: the benefits of jogging. He then went back to his sources and found additional information on that more limited topic. After discarding the irrelevant notes and taking new ones, he found that he could sort the notes he now had into four main categories: weight control, muscular development, psychological health, and cardiovascular fitness. Note the balanced outline (p. 150) that he eventually made.

ORGANIZING NOTES IN A COMPUTER FILE

How you go about using a computer to help you organize your material will depend on the particular word-processing program you use. For this reason, it is important that you study your program carefully to learn what it can do for you.

If you have used a word processor to take notes, jot down ideas, or make a plan for your paper, you may want to print out your files so that you can easily read them and decide what is useful and what you want to discard. If you have doubts about whether you will use certain notes, you may want to move them to a new file entitled "maybe." Delete only material that is *clearly irrelevant* to your topic as you have focused and refined it.

As you read through your hard copy, look for ideas and facts that belong together, creating categories as you go. If you create a code—give subheadings a letter (A, B, C) or underline different aspects of the topic with different colored highlighters—it will soon be clear which notes belong together, which subheadings are adequately covered, and which you need to find more information about. Also look for key phrases, particularly effective points, and details that will effectively reinforce what you want to say. You may at this point want to go back to the computer and move your notes around so that those that belong to the same category are grouped together in an order that makes sense.

If you are comfortable editing and organizing your notes directly on the computer, devise a way to mark sections that you want to delete and those you want to move to a "maybe" file. You may also create a method for marking notes that belong in the same category so that you can easily move them to the same part of the file. If you are using a program with split-screen or window feature, you can read your notes on one side of the screen while listing key points or ideas on the other side, marking items on the list with a letter or symbol that you insert in the text.

Testing Your Hypothesis

Most people begin a research project with some idea of what they will find. Michael Gold, for example, expected to find that the success of *Rebel Without a Cause* was due to the charisma of its leading actor, James Dean, but he discovers that many other factors contributed to the film's success. This discovery leads him to discard a single hypothesis, to raise a number of questions, and to keep an open mind.

LISA LEE

Lisa began her research on animals in the rain forest with the notion that the plant/animal relationship is one-sided. She thought that while trees are useful to animals, providing them with shelter, food, and a place of safety from predators, only a few animals assist plants, mainly by pollinating them. Lisa soon discovers that this assumption, or implied hypothesis, is inaccurate, and that many animals are essential to the survival of plants. She then develops a working hypothesis that the plants and animals are mutually interdependent.

Although Lisa takes notes from articles in the library, she also photocopies some articles. As soon as she has identified information relevant to her topic, she enters notes into a computer file.

Before you begin to outline your findings, you should pause and ask yourself whether you still have one or more working hypotheses or a preliminary thesis that you think your findings will demonstrate. If so, write it out, and then go back to your sorted notes and test it. If Michael Gold had written out his original hypothesis—that *Rebel's* success is due to its leading actor—then he would easily have seen that his research could not support that statement. It is a good idea to make a list of any preconceived ideas you have and to test them against your notes to make sure that you do not distort your findings in order to prove yourself right. Ask yourself the following questions:

Testing Your Hypothesis: A Checklist

1. What did I expect to find when I began research?
2. What did I actually find?
3. If these two are different, what led me to change my mind?
4. If they are the same, have I ignored any evidence that might suggest a different conclusion?

It is possible that your original expectations and your conclusions will be the same, but most researchers find that their original ideas are altered more than once. This of course does not always happen in the systematic way suggested by the list of questions above, since a single article or even a sentence in a text may change your way of thinking.

Developing a Controlling Idea or Thesis Statement

You will be able to control and shape your material more effectively if you can explain in a sentence or two exactly what your paper will be about. This statement of what you intend to demonstrate in your paper is the thesis, and everything in your paper should contribute to that goal.

THE THESIS STATEMENT

After you have sorted your note cards and decided that you have enough material to write a report, you may want to write out what you think will be your thesis statement, the controlling idea of your paper.

After he sorts notes and before making an outline, Michael writes:

> Rebel Without a Cause was created over a period of years,
> developing from the dedicated collaboration of many people who
> brought different points of view and experiences to the
> project, and it influenced the behavior and feelings of a large
> number of young people who were united by their infatuation
> with James Dean.

By keeping this statement in mind both when he outlines his material and when he starts writing his first draft, Michael is able to decide which notes are relevant and which, though they are interesting, should be set aside. Trying to stick to a controlling idea makes it easy for Michael to discard notes concerning Dean's irrational behavior and his similarity to Marlon Brando.

After he writes a first draft based on this controlling idea, Michael examines what he has written, revises it—bringing the information about the Dean cult to the beginning—and writes a new thesis sentence:

> Rebel Without a Cause was really the product of the
> imagination, the creative energy, and the plain hard work of a
> group of people--the director, writers, actors, and technical
> experts--who compose the community of a film.

This thesis allows Michael to use the information about the Dean cult in his introduction, to qualify it in the fifth paragraph, and to focus in the remainder of the paper on the various people who contributed to creation of the film. He is able to use the information about the film's interpreters in a final section leading up to the conclusion.

Not everyone is able to identify a controlling idea after sorting note cards. Some students need to write out an introductory paragraph before they can identify a single thesis or main idea that directs the progress of the finished product. Others discover a controlling idea only after they have begun writing.

Some students, like David Harris, cannot reduce their findings to a single sentence, and they have to settle for a summary paragraph. The process of trying to get down your first ideas may help you to discover an approach to your topic and a way of relating the different aspects of your study to each other. The first draft of an introductory paragraph may simply be a way to get started. After you have written it, you may be able to sketch out a preliminary outline. Later you may want to revise it and incorporate it into a more polished introduction.

EXPOSITORY OR PERSUASIVE THESIS

The controlling idea or thesis statement of a research paper may be expository or persuasive, or a combination of the two. An **expository** thesis simply states what the paper is about in a sentence that suggests that what follows will be interesting and informative. A **persuasive** thesis also states what the paper is about, but in a manner that shows that the author is taking a stand, making an argument, hoping to change the reader's beliefs or move the reader to action.

Linda Orton's thesis statement in her paper about Eleanor Roosevelt is expository:

Her many activities included work to improve the lot of
disadvantaged women and to help all women develop their potential.

This precise statement alerts the reader that the rest of the paper will provide information about Eleanor Roosevelt's work for women.

Not every paper includes a single-sentence thesis statement. Because Lisa Lee's paper follows a scientific format, her main points are summarized in the abstract at the beginning (see p. 290). She could combine these, however, into the following thesis statement:

Whether a seed will grow to a mature tree depends on features of its
parent, the treatment it receives from animals, and the availability
of the space and light necessary for growth.

David Harris's thesis statement is the first step in his attempt to persuade his readers to take a particular point of view:

Child psychiatrists, pediatricians, educators, and legislators are
becoming increasingly aware that the threat of a nuclear explosion
is affecting the psychological welfare of the world's children, and
many have concluded that they must do something and encourage others

to respond to the problem. Although there is much to learn about
how to deal with children's fears of a nuclear disaster, those
responsible for the welfare of children must act now to educate
themselves and to provide children with the information and
reassurance they need to grow up in the nuclear age.

This more complex statement of intent sets up the argument that will
follow as David brings forth the evidence to persuade his reader that there
is a problem and that action must be taken to solve it.

Michael Gold's thesis is a combination of persuasion and exposition:

Rebel was really the product of the imagination, the creative
energy, and the plain hard work of a group of people—the producer,
director, writers, actors, and technical experts—who compose the
community of a film.

In his paper Michael Gold puts together the story of all the people who
helped to create the film, and at the same time he argues against the idea
that James Dean himself was responsible for the film's success.

Many good research papers have both expository and persuasive elements, but there can be dangers in overemphasizing either mode. By
writing a purely expository paper, you may leave your reader thinking "So
what?" Some students work very hard researching a topic, but they fail to
present the material in a way that convinces readers of its importance.
Their papers are nothing more than a collection of facts.

One effective form of persuasion is the presentation of interesting facts
in such a way that readers are able to reach their own conclusions. Lisa Lee
presents her findings objectively without using excessive emotional ap-
peals. Her readers can easily conclude that the protection of tropical animal species is essential to the preservation of plant life. The first step in
many persuasive projects is to educate, to give people the facts they need
to understand the importance of a subject.

A straightforward scientific paper like Lisa's usually does not pull on the
heartstrings. A paper whose intent is to move people to action immediately
might include more imaginative elements to motivate readers—a description, for example, of an animal watching its habitat destroyed by fire. When
you use such persuasive strategies, you will want to be as careful with facts
as you are in an objective scientific paper. Lisa Lee, however, also does more
than simply lay out the facts; she makes it clear that what she has to say is
important and that her readers should be interested. If you are genuinely
interested in a subject—as were all the students whose papers are in this

text—then you will be able to make that subject interesting to your readers. Almost all successful persuasive writing requires careful research and thoughtful presentation of research findings.

There are some dangers to conducting research with the intention of using it to write a persuasive paper. You may be tempted to oversimplify a complex subject, to select only the evidence that proves a thesis and ignore the rest. You probably should not begin a persuasive paper until you yourself have been persuaded by what you have found.

Writing an Introduction

There are no hard and fast rules about when you should write the introduction to a paper, but some students who have difficulty organizing material find that the effort to write an introduction results in a kind of unconscious organizing. The draft of an introduction may serve as a skeleton outline that, as you review your notes, you can elaborate and develop. It is usually a good idea to draft an introduction very early on, to analyze the main points in an introduction, and then to determine what should be eliminated and what needs to be expanded. Give yourself time for this process to take place. After you have reviewed and sorted your note cards, and perhaps even after you have constructed what you think is your thesis sentence, take a clean notebook and go off by yourself and begin writing. What comes out may surprise you and may help you shape your paper. A preliminary draft of an introduction can be useful even if you discard it later and write another.

Although you may use more than one paragraph for the introduction to your paper, your first paragraph must do double duty. It must help announce what the paper is about, and it must get the reader's attention. Readers will probably continue to read if they are convinced that what they will learn from the paper is both interesting and important.

Following the Standard Outline Format

The standard outline format that is used in most disciplines is simple and logical. It alternates between numbers and letters, using Roman numerals for major categories of a paper, capital letters for the subheadings under the major categories, Arabic numbers for details under the subheadings, and lower-case letters for any breakdown of the details. Each subordinate heading is indented, beginning immediately under the first letter of the first word of the larger category. You should be able to adapt this pattern to any topic:

I. [First major category]
   A. [Subheading]
   B. [Subheading]
II. [Second major category]
   A. [Subheading]
     1. [Detail]
     2. [Detail]
       a. [Breakdown]
       b. [Breakdown]
   B. [Subheading]
III. [Third major category]

Another form—often used in technical writing or for papers in business and the sciences—is the decimal outline:

1. [First major category]
   1.1. [Subheading]
   1.2. [Subheading]
2. [Second major category]
   2.1. [Subheading]
     2.1.1. [Detail]
     2.1.2. [Detail]
       2.1.2.1. [Breakdown]
       2.1.2.2. [Breakdown]
   2.2. [Subheading]
3. [Third major category]

Many topics can be organized using only one level of subdivisions under the major categories. An outline that includes even minor details is more than a plan; it is really a distilled version of a complete paper that will later be cast in readable prose. A very detailed outline sometimes requires as much work as a rough draft.

OUTLINING YOUR MATERIAL

There are different ways of thinking about outlining. For some writers the outline is a strict plan carefully structured before drafting of the paper begins. For others, outlining is a process of discovery that changes as they draft and revise. Michael Gold combines the process of drafting and outlining, David Harris works out his paper in a complete sentence outline before he begins his first draft, and Lisa Lee organizes her paper according to a scientific format. For her work on *The Color Purple*, Carla Medina decides that her paper will have three parts and an introduction (see p. 169). Her outline for the Huck Finn paper is ordered chronologically as she traces first one side and then the other of the controversy about the novel (see p. 321). Instructors vary in their requirements about outlines. Some teachers may not even ask to see your outline, some may want only the final outline, and still others may want to check the drafts of outlines in order to advise you as you organize the paper. Keep in mind that an outline is a tool to help you shape your material, not a hurdle that you must get over to meet a requirement. If you are having trouble making an outline, you may need to reconsider your thesis statement and to reexamine your sources to find out what you have really learned.

CONSTRUCTING AN OUTLINE

An outline is both an organized description of your research findings and a plan for the report you will write about your research. An outline of what you have found may reveal irrelevant material or point to aspects of your topic that need more research. A final outline of what you intend to write about may go through several stages as your ideas develop. Most people are able to construct an adequate plan using words or, at most, phrases to indicate the main points or topics they plan to cover. A sketchy topical outline allows you to develop ideas as you compose, whereas a detailed sentence outline requires that you develop your ideas primarily in the outlining process. Some people, however, do prefer to organize their material in complete sentences before they begin to compose.

The kind of outline you use should be determined by the subject you have researched, the amount of factual evidence you have to support your points, and the nature of your own thought processes. For most people, there is an interaction among writing, thinking, and organizing. As you proceed with the writing of a paper, you will probably revise your outline more than once, rearranging the order of topics, adding evidence, deleting irrelevant material.

BALANCING AN OUTLINE

Your paper will probably be more effective if you try to present your findings so that the different parts are about the same length. If you are researching two books, for example, you should give approximately the same space to each. The student who once had such a hodgepodge of miscellaneous material on the subject of running eventually focused his study and constructed this perfectly balanced outline:

THE BENEFITS OF RUNNING

```
  I. Weight Control
     A. Aids self-control
     B. Expends calories
     C. Suppresses appetite
     D. Encourages a healthy diet
 II. Muscular Development
     A. Improves tone
     B. Enhances contours
     C. Increases strength
     D. Improves endurance
III. Psychological Well-Being
     A. Aids sleep
     B. Inhibits depression
     C. Increases strength
     D. Intensifies vitality
 IV. Cardiovascular Fitness
     A. Strengthens heart
     B. Lowers blood pressure
     C. Changes blood lipids
     D. Improves circulation
```

The parts of an outline are often not as symmetrical as they are here, where each category has an equal number of subcategories. Research findings may not fall into categories with equal and parallel subheadings, and it is a serious mistake to try to force your material into a neat outline. To do so is to distort your findings and to suggest a false logic and even false conclusions. It is much better to have a sketchy, unbalanced outline that is an accurate reflection of your findings than a neat but misleading one. But an outline that is very unbalanced may indicate serious problems in organization.

Some topics can be planned from the beginning in such a way that the findings will necessarily suggest a balanced outline. For example, a student who wanted to learn something about jazz and who decided to study two representative musicians from four cities where jazz has flourished constructed the following outline:

I. New Orleans
   A. King Oliver
   B. Sidney Bechet
II. Chicago
   A. Tommy Dorsey
   B. Glenn Miller
III. New York
   A. Dizzy Gillespie
   B. John Coltrane
IV. San Francisco
   A. Gerry Mulligan
   B. Chet Baker

This outline is geographical in that each main category is a city where jazz was important, but there is also a chronological principle at work: jazz began in New Orleans, moved up the river and on to Chicago, then became popular in New York, and finally emerged on the West Coast. Often, as with the jazz outline, the best organizing principles for research findings are inherent in the topic and in the way the research is conducted. An anthropologist studying the economic significance of various animals in a peasant community might naturally order her findings by reporting on one animal at a time, moving from the least important to the most important. Many students, however, begin to explore a subject without a fixed idea of what they want to find out; and in such cases, it is best to keep an open mind about how to organize research findings, allowing, as Michael Gold does, the material itself to suggest its own order.

USING AN ORGANIZING PRINCIPLE

There is usually more than one way to organize the same material. You might, for example, shape your findings by ordering events as they happened, by showing how two or more elements are alike and different, by making general statements and then supporting them with concrete evidence, or by setting up a problem and demonstrating solutions. With the exception of the opening paragraphs that deal with the cult that developed after Dean's death, Michael Gold largely organizes his material chronologically, telling the story of the making of *Rebel Without a Cause* as it happened. Carla Medina organizes her discussion of *Huck Finn,* around the two arguments, discussing the novel's critics first, then its defenders. Within these two categories she organizes her discussion chronologically.

David Harris orders his paper according to logic, moving from an explanation of the problem to a discussion of the solution. Lisa Lee, on the other hand, organizes her material using the guidelines of a scientific format. Your organizing principle may emerge unconsciously as you struggle with your material, and a carefully constructed thesis will usually call for one or another treatment. Michael Gold's research focuses on a process and therefore invites a temporal ordering.

REVISING AN OUTLINE

MICHAEL GOLD

Michael organizes his study of *Rebel Without a Cause* rather easily. He first watched a videotape of the film and read the book that gave it a title. After a period of reading, taking notes, photocopying articles, and marking relevant passages, Michael categorizes his notes and writes his first preliminary thesis sentence:

> Rebel Without a Cause was created over a period of years,
> developing from the dedicated collaboration of many people who
> brought different points of view and experiences to the
> project, and it influenced the behavior and feelings of a large
> number of young people who were united by their infatuation
> with James Dean.

He decides that he can organize his paper chronologically, telling the story of the creation of the film from beginning to end. He then sorts his cards into stacks representing those people who contributed to the film's production, those who were influenced by it, and those who have interpreted it. He arranges them chronologically and produces the following outline:

```
     THE COMMUNITY OF A FILM: REBEL WITHOUT A CAUSE


  I. The Beginning
     A. Robert Lindner's Rebel Without a Cause
     B. Warner Brothers' purchase
     C. Lindner's contribution
 II. The core community
     A. The director
     B. The producer
```

```
        C. The musical director
III. The screenwriters
        A. Problems
        B. Leon Uris
        C. Irving Shulman
        D. Stewart Stern
 IV. The actors
        A. James Dean
            1. Relationship with Ray
            2. Improviser
        B. Natalie Wood
        C. Supporting actors
  V. Influence
        A. The original fans
        B. The Dean cult
        C. The interpreters
        D. Conflicting views
        E. Problems of evaluation
```

When revising the first draft based on this outline, Michael decides to rearrange his material. By moving the information about the Dean cult to the introduction, Michael can stress that what many people know about the film—James Dean and his impact—is only part of the story. Studying his outline, he retitles the other categories and rearranges the material, emphasizing the different stages of the film's development in a more effective way. His new outline looks like this:

```
  I. Rebel's followers and creators
        A. Rebel's impact
        B. The Dean cult
        C. The creators
 II. A collaborative effort: the beginning
        A. Robert Lindner and Warner Brothers
        B. Nicholas Ray
III. The writers
        A. Odets and Uris
        B. Shulman
        c. Stern
 IV. The actors
        A. James Dean
```

```
       B. Natalie Wood
       C. Others
   V. The interpreters
       A. Conflicting views
       B. Problems of evaluation
  VI. Rebel's place in film history
       A. Appropriate categories
       B. Need for reevaluation
```

LISA LEE

After Lisa has checked out several books, read and photocopied more than a dozen articles on seed dispersal, highlighted relevant passages, taken notes both on cards and in a computer file, and carefully recorded information from books that she would soon have to return to the library, she prepares to organize her material. She prints the notes she has on a computer disk and then clears her desk. She then assembles all of her sources and classifies them into four general categories: introductory material, plants, animals, and environmental factors. She enters all her references into a computer file, using the correct bibliographic style.

With all this material organized in front of her, Lisa opens a computer file and constructs an outline. Following a format recommended for scientific papers, she decides that her paper will have seven parts: an abstract, an introduction, a discussion of the methods she used to find her materials, three main parts in which she explains her findings, and a conclusion. Since an abstract and conclusion cannot be written until the main body of the paper is complete, Lisa does not subdivide them. A version of this outline is incorporated into her highly structured paper.

```
   I. Abstract
  II. Introduction
       A. State of research
       B. Various methods of seed dispersal
 III. Research methods
       A. Search of indexes
       B. Examination of lists of references
       C. Focus of studies used
```

IV. How plants facilitate dispersal
   A. Schedule of ripening
   B. Influence of disperser's feeding behavior on ripening
   C. Size of fruit crop
   D. Availability of fruit during times of scarcity
V. Factors determining a disperser's effectiveness
   A. Degree to which digested seeds survive
   B. Rate of passage through the gut
   C. How the animal handles seeds while eating fruit
   D. Failure to retrieve hoarded seeds
VI. Other factors that impact the fate of a seed
   A. Presence of seed predators
   B. Number of seeds in dung pile
   C. Adequate light and space: treefalls
VII. Conclusion

Lisa is now ready to begin drafting her paper. As soon as she finishes this outline, she opens a computer file and begins.

WRITING A SENTENCE OUTLINE

DAVID HARRIS

At his instructor's suggestion, David writes a sentence outline, an exercise that was very helpful since he is forced to think through his entire paper before he writes the first draft. By putting down his main points in complete sentences, David is able to gain control over a very complex subject:

I. The psychological effects of the nuclear threat on children are considerable.
   A. A significant number of children experience serious worry about nuclear weapons.
   B. The psychological effect of the nuclear threat varies with age, social class, and parental attitudes.
   C. Children in countries with nuclear weapons and those from non-nuclear nations seem to have comparable levels of concern.

II. The fear that children experience is a normal,
    appropriate emotional response to danger with serious
    consequences for some.
    A. Some live with a sense of futurelessness.
    B. Futurelessness causes some to live for the moment.
    C. Living for the moment may result in self-destructive
       behavior.
    D. It causes others to live a double life.
III. Children need help from responsible adults in dealing
    with the nuclear threat.
    A. Children lack defense mechanisms to deal with fears.
    B. They are holding adults responsible.
    C. They must be given hope.
IV. There is no single solution to the nuclear threat or to
    the problems it creates for young people, but one
    significant aspect of any set of solutions must be
    education.
    A. Young people want more information.
    B. Educators and other responsible adults must end their
       own denial of the problem and learn more about the
       effects that living in the nuclear age is having on
       today's children.
    C. Adults must begin by sharing knowledge with the young.
    D. Although further research is needed, educators and
       parents must act on what is already known.

The hard work is over for David now, and he is able to draft his paper with ease.

Activities

A. Read the short paper about Eleanor Roosevelt at the end of chapter 8 and sketch out an outline of the main points.

B. Turn to page 308 and read Carla Medina's paper "The Voices of *The Color Purple.*" Outline her main points. Is there another way she might have organized the same material?

C. Consider the branching diagram on page 16 that Lisa Lee uses to recall what she already knows about environmental issues. Translate the topics on the diagram to a standard outline format. Which categories are incomplete? What might you add? Can you add subheadings?

D. Look back again at the encyclopedia article on pages 36–38. Outline the main points using either a standard outline or a branching diagram.

Project Activities

A. Sort your notes into categories and eliminate those not obviously related to your topic.

B. Is there more than one way to organize your notes? Choose the one that seems best and sketch out an outline of your findings.

C. Write out a statement of what you intend to demonstrate in your paper. Do you expect to write an expository or a persuasive paper?

D. If you plan to write a persuasive paper, sort your notes, choosing those that will most effectively advance your argument.

COMPOSING AND REVISING

8

You begin writing your paper the first time you paraphrase a written source or jot down a summary after an interview. By the time you sit down with a clean sheet of paper, several stacks of notes, and an outline, you will already have written drafts of small parts of your paper. Nevertheless, the task of taking this raw material and crafting it into smooth, readable prose lies ahead. Even though you may have an outline that seems orderly enough, you still must arrange the bits and pieces that you have collected into logical sentences and paragraphs, creating a coherent pattern. Shaping your material requires constant attention to the way one sentence relates to another, as well as to how each relates to the whole. From the beginning, it is good to make your points as clearly as possible, using all the transitions, definitions, and explanations that are necessary for meaning.

Getting Started

Before you start to write, try to have the materials, the space, and the time you need to write at least three hundred words—a good beginning.

Many writers like to compose first drafts in longhand, using a pencil for easy erasure. If, however, you write best with a favorite pen, by all means use it. A long legal pad is good for drafts because you can use every other line, leaving space for revision, and still have several sentences on a page.

158

Find a surface—a large desk, a dining room table, or a card table—where you can line up your note cards, stack books, and lay out your writing materials. You will save time if you find a place where you can leave these materials until your paper is complete; but if roommates, family members, or others are likely to distract you, it may be best for you to pack up and head for the library.

You will probably get more done if you can allot at least three hours for a writing session. If possible, allow yourself a little more time than you think you will need and plan to take a break after about an hour and a half or when you get tired.

USING A WORD PROCESSOR

If you have access to a personal computer and are familiar with a good word-processing program, you will do well to use it as early in the composition process as possible. Though some writers prefer to write their first drafts in longhand, there are many advantages to beginning the composition process directly on a computer. Whether you are going to use a computer from the beginning or after your project is well underway, you may want to consider the following recommendations:

1. If you have your own personal computer, you will be able to work on it whenever you like, but you should make sure that your computer and printer are in good working order before you begin. You don't want to find out on the morning your paper is due that the printer is broken or needs a ribbon or ink.

2. If you are using a computer that belongs to a friend or one in the computer center, plan ahead to make sure it's in good condition and available at times you can use it.

3. Decide which word-processing program available to you is most suited to your project. A program with split-screen or window capability is especially useful.

4. If you are using an unfamiliar program, study it carefully and practice composing before you begin your paper.

5. If you are using a program that you have used before, review the manual to make sure you know what it can do for you.

6. Make sure that you know how to indent, delete, and insert words and passages; move blocks of texts within a file and from one file to another; and save, copy, and delete files. Practice the format

commands—underlining, spacing, setting margins, and numbering pages. Finally, print a file and study the results.

7. If you already know how to use these features of a word processor, you may use it for recording sources, taking notes, organizing findings, and outlining or planning a paper. If you do so from the beginning, you can move ("cut and paste") material from a note file directly into the paper.

8. Once you are confident that you can use a word-processing system, you will want to use it for composing the draft even if you have not used it for earlier stages of the process. In this case, you may want to make space next to your computer to lay out your note cards organized into categories.

9. As soon as you have completed a draft of your paper, you may want to print out a hard copy since many writers find they can make revisions more effectively on a printed copy than on the computer monitor.

10. After you make revisions on the hard copy of your draft, you will then make the same changes on the disk. As you do so, you will probably make other revisions. Many students find that they print and revise several times before completing the final paper.

COMPOSING ON A TYPEWRITER

A portable typewriter is a valuable research tool that you can use at your own desk or in designated sections of most libraries. If you are a good typist—or even just a fair one—you may prefer to compose your first draft on a typewriter, triple spacing to provide adequate space for revision. Even if you mark through passages as you compose, a typed draft is more legible than a handwritten one. Many writers combine handwritten composition with typing, from time to time jotting down sentences by hand and then incorporating them into a typescript.

Imagining the Reader

All writers need to consider for whom they are writing. Scholars who write for professional journals assume that their readers are people like themselves, specialists who share a vocabulary and a common body of knowledge. Microeconomists, behavioral psychologists, or medieval historians might report their research in a way that only others in their fields can read with ease. In the course of your research, you may have found articles or books that you could not make much sense out of simply because their authors used many words you did not understand.

Most students, however, do not write up their research findings for specialists. Unless your instructor specifies a reader for you, it is usually advisable to think of your audience as someone who wants to learn about your topic, but who knows little about it. You may find it helpful actually to imagine a particular person who fits that description, a classmate or family member who is interested in what you are learning but who has no context or special vocabulary for understanding it. Michael Gold, for example, does not write for movie buffs only, but for anyone who has even a slight interest in movies. He imagines a reader who may not even have seen *Rebel Without a Cause*.

BEING CONSISTENT

From the beginning, you want to strive for consistency—selecting a verb tense, a level of word choice, and a tone that you carry throughout your paper. You should also be consistent about the mechanics of writing. When there are variant spellings of a word, for example, choose one and use it consistently; or when you are documenting your sources, choose one style of documentation and use it throughout the paper.

DEVELOPING A READABLE STYLE

Your main consideration when you choose your words and construct your sentences should be **readability.** You want to write so that others can understand what you have to say as easily as possible. Some students are tempted to use a specialized vocabulary or long but obscure words because they want to sound intelligent; but it is best to concentrate on communicating what you know clearly rather than on showing off what you have learned.

What you write will be more readable if you create a voice that is natural to you, so that when you read what you have written, it sounds like you when you are trying to explain something that is important. Of course you will not use slang, which is often natural to informal speech, but which is also often vague and imprecise. One way to test the voice of what you have written is to read out loud or, even better, into a tape recorder. If your voice sounds pretentious or insincere, you will probably want to work on your style. Once you have completed a portion of your paper, read it carefully and ask yourself the following questions:

Developing a Readable Style: A Checklist

1. Have I used long words where shorter ones would have been just as effective?
2. Have I been general where I could have been specific?
3. Have I tried to show off what I know rather than to say clearly and precisely what I mean?

If the answer to even one of these questions is yes, you probably need to try more consciously to compose sentences and paragraphs that others can read with ease.

As you are composing your paper, take care to avoid sexist language. Writing prose that does not use sexist language is easy if you follow these guidelines:

Watching Out for Sexist Language: A Checklist

1. Use masculine pronouns only to refer to individual men or to groups of people that are *exclusively* male.
2. In order to avoid the awkward "he or she" and "his or her," consider changing singular nouns to plural as in the example below:
   A student who finishes his or her project early . . .
   Students who finish their projects early . . .
3. Use nouns that are not gender-specific: *server* instead of *waiter*, *firefighter* instead of *fireman*, *spokesperson* instead of *spokesman*.

The National Council of Teachers of English has drawn up guidelines for avoiding sexism in writing. To order a copy of them, ask for *Guidelines for Nonsexist Use of Language in NCTE Publications* (NCTE, 1111 Kenyon Road, Urbana, IL 61801. Stock No. 19719).

Planning Ahead

Budgeting time is important at every stage of research, and it becomes crucial as you begin to write. Not only do you need time for composition, revision, and typing, but you need adequate time in between these steps. When your first draft is finished, it is a good idea to set it aside before you revise it. When you come back to a draft after some time, you will usually be able to see where it needs improvement. The time required for writing papers varies enormously, but the schedule below is adequate for most people writing a paper of approximately ten pages.

Planning Ahead: A Checklist

1. Writing the first draft: two to three days or five three-hour sessions
2. Laying the first draft aside: one day
3. Revising and typing the second draft: one day
4. Laying it aside: one day
5. Revising and typing the finished paper: one day

Writing the First Draft

Whether you write in longhand, use a typewriter, or compose on a word processor, writing your first draft should be a process of trying out alternatives, marking some out, and starting over again and again. Even if you are working from a detailed outline, you will probably experiment with different ways of presenting your research as you write. A handwritten or typed first draft should in fact be messy, reflecting numerous efforts to improve your writing—to say it better—as you compose. The way in which you introduce your sources and give credit for information can, however, help you present your findings and argue your thesis.

WRITING IN YOUR OWN VOICE

Think of your paper as being mainly written in your own voice. You are explaining in your own words what you have learned and what you have concluded. Whenever you paraphrase or summarize the words of the writers whose articles and books you have studied, you must try to do so in a way that is natural to you, in words that you might use, while being careful to indicate your sources in the text of your paper so that it is perfectly clear which are your thoughts and ideas and which are those of others.

CITING SOURCES AS YOU COMPOSE

From the beginning, cite each source as you use it and make sure that you have all the information needed for a complete citation in the bibliography. Every quotation, every paraphrase, every fact that you have learned in your research should be identified in the text of your first draft. Sometimes you may want to begin a paragraph or a sentence with the name of the author or authors of a source you are using:

```
Joseph Lash concludes that . . .
Tamara K. Hareven offers another view.
Bernard Bailyn et al. explore . . .
Davidson and Lytle demonstrate that . . .
```

Always cite the page number when you refer to a part of a source rather than the whole and place the page number of the source at the end of a clause or sentence as you compose:

```
In Eleanor and Franklin, his best-selling Pulitzer Prize-winning
biography, Joseph Lash explains Eleanor Roosevelt's role in the
League of Women Voters (355).
```

```
As Eleanor Roosevelt has written, "It is probably the sense of being
really needed and wanted which gives us the greatest satisfaction
and creates the most lasting bond" (308).
```

When you do not mention the author's name in the text, include it in the parenthetical reference along with a page number:

```
During Franklin's convalescence, Eleanor assumed the responsibility
of keeping the Roosevelt name before the public (Hareven 20).
```

Always make it clear where a paraphrase ends by putting the page number at the end of several sentences or a paragraph taken from the same part of a source. See the first full paragraph on page 179.

Note how sources are cited in the sample paper at the end of this chapter, and see page 164 for further examples of ways to introduce sources.

If you are writing a paper using the APA style or the citation-sequence system of documentation recommended by the CBE style manual, you will include other information in the text of your paper as you compose—date of publication for APA and a number for each source in the number system. See chapter 12 for APA and chapter 13 for CBE style.

The following rules assume that you are using the documentation style recommended by the Modern Language Association, but the principles apply to other styles of documentation as well. These rules should help you with the technical aspects of integrating sources into a coherent text. For examples, see the marginal notes in the short paper at the end of this chapter.

Citing Sources: A Checklist

1. Make perfectly clear the exact source of all material except facts of general knowledge and your own ideas and conclusions.
2. Indicate sources within the text when you can do so smoothly and always when you need to clarify which are your own ideas and which you owe to someone else. When you refer to material from a particular page number of a written text, you will have to give the page number—in parentheses or in a note.
3. After direct quotations indicate the source either in parentheses or with a note number that will correspond to a note at the bottom of the page or on the endnote page or to an item in your list of sources.
4. Place references after paraphrased material in such a way that there is no doubt about the source. In paragraphs that depend entirely on a few pages of a single source, cite the source at the end of the paragraph.
5. When you use two or more sources in a paragraph, use as many citations as are necessary for clarity.

If your paper requires either explanatory or documentary footnotes or endnotes, indicate in your draft where you expect to place the note, using an asterisk, a circle, or some other code. In the margin, place the page number and any other information necessary to write a complete note later. Since revising often includes rearranging, you should number the notes only when you are ready to type the final copy.

INTEGRATING QUOTATIONS WITH YOUR OWN WORDS

Learning how to combine your own words with someone else's is as necessary as learning the technicalities of documentation. The best guide for doing this effectively is again your own voice. Quote only when it is important to capture another person's voice or exact words, and know enough about your subject so that you can smoothly move from your own ideas and words to those of another person. Remember, this is *your* research paper. The sources you use and the quotations you include are intended to back up and explain your thesis. You are not just compiling data—you are interpreting and reporting your findings.

You may choose to quote a word, a phrase, a sentence, or several sentences, but in any case, you should retain the exact spelling and punctuation of the original. When you use quotations, it is important that you do so smoothly, making sure that your sentence is grammatically correct and that any quoted material appears exactly as it does in the original. Short quotations—not more than four lines—should be incorporated into the text of your paper. They may be integrated in a variety of ways:

At the beginning of a sentence:

> "The very best of human possibilities," according to George Eliot in Daniel Deronda, is "the blending of a complete personal love in one current with a larger duty" (685).

Following an introductory clause:

> A character in George Eliot's Daniel Deronda refers to marriages as "all the wondrous combinations of the universe whose issue makes our good and evil" (812).

With an introductory clause followed by a colon:

> Joseph Lash stresses the complexity of Eleanor Roosevelt's
> character: "She was the teacher, the moralist, the dreamer, but she
> was also highly practical" (386-87).

Combined with paraphrase in the same sentence:

> Lash argues that because of Franklin's career, Eleanor's "proddings
> and probings had to be carried on in a way that would not embarrass
> him politically" (387).

Note how short quotations are integrated into the sample paper at the end of this chapter (pp. 178–83).

Long quotations of more than four typed lines are usually set off with a colon with no quotations marks and indented ten spaces from the left margin. The right margin does not change. Do not add extra space before or after the quotation, but simply double-space throughout. If the long quotation is all from one paragraph, do not indent further (see the long quotation on page 180), but if you are quoting two paragraphs, indent the first line of each three more spaces:

> Dickens's descriptive power is evident in the opening lines of
> Little Dorrit:
>
>> Thirty years ago, Marseilles lay burning in the sun,
>> one day. A blazing sun upon a fierce August day was no
>> greater rarity in southern France then, than at any other
>> time. . . .
>> There was no wind to make a ripple on the foul water
>> within the harbour, or on the beautiful sea without. The
>> line of demarcation between the two colours, black and
>> blue, showed the point which the pure sea would not pass;
>> but it lay as quiet as the abominable pool, with which it
>> never mixed.

AVOIDING PADDING

You may be tempted to pad a research paper, to put in all the interesting bits of information you have found, even when they do not directly relate to the main idea of the paper. If your instructor has asked for a paper of a particular length—perhaps ten pages—you may at first feel that you cannot possibly write so much on your topic and that you therefore will have to use all your notes.

Before she focused her paper on factors determining the effectiveness of seed dispersal of tropical trees in Central America, Mexico, and Peru, Lisa read and finally eliminated a number of interesting articles that were not directly relevant to the points she wanted to make: about crabs and even fish that disperse seeds, about the ways monkeys seem to organize themselves into groups according to the amount of food available in a given area, and about the germination rates of seeds that have passed through the digestive track of pygmy chimpanzees in Africa. After carefully sorting out this material, she places it in a separate file labeled "Sources not used." She is then able to write a clear, uncluttered paper.

Revising

By writing every other line on long sheets of paper—such as legal pads—or by triple- or at least double-spacing a rough typed copy, you will have adequate space for revising sentences and words, but revising paragraphs and the overall structure will sometimes require rewriting on separate paper and cutting up the sheets you have written and rearranging them. Every time you read through your paper, you will probably make minor changes in words and sentences, but the larger structural changes need to be made systematically.

Revising on a word processor is both easy and fun. The cutting and pasting happens simply by giving the computer a command and striking a key. You can of course eliminate words, add words, move sentences and paragraphs, and check your spelling. If you think you want to save parts of your draft, you can open a file (labeled "Extra") and store them for later.

If you compose your paper on a word processor from the beginning, you will probably revise all along. When you are ready for a systematic revision of a completed draft, you will probably print out a copy that you read carefully, perhaps in a comfortable chair with pencil in hand.

EVALUATING ORGANIZATION

Once you have written a first draft, you should examine it to see if it really reflects what you intended to say. The first step is to compare your preliminary outline—the one you made before you began to write—with an outline of what you have written. The surest way is to go through your draft and to write down in abbreviated form—words and phrases—what you have actually written, making a new outline of the draft itself. Then consult your original plan. Are they the same? Which is better?

CARLA MEDINA

Carla has decided to organize her paper on *The Color Purple* by first treating the critical reception of the novel, then analyzing the ways Celie speaks and gives voice to others, and finally considering how Celie's ability to speak for herself and others is related to her development as a person.

Once Carla has decided how to organize the major points she wants to make, she is able to write the first draft and prepare her list of references in two days. Since Carla composes the whole paper directly on a word processor, she prints out the paper and sets it aside.

After reading her first draft of the paper, Carla decides to add a paragraph describing the novel's form and content so that what she says about the novel's voices will make sense to someone who has not read the novel. (See the second paragraph of her paper on p. 308.)

REARRANGING THE PARTS

Rearranging may require drastic methods: taking a paragraph from the middle and putting it in the introduction, for example. Sometimes you can indicate changes in the margins, but often you will want to make the change by cutting up your manuscript and pasting or taping sections on new sheets, leaving space for writing transitions to connect one part to another. Even if you are working with a word processor, you will often find it easier to do major rearrangement on your printed copy in this fashion before entering it onto your disk or tape. Numbering the pages of your draft, even though you know these will not be the final page numbers, makes it easier to change or add material during revision. If, for example, you write a paragraph that you want to insert in the middle of page 12, number it 12a and place it after the original page 12, indicating clearly in the text where you want to insert it.

You may be reluctant to strike through sentences and paragraphs that you have worked so hard to write, but most rough drafts include extra words, sentences, and even larger units that you later admit are really not necessary. You may have to force yourself to mark through repetitive or irrelevant passages. Tell yourself that your writing will be more effective if it is not repetitious and if each part contributes to the whole. Then read through your draft looking for what you can strike through without weakening your meaning. Notice how Michael Gold cuts the passage below from forty to twenty-two words:

ORIGINAL

```
According to Kreidl, it was Leonard Rosenman, the musical director
of Rebel, who suggested the thirty-one-year-old Stewart Stern as a
replacement for Shulman. At last, Ray had found a collaborator with
whom he could work until the film was finished.
```

REVISION

```
Leonard Rosenman, the musical director of Rebel, suggested the
thirty-one-year-old Stewart Stern, who worked with Ray until the
film was finished.
```

Since Michael's preceding paragraph ends with a statement about the break between Shulman and Ray, there is no need to repeat it, and nothing is lost with the other cuts (see p. 243).

Lisa Lee cuts her paper by eliminating largely speculative material about co-evolution of plants and animals since the studies she read on this subject did not really contribute to the points she wants to make. In the following passage, she paraphrases a quotation that seemed confusing, and she retains the one that seems most understandable.

ORIGINAL

```
John Terborgh, for example, suggests the possibility that the
keystone plant species may "act over evolutionary time as decisive
factors in the evolution of whole faunal assemblages," but he urges
that this possibility "be regarded as wide-eyed speculation."
```

John Terborgh suggests that keystone plant species may determine how
groups of animals act over time, but he urges that this possibility
"be regarded as wide-eyed speculation."

CLARIFYING MEANING

Ask yourself if you have expressed what you want to say as clearly as possible, and then reread your paper from the point of view of an interested reader who does not know very much about your topic. Sometimes what is clear to you may not be clear to someone else. Because you have become familiar with a topic, you may find it difficult to decide whether what you have written will make sense to someone who has not studied the same material.

IMPROVING PARAGRAPHS

The goal of all revision is clarity. When you examine a paragraph to see what improvements you can make, first identify the main idea and then decide if you have developed it as clearly as possible. Do you need more explanation? Is there irrelevant material that belongs elsewhere or not in your paper at all? Is the order effective? Sometimes when you have doubts, you may want to write another version and choose between the two.

IMPROVING SMALLER UNITS

Although you will probably change some sentences and words as you revise the larger units of your paper, it is advisable to go through it at least once just to improve diction (word choice) and sentence structure. The following list suggests a procedure for revising that you may find helpful:

1. *Examine the length of your sentences.* If most are approximately the same length, try to achieve more variety either by combining short sentences or by breaking down long ones.

2. *Check for active voice.* Whenever possible, structure sentences so that the subject is followed by an active verb. Note the following example from Michael Gold's paper:

Rebel was directed by Nicholas Ray.

Nicholas Ray directed Rebel.

You can easily locate passive verbs by looking for "is," "was," and other forms of the verb "to be." (But the passive voice is not taboo. It can be used effectively both to vary sentence structure and to emphasize the object rather than the subject—as I have done in this sentence. Instead of beginning another sentence with "You can use," I decided to emphasize the passive voice.)

3. Note whether you have stretched out your sentences with unnecessary clauses or phrases. If so, these examples may help you revise:

ORIGINAL

The difficulty of dealing with screenwriters who are uncooperative often delays the production of a film.

REVISION

Uncooperative screenwriters often delay film production.

ORIGINAL

James Dean's fans were characterized by an excessive degree of sentimentality regarding his memory.

REVISION

Dean's fans sentimentalized his memory.

4. Decide if the verb forms are unnecessarily complex, as in the following sentence:

ORIGINAL

Rebel Without a Cause was to have been based on a book by Robert Lindner.

```
Robert Lindner's book was the original inspiration for Rebel Without
a Cause.
```

5. Look out for excessively long or vague words. Whenever you can, substitute a short, easily understood word for an unnecessarily long or obscure one.

```
Eleanor Roosevelt endeavored to improve living conditions for
indigent people who were deprived of the benefits of society.
```

```
Eleanor Roosevelt worked to improve the lives of the poor.
```

6. Check for repetition. Do you use certain words repeatedly? If so, search for good synonyms to provide some variety. You may find a thesaurus, a dictionary of synonyms, or a regular dictionary helpful to remind you of other appropriate words. But, of course, you should never use a word unless you are confident that its meaning will be clear to your reader.

Revising for the Last Time

Ideally, you should consolidate your revisions in a second draft, preferably a rough typed copy. If you set this second draft aside for a day and then come back to it, you will certainly find that there are more changes you want to make. Once again you will want to examine the organization, the transitions, the paragraphing, the sentences, and the choice of words, making changes directly on the draft. Some students run into difficulty at this stage. They are unable to complete their revisions because they feel there is always more to be done, always something more they can do to improve their paper. While it is true that no writer ever produces the perfect paper, there must come a time when you realistically judge that you have done all you can to improve the paper in the time allowed. Three important steps in revision remain:

Revising for the Last Time: A Checklist

1. Check and correct spelling, looking up any words of which you are unsure.
2. Check and correct punctuation, reading through once concentrating on punctuation and capitalization. Use the rules in chapter 10 for guidance.
3. Make final alterations in the documentation. If you are using documentary notes—a number after each reference corresponding to an endnote placed after the main body of your paper or to a footnote placed at the bottom of the page—you are ready to put in the numbers as soon as you are sure that there will be no more rearranging, deleting, or adding of material. This is usually one of the last steps before you type the final copy. It is also a good idea to check your sources against your note cards to see if you have made any errors in page numbers, quotations, or other details.

Examples of Revision

The following passages show the process of revision. The typed passages were taken directly from rough drafts, and the revisions are indicated in longhand.

1. From Michael Gold's paper:

~~It was~~ Leonard Rosenman, the musical director of <u>Rebel</u>, ~~who~~
suggested the thirty-one-year-old Stewart Stern *who worked* ~~as a replacement for~~
~~Shulman. At last~~ *with* Ray had found a collaborator ~~whom he could work~~
~~with~~ until the ~~end. Apparently it was Stern who synthesized the~~ *film was finished, bringing together*
the ideas of previous writers with his own. ~~various ideas that fed into the finished script.~~

Note how Michael has reduced the number of words, simplified the language, and generally made the original passage more readable.

2. From David Harris's paper:

is no single solution to the nuclear threat or do
There ~~must be many approaches to solving~~ the problems that ~~the~~
it   *but*
~~nuclear threat~~ causes for children and adolescents, ~~and~~ one ~~solution~~
significant aspect of any set of solutions   *Although some people argue*
~~must be education. There are those who think~~ that ~~young people~~
youth
(should be shielded from the horrible facts of the nuclear threat, ~~and~~

~~of what a nuclear war would be like, but~~ most people realize that it
even small children
is impossible to shield ~~them~~ from that knowledge.

Note how David has clarified his argument.

3. From Lisa Lee's paper:

species of
Countless trees in ~~regions of the world known as~~ tropical rain

forests depend on the activities of animals for ~~their own~~ survival.
carry pollen,
Animals ~~serve trees by their pollination activities;~~ by eat~~ing~~

insects that prey on leaves and bark, and ~~by~~ transport~~ing~~ seeds to

locations in the forest where they may have a chance to germinate;

some will grow to saplings; and a few, maybe only one from a

solitary tree, will find the space and light necessary ~~for it to be~~

~~able~~ to soar to the top of the forest.

Note how Lisa has removed unnecessary words, divided the second sentence, and expressed the activities of animals as three parallel verbs: carry, eat, and transport.

LINDA ORTON

COMPOSITION

The decision to focus on Eleanor Roosevelt's efforts to help women allows Linda to direct her reading, but when she finishes her research, she finds that she has taken notes in several areas that do not directly relate to her chosen topic. Yet she still thinks she might be able to use some of that very interesting information. Her first rough draft includes information about Roosevelt's parents and her education, as well as speculation about what motivated her to live as she did. This first draft is too long and unorganized.

Linda decides to cut the parts about Roosevelt's childhood and her psychological development. She is then able to concentrate on Roosevelt's public accomplishments. Her second draft, however, is still not focused enough.

REVISION

Revision often involves excluding information that may be very interesting, but that is really irrelevant to the research topic. The passages below show Linda revising by eliminating material that is not directly related to her topic.

ORIGINAL

Among the young men who were attracted to Eleanor was Franklin Roosevelt. Soon they were secretly engaged. Their engagement coincided with Eleanor's increasing interest in social reform, which resulted in her going to work in a settlement house in one of New York's slum districts.

REVISION

In 1902, at about the time she became involved with Franklin, Eleanor began to work as a volunteer at the Rivington Street Settlement House in one of New York's slum districts.

For some years after she was married, Eleanor's life was filled with raising her five children, meeting the demands of her domineering mother-in-law, and running a complicated household.

For some years after she was married, Eleanor was occupied with family obligations.

Linda finally decides to outline the main points that have to do with Eleanor Roosevelt's public activities on behalf of women. When she does this a clear thesis sentence emerges:

Her many activities included work to improve the lot of disadvantaged women and to help all women develop their potential.

STEPS LEADING TO LINDA'S PAPER

1. Is asked to write a short research paper exploring the work of a public figure; reads the article on Eleanor Roosevelt in the *Encyclopedia Americana* (p. 21).
2. Consults the card catalog under "Roosevelt, Eleanor" and finds three books about Roosevelt's concern for women's issues (p. 61).
3. Uses the *New York Times Index* to find several articles about Roosevelt's work for women (p. 63).
4. Decides to focus on Roosevelt's efforts to help women and directs her note taking accordingly; writes a first draft, focuses her topic, and revises her paper (p. 176).

Thesis sentence

Orton 1

Linda Orton
Professor Shostak
English 102
25 October 1991

Eleanor Roosevelt: Blazing a Trail for Women

Eleanor Roosevelt was the First Lady of the United States for some twelve years, but she was much more than that. Long before she became First Lady, she was working for a better society: Her many activities included work to improve the lot of disadvantaged women and to help all women develop their potential. In 1902, at about the time she became involved with Franklin Roosevelt, she began to work as a volunteer at the Rivington Street Settlement House in one of New York's slum districts. There she taught young women who could not regularly attend school because of their long working hours. This experience, Eleanor's first extended contact with poverty and its demands, helped shape her social conscience, according to Joseph Lash (E&F 98); it also exposed Franklin to real poverty for the first time (E&F 135).

For some years after she was married, Eleanor was occupied with family obligations. As Franklin's career developed, she assumed more of the responsibilities of the wife of a government official. During this time, she did not join the widespread movement to help women get the vote. Even when Franklin voiced his support for women's suffrage in 1911, Eleanor "considered men superior beings" (E&F 173), and she remained--in Joseph

MLA citation style

178   COMPOSING AND REVISING

Orton 2

Lash's words--"anti-suffragette, and vigorously so" (E&F
168).

 World War I offered Eleanor the opportunity to re-
enter public life. As head of the Naval Department
knitting project, she supervised more than forty groups
of women who knitted woolen clothing for soldiers (E&F
213). In the first volume of her autobiography, This Is
My Story, Eleanor writes that it was her war work and
her activities immediately following the war that caused
her to change her ideas about women's suffrage: "Soon
after [ratification of the Nineteenth Amendment] I
undertook work which proved to me the value of the vote.
I became a much more ardent citizen and feminist than
anyone . . . would have dreamed possible" (297).

 After the war, Eleanor took projects specifically
concerned with bettering the lot of women and helping
them develop their full potential. Her interest in
education led her to purchase Todhunter, a school for
girls. There she taught a variety of subjects and
struggled to help her students see beyond their own
narrow world (E&F 306-8). During this time, she
continued to work for social reform, specifically for
shorter working hours and better working conditions for
women. Her concern for women's welfare and an
increasing recognition of her abilities helped her to
rise rapidly to responsible positions in several
organizations, including the Women's Trade Union League
and the League of Women Voters (E&F 281).

 Eleanor found that the various parts of her rich

Note use of ellipsis points to indicate
omission from quotation.

A SAMPLE SHORT PAPER 179

Quotation of more than four typed lines is
indented ten spaces.

life enhanced each other. Through her work in women's
organizations, she made friends and learned skills that
proved invaluable in her later work:

> Eleanor not only made friends but she learned
> by doing, a title she used in one of her last
> books. These friendships and activities did
> not replace but supplemented her life at home,
> running a large household and bringing up five
> children to whom she had to be father as well
> as mother. (Love, E 85)

This incredibly competent woman, however, was more than
teacher, social reformer, and homemaker.

After Franklin contracted polio in August 1921,
Eleanor's activities took a pronounced political turn.
During his convalescence, she assumed the responsibility
of keeping the Roosevelt name before the public (Hareven
20). But she did not give up her work to help women
play a significant role in society.

Eleanor began to see suffrage as a means for
achieving specific goals: Having gained the vote, women
now had the duty to work for political power and to work
for social reform through the system. In 1921 Eleanor
joined the women's division of the New York Democratic
State Committee. Other members quickly recognized her
organizational abilities, and she soon headed the
division's finance committee (Hareven 26-29).

Joseph Lash concludes that by 1924 Eleanor
Roosevelt was one of the leading politicians of the
state of New York (Love, E 86). On 16 April of that

Only a single parenthetical reference is
needed since all facts in paragraph are
from the same source.

Page reference is unnecessary with a newspaper article.

year, the New York Times reported that she had helped win the fight for the right of women to choose their own representatives at the state convention ("Democratic Women Win"). She also worked to incorporate issues of concern to women in the New York State Democratic platform (Love, E 88). The following year, Eleanor took part in the fight before the New York State legislature for a forty-eight-hour work week for women ("Women at Odds"), and she continued to battle industrial lobbyists on this issue in 1926 and 1927 (E&F 310).

During these years, Eleanor Roosevelt worked to increase women's involvement in national politics. In 1924 she led the struggle to include women's issues in the Democratic platform at the National Convention ("Democratic Women to Help"). In 1928 she headed the bureau of women's activities of the Democratic National Committee and directed the national women's campaign for Al Smith, the party's nominee for president ("Mrs. F. D. Roosevelt").

In 1928 Franklin was elected governor of the state of New York, and Eleanor found herself with new responsibilities as the wife of the governor. While she felt that she should no longer hold official positions in certain organizations, especially within the Democratic party, Eleanor continued to work for women's rights and social reform (Rice 5). On a national radio broadcast in 1929 called "Women in Politics," she advised women to get involved in politics and to "work a little harder than men" since they "have a new trail to

Even though some lines may appear short, try not to hyphenate words at the ends of lines.

Final paragraph is Linda's own conclusion.

blaze" ("Mrs. Roosevelt Prepares").

Eleanor Roosevelt is widely recognized for her aggressive and creative approach to her responsibilities as the wife of the president of the United States. A little investigation reveals, however, that she was an independent thinker and a leader in her own right. She blazed many trails through the wilderness of social injustice; her work with women and for women formed one of those trails.

Orton 6

Works Cited

"Democratic Women to Help on Platform." <u>New York Times</u>
    31 Mar. 1924: 2.

"Democratic Women Win." <u>New York Times</u> 16 Apr. 1924: 2.

Hareven, Tamara K. <u>Eleanor Roosevelt: An American</u>
    <u>Conscience.</u> Chicago: Quadrangle, 1968.

Lash, Joseph P. <u>Eleanor and Franklin</u>. New York: Norton,
    1971. Referred to in the text as <u>E&F</u>.

---. <u>Love, Eleanor</u>. Garden City: Doubleday, 1982.
    Referred to in the text as <u>Love, E.</u>

"Mrs. F. D. Roosevelt Urges Peace Work." <u>New York Times</u>
    4 Aug. 1928: 4.

"Mrs. Roosevelt Prepares to Unite Democratic Women." <u>New</u>
    <u>York Times</u> 9 Nov. 1929: 25.

Roosevelt, Eleanor. <u>This Is My Story</u>. New York: Harper,
    1937.

Rice, Diana. "Mrs. Roosevelt Takes on Another Task."
    <u>New York Times</u> 2 Dec. 1928, sec. 5: 5.

"Women at Odds on 48-Hour Bill." <u>New York Times</u> 26 Feb.
    1925: 23.

Activity

Note the thesis sentence of Michael Gold's paper on *Rebel Without a Cause* beginning on page 237. How much can you cut out of the paper that does not directly relate to the thesis? Hone your revision skills by trying to shorten this paper.

Project Activities

For Students Who Have Organized Their Notes

A. Write a paragraph—perhaps one that would be appropriate as an introductory paragraph to your research paper—that explains the main findings of your research. Set it aside and come back later to revise it.

B. Write a sentence that reduces your findings to a single controlling idea.

C. Imagine your readers. Write a paragraph in which you indicate the kind of readers you are writing for—how much they know about your topic, how interested they are, and what you will need to explain for your research to make sense.

D. Compose a rough draft, skipping lines to leave room for revision.

E. If you have composed your first draft on a word processor, print out a hard copy and set it aside for later.

For Students Who Have Finished a Draft

F. After setting your draft aside for at least a few hours, go over it and mark passages that need to be reorganized, sentences that can be improved, and words that should be replaced.

G. Go through your draft and cut unnecessary words and shorten lengthy sentences.

H. Reread the section on revising in this chapter, make a checklist for revising your own draft, and go through your paper again, doing all you can to improve it.

DOCUMENTING SOURCES

9

There are different ways to document written reports of research findings, but all have the same purpose: to make the source of such findings perfectly clear to the reader. The differences in documentation styles are mainly small details of capitalization, underlining, and spacing, but it is important that you use a style that is appropriate for your subject and acceptable to your instructor. It is also important to use only one style for each research paper and to be consistent about the smallest details so that your reader will know exactly what each item means.

Choosing a Documentation Style

The style used in this chapter—known as the MLA style since it is recommended by the Modern Language Association—is appropriate for papers in English, philosophy, history, and other disciplines in the humanities; and it will be acceptable to some instructors whatever your topic might be. For his paper on *Rebel Without a Cause,* Michael Gold follows the style recommended by the Modern Language Association. He compiles a list of sources and cites all references in an abbreviated form in parentheses in the text of his paper. Carla Medina's papers also use the MLA style. Appendix A shows how to document Michael's paper using footnotes.

When necessary, other instructors will direct you to a style commonly used by researchers in the particular subject you are studying. David Harris follows the author/date system recommended by the *Publication Manual of*

Planning Ahead for Documentation: A Checklist

To make it easy to assemble your final list of sources, you will want to do the following in advance:

1. As soon as you have chosen a topic, decide which documentation style is appropriate so that you can record the information in the correct form from the beginning. You may want to consult your instructor before making the final decision. For the APA style, consult pages 253–59, and for the scientific number system, or CBE style, see pages 282–86.
2. Take down all relevant information—author, title, volume number, publisher, date, page numbers, etc. about each source as you find it in a catalog, index, or bibliography.
3. If you find sources from a computerized index or a CD-ROM that is connected to a printer, print out the citation and then check it against the actual source. Keep in mind that indexes sometimes contain errors.
4. When you locate the actual source, double check the details of the citation.
5. If you photocopy an article, note the publication information on your copy, making sure to record titles of both the periodical and the article, authors, dates, volume and issue numbers, page numbers and sections (for newspapers), and whether the periodical is paginated for each issue or continuously through the volume.
6. Before you return a book you have borrowed from the library, make sure you have correctly recorded all the information you need for documentation.
7. If you are using a computer, keep a file for your list of sources and record them using the correct documentation style.

the American Psychological Association. David also provides a complete list of references at the end of his paper—with some slight differences of details from those used by Carla and Michael. He identifies the author, the publication date, and, when appropriate, the page number in the text of his paper, using parentheses when needed. Lisa Lee uses the citation-sequence, or number, system recommended by the Council of Biology Editors and the National Library of Medicine.

Style manuals sometimes used for other disciplines include:

CHEMISTRY

American Chemical Society. *Handbook for Authors of Papers in American Chemical Society Publications.* Washington: American Chemical Soc., 1978.

GEOLOGY

United States Geological Survey. *Suggestions to Authors of the Reports of the United States Geological Survey.* 6th ed. Washington: GPO, 1978.

LINGUISTICS

Linguistic Society of America. *LSA Bulletin,* Dec. issue, annually.

MATHEMATICS

American Mathematical Society. *A Manual for Authors of Mathematical Papers.* 7th ed. Providence: American Mathematical Soc., 1980.

PHYSICS

American Institute of Physics. Publications Board. *Style Manual for Guidance in the Preparation of Papers.* 3rd ed. New York: American Inst. of Physics, 1978.

All four students were careful to be consistent, that is, to cite the same kinds of sources in the same way each time they were used. If you understand the conventions used in all four papers, you will have two valuable skills: the ability to document appropriately any paper you write and the ability to interpret the documentation of articles and books that you read.

Deciding What to Document

As you write your paper, you should keep in mind from the beginning that *literally everything you take from your sources must be documented.* Not only must you make perfectly clear to your readers the exact source of quotations and paraphrases of your sources, but also where you have found ideas, concepts, and the smallest facts. You must give credit for a concept like the relationship of a film to the culture that produced it as well as for a fact such as the particular kind of sports car that James Dean drove. The only material that does not need documentation is information that most people would consider to be general knowledge—widely known facts, such as the fact that Dean was a famous movie actor.

PARENTHETICAL AND TEXTUAL DOCUMENTATION

A list of works cited at the end of the paper must be supplemented by references both in the running text of the paper and in parentheses at the end of sentences and paragraphs. How you cite sources within your paper should be determined by what you want to stress, the need to make your references as clear and concise as possible, and your effort to vary sentence structure to avoid boring repetition. Sometimes you may choose to mention the author's name at the beginning of a sentence or paragraph; at other times, you may place the author's name along with the page number of a source in parentheses at the end. Place the parenthetical reference at the end of a clause or sentence. When all of the information in a paragraph comes from the same part of a single source, you may place the parenthetical reference at the end of the paragraph.

In every case, you should make it clear which source you are citing. For example, if there is only one work in the bibliography by an author, then you need only cite the author's name and a page number. If there are two sources by the same author, however, you must include both the author's name and the title—or shortened title—of the work to which you are referring. For each source you cite, the parenthetical citation combined with any information in the text identifying the source should be as brief and unambiguous as possible, making it perfectly clear to the reader which item in the bibliography is being cited. The first item in a bibliographic citation—author, editor, translator, speaker, performer, director, title, or some other entry—must appear either in the text or in parentheses in order for readers to find it easily.

The following sentences suggest various ways to document your sources within the text of the paper.

Author's Name in the Text   MLA method

Stephen B. Oates goes even further in exploring the consequences of childhood experiences on Martin Luther King, Jr.'s development (1-17).

Give exact pages

Note: When there is only one work by an author in the list of works cited, it is not necessary to mention the title in the text.

In <u>Eleanor and Franklin</u>, his best-selling, Pulitzer Prize-winning biography, Joseph Lash explains Eleanor Roosevelt's role in the League of Women Voters (355).

Note: To stress the importance of a source, use the title in the text.

Author's Name in a Text Using More Than One Source by That Author

Joseph Lash concludes that by 1924 Eleanor Roosevelt was one of the leading politicians of the state of New York (<u>Love, E</u> 86).

Note: When there are two or more sources by the same author in the list of works cited, indicate the title, or an easily understood abbreviation of the title, in the parenthetical reference.

Author's Name in Text Preceding a Quotation

The film has what Kreidl calls "a disparate smattering of different vocabularies from different sources" (86).

Author's Name in Parenthetical Reference

Once the actors went to work, the script continued to evolve, with James Dean, in particular, creating as he acted (Kreidl 86).

Author's Name in Parenthetical Reference When There Is More Than One Citation by the Author

After the publication of her first book, it became clear that Eleanor Roosevelt would have considerable influence on women's efforts to gain political power (Lash, <u>E&F</u> 517).

Author's Name Introducing an Indented Quotation

Ezra Goodman wrote of the public response to the death of James Dean:

> The U.S. is currently in the throes of a movie fan craze for a dead man that surpasses in fervor and morbidity even the hysterical mass mourning that attended the death of Rudolph Valentino in the dim past of the movies. The object of this posthumous adulation is James Dean . . . who died at 24 in the wreck of his Porsche sports car a year ago this month. (75)

Volume Number Mentioned in Text

In the fifth volume of <u>Children of Crisis,</u> Robert Coles tells the story of a young girl who had the habit of staring absently at a cemetery (549).

Volume Number in Parenthetical Reference

Robert Coles tells the story of a young girl who had the habit of staring absently at a cemetery (5: 548-51).

More Than One Author's Name in Text

Davidson and Lytle note the difficulty historians have explaining the decisions that led to the bombing of Hiroshima (353).

Note: For sources with three authors, use all three last names; for more than three authors, use the last name of the first followed by et al., as in the list of works cited.

More Than One Author's Name in Parenthetical Reference

Historians attempting to explain the events leading up to the bombing of Hiroshima are faced with a formidable task (Davidson and Lytle 319-53).

A Work Listed by Title

Eleanor Roosevelt took part in the fight before the New York State legislature for a forty-eight-hour week for women ("Women at Odds").

Note: There is no need to include the page number either for articles that are only one page long, since the page is included in the bibliography, or for alphabetized sources, such as dictionaries or encyclopedias.

An Article Listed by Title from a Periodical Mentioned in the Text

On 16 April of that year, the <u>New York Times</u> reported that she had helped win the fight for the right of women to choose their own representatives at the state convention ("Democratic Women Win").

An Entire Work

In the first volume of her autobiography, <u>This Is My Story,</u> Eleanor Roosevelt explains how she changed her mind about suffrage and became an advocate for women's rights.

Note: To cite an entire work rather than a particular part, it is preferable to use the author's name in the text. In such cases, there is no need for a parenthetical reference.

More Than One Work in a Single Parenthetical Reference

In recent years, scholars have examined the place of <u>Rebel Without a Cause</u> in American film history (Biskind; Cook 427).

Note: Cite each work exactly as if it were cited alone; separate citations with a semicolon.

The List of Sources or Bibliography

The following form for the list of sources—also called the bibliography—is based on the *MLA Handbook* (1988). For advice on using the APA style (1983), turn to chapter 12. For the citation-sequence system, turn to chapter 13.

WHAT TO INCLUDE

To decide what to include in a list of sources, sort your bibliography cards into three stacks:

I. those you actually cited in the text of your paper;
II. those that helped you understand your topic, but that you did not actually cite
III. those that you either did not consult or that were not helpful.

Eliminate the third category. In some cases, you may decide to list only those works you actually cited; and in others you may want to include the second group, whether as part of a single alphabetized list or as a separate list, by dividing your sources into "Works Cited" and "Other Works Consulted."

HOW TO ARRANGE YOUR SOURCES

Sources should be listed alphabetically by the last name of the author or, when there is no author, by the first word of the title, excluding *a, an,* or *the.* When you have more than one work by the same author, give the name in the first entry only. For his or her other works, substitute three hyphens and a period for the name and arrange the titles alphabetically. Occasionally, you may be instructed to separate your sources according to books, articles, and other sources; to arrange them chronologically according to publication date; or to present them in the order that they appear in the text.

A list of sources is placed at the end of a research paper—after the notes or, for papers that do not have endnotes, immediately after the last page of the text. Begin the list on a new page with a title, "Works Cited," one inch from the top. Skip two lines, and start each entry flush with the left margin. Lines after the first of each entry are indented five spaces, and the entire list is double-spaced. Do not number the items unless you are consistently following the citation-sequence system (see chapter 13).

A complete list of sources placed at the end of your paper will allow you to clarify your sources simply by placing a shortened form of the citation—the author's last name, a brief title, or an abbreviation—in parentheses in the appropriate place in the text of your paper.

When you quote frequently from the same text, you may want to use an abbreviation: *S* for *Sula* or *MSND* for *A Midsummer Night's Dream*. Indicate this abbreviation at the end of the bibliographic citation: "Referred to in the text as *MSND*."

Compiling a List of Sources

Every book in your list of sources should include any of the following information that is available: ***author, title, place of publication, publisher,*** and ***date of publication.*** Many sources will require additional information such as multiple or corporate authors, the name of an editor or translator, the edition, the part of a work cited, or other particular information needed to identify the exact source used. In addition to books, you may need to list portions of books, periodicals, other written sources, and non-print sources as well. The following list of examples should provide you with a model for documenting any item you need to include in your list of sources.

A Book with One Author

```
Fish, Stanley.  Is There a Text in This Class?  Cambridge: Harvard
     UP, 1980.
```

Two or More Books by the Same Author

```
Lash, Joseph P.  Eleanor and Franklin.  New York: Norton, 1971.
---.  Love, Eleanor.  Garden City: Doubleday, 1982.
```

Note: If the author of one book is also the first of two or more authors of a following book, you must repeat the name, since the three hyphens stand only for the author of the preceding source:

```
Ellmann, Richard.  James Joyce.  2nd ed.  New York: Oxford UP, 1982.
---, ed.  The New Oxford Book of American Verse.  New York: Oxford
     UP, 1976
Ellmann, Richard, and Robert O'Clair, eds.  The Norton Anthology of
     Modern Poetry.  2nd ed.  New York: Norton, 1988.
```

A Book with Two Authors or Editors

```
Ehrlich, Paul R., and Anne H. Ehrlich.  Healing the Planet.
     Reading: Addison, 1991.
Pryse, Marjorie, and Hortense J. Spillers, eds.  Conjuring: Black
     Women, Fiction, and the Literary Tradition.  Bloomington:
     Indiana UP, 1985.
```

A Book with Three Authors

```
Kahn, Herman, William Brown, and Leon Martel.  The Next 200 Years.
     New York: Morrow, 1976.
```

A Book with More Than Three Authors

```
Bailyn, Bernard, et al.  The Great Republic: A History of the
     American People.  Lexington: Heath, 1977.
```

Note: The abbreviation "et al." stands for "and others."

A Book with a Corporate Author

```
U.S. Department of Energy.  An Assessment of Thermal Insulation
     Materials.  Washington: GPO, 1978.
```

Note: GPO is an abbreviation for Government Printing Office.

A Book with an Anonymous Author

Writers' and Artists' Yearbook, 1980. London: Adam and Charles
    Black, 1980.

A Book with an Author Using a Pseudonym (a Fictitious Name)

Innes, Michael [J. I. M. Stewart]. Going It Alone. New York: Dodd,
    1980.

Note: The author's real name may be supplied in brackets.

A Scholarly Edition

Dickens, Charles. Oliver Twist. Ed. Kathleen Tillotson. The
    Clarendon Dickens. Oxford: Clarendon, 1966.

Note: If the work of the editor is being discussed, this should be cited
as follows:

Tillotson, Kathleen, ed. Oliver Twist. By Charles Dickens. The
    Clarendon Dickens. Oxford: Clarendon, 1966.

A Work in a Series

Reiman, Donald H. Shelley's "The Triumph of Life": A Critical
    Study. Illinois Studies in Lang. and Lit. 55. Urbana: U of
    Illinois P, 1965.

A Single Work Published in More Than One Volume (with Continuous Pagination)

Johnson, Edgar. Sir Walter Scott: The Great Unknown. 2 vols.
    London: Hamilton, 1970.

A Book That Is Part of a Multivolume Work with a Single Title

Kettle, Arnold. An Introduction to the English Novel. Vol. 2.
    London: Hutchinson U Library, 1953. 2 vols.

A Book That Is Part of a Multivolume Work by One Author When Each Volume Has a Separate Title

Coles, Robert. Privileged Ones. Boston: Little, 1977. Vol. 5 of
    Children of Crisis. 5 vols. 1967–77.

A Book That Is Part of a Multivolume Work When Each Volume Has a Separate Title and Author

Stewart, J. I. M. Eight Modern Writers. Oxford: Oxford UP, 1963.
    Vol. 12 of Oxford History of English Literature. Gen. eds.
    John Button and Norman Davis. 12 vols. 1945–86.

A Book with Different Authors for Each Chapter and a Single Editor

Hoffman, Daniel, ed. Harvard Guide to Contemporary American
    Writing. Cambridge: Harvard UP, 1979.

A Reprint of an Older Edition

Hurston, Zora Neale. Their Eyes Were Watching God. 1937. Urbana:
    U of Illinois P, 1978.

Note: The date, but not the publisher, of the first edition is given immediately after the title.

A Paperback Reprint of a Hardback Edition

Conway, Jill Ker. The Road from Coorain. 1989. New York: Vintage,
    1990.

A Revised Edition

Ellmann, Richard. James Joyce. 2nd ed. New York: Oxford UP, 1982.

A Revised Version of a Work of Literature

Fowles, John. The Magus. Rev. version. Boston: Little, 1977.

A Translation

Homer. The Iliad. Trans. Richmond Lattimore. Chicago: U of
    Chicago P, 1951.

Note: If the work of the translator is being discussed, this should be cited as follows:

Lattimore, Richmond, trans. The Iliad. By Homer. Chicago: U of
    Chicago P, 1951.

```
Bible
Bible, Revised Standard Version
Old Testament
Talmud
Koran
Song of Solomon
```

Note: Sacred writings are neither underlined nor placed in quotation marks. Unless otherwise indicated, references to the Bible or books of the Bible are assumed to refer to the King James Version. Indicate the particular book, chapter, and verse of the Bible in parentheses in the text of your paper:

```
(Gen. 20:1-17)
```

(See pp. 209–11 for abbreviations of biblical works.)

PARTS OF BOOKS

An Article, Essay, Chapter, or Other Part of a Book with a Single Author

```
Lessing, Doris. "The Temptation of Jack Orkney." Stories. New
    York: Knopf, 1978. 564-625.
```

An Introduction, Afterword, Preface, or Foreword to a Book Written by Someone Other Than the Book's Author

```
Walker, Alice. Afterword. I Love Myself: A Zora Neale Hurston
    Reader. Ed. Alice Walker. Old Westbury: The Feminist Press,
    1979. 297-313.
```

A Previously Published Essay or Article from a Collection of Writings by Different Authors

```
Said, Edward W. "An Ideology of Difference." Critical Inquiry 12
    (1985): 89-107. Rpt. in "Race," Writing, and Difference. Ed.
    Henry Louis Gates, Jr. Chicago: U of Chicago P, 1986. 35-58.
```

An Essay or Article from a Collection of Works Not Previously Published

```
Brutus, Dennis. "English and the Dynamics of South African Creative
    Writing." English Literature: Opening up the Canon. Selected
```

Papers from the English Institute, 1979, New Series 4. Ed.
Leslie A. Fiedler and Houston Baker, Jr. Baltimore: Johns
Hopkins UP, 1981. 1-14.

A Short Story or Poem from an Anthology

Herbert, George. "The Flower." <u>Seventeenth-Century Prose and
Poetics</u>. Ed. Alexander M. Witherspoon and Frank J. Warnke.
2nd ed. New York: Harcourt, 1963. 857.
Pope, Alexander. "The Rape of the Lock." <u>The Norton Anthology of
World Masterpieces</u>. Vol. 2. Ed. Maynard Mack et al. 6th ed.
New York: Norton, 1992. 306-26. 2 vols.

A Novel or Play from an Anthology

Morrison, Toni. <u>Sula</u>. <u>The Norton Introduction to the Short Novel</u>.
2nd ed. Ed. Jerome Beaty. New York: Norton, 1987. 617-96.

Afterword, Preface, Introduction, or Other Editorial Comment on Individual Pieces in a Collection

Beaty, Jerome. Afterword to <u>Sula</u>. <u>The Norton Introduction to the
Short Novel</u>. 2nd ed. Ed. Jerome Beaty. New York: Norton,
1987. 697-702.

An Unsigned Article in a Widely Known Reference Work

"Solar Energy." <u>The Random House Encyclopedia</u>. 1990 ed.

A Signed Article in a Widely Known Reference Work

Suber, Howard. "Motion Picture." <u>Encyclopedia Americana</u>. 1981 ed.

An Article in a Specialized, Less Familiar Reference Work

Monro, D. H. "William Godwin." <u>The Encyclopedia of Philosophy</u>.
Ed. Paul Edwards. 8 vols. New York: Macmillan, 1967.
Roberts, John W. "James Baldwin." <u>Dictionary of Literary
Biography</u>. Vol. 33. Ed. Thadious M. Davis and Trudier Harris.
Ann Arbor: Gale, 1984. 134 vols. to date. 1978-.

Note: Since the entries are alphabetical, it is not necessary to provide
page numbers.

A Signed Article from a Daily Newspaper Divided into Sections Paginated Separately

Benjamin, Milton R. "U.S. Is Allowing Argentina to Buy Critical
A-System." Washington Post 19 July 1982: A1+.

Note: For newspapers divided into sections with the section designa-
tion used as part of the page number, give the page number as it appears
on the page (see the example above). For newspapers that are paginated
continuously, give date, edition if there is one, and page number (see *A
Signed Article from a Daily Newspaper,* below). For newspapers divided into
numbered sections, give date followed by a comma, then the abbreviation
"sec." and the section number, a colon, and page number (see *An Unsigned
Article from a Daily Newspaper,* below).

Note: Use " + " for an article that begins in one part of a periodical and
continues elsewhere.

A Signed Article from a Daily Newspaper Paginated Continuously

Passell, Peter. "Czechs Tread Minefield on the Way to Capitalism."
New York Times 18 Apr. 1992, natl. ed.: 17+.

Note: Some newspapers are published in more than one edition, and
the pagination varies from one to another. Indicate the edition if it is
specified on the masthead at the top of the first page.

An Unsigned Article from a Daily Newspaper

"Soviet Group Presses for Broader Arms 'Dialog.'" New York Times 5
Sept. 1982, sec. 1: 16.

A Signed Article from a Weekly Magazine or Newspaper

Bettelheim, Bruno. "Reflections: Freud and the Soul." New Yorker 1
Mar. 1982: 52+.
Lewis, James. "Jobless Reality Fails to Impress Thatcher's
Cabinet." Manchester Guardian Weekly 5 Sept. 1982: 3.

An Unsigned Article from a Weekly Publication

"Computers." Time 2 Aug. 1982: 72.

A Serialized Article

Broad, William J. "Science Showmanship: A Deep 'Star Wars' Rift."
New York Times 16 Dec. 1985, natl. ed.: 1+. Pt. 2 of a series
begun on 15 Dec. 1985.

Note: If author and title are the same for all the articles in the series,
give only one citation, indicating the dates and pages at the end. With the
same author and different titles, give separate citations, using three hyphens in place of the author's name for all citations after the first. With
different authors, give separate citations.

A Signed Editorial

Smith, Gerard. "Toward Arms Control." Editorial. New York Times
29 June 1982: A23.

An Unsigned Editorial

"Tuition Subsidies Are Not Benign." Editorial. New York Times 3
July 1982: 20.

An Article from a Monthly Magazine

Greider, William. "The Education of David Stockman." Atlantic Dec.
1981: 27-54.

An Article in a Journal with Pages Numbered Continuously Through Each Volume

Gelfant, Blanche H. "Mingling and Sharing in American Literature:
Teaching Ethnic Fiction." College English 43 (1981): 763-72.

Note: The numbers after the title of the journal refer to the volume
number, the date, and the pages of the article cited.

An Article in a Journal That Numbers Pages Separately for Each Issue

Biskind, Peter. "Rebel Without a Cause: Nicholas Ray in the
Fifties." Film Quarterly 28.5 (1974): 32-38.
Sprague, Claire. "Dialectic and Counter-Dialectic in the Martha
Quest Novels." Journal of Commonwealth Literature 14 (1979):
39-52.

Note: The numbers following the journal title refer to the volume (28) and issue (5).

Note: Where there is no volume number, treat the issue number as though it were a volume number.

A Signed Review with a Title

Berger, Peter L. "A Woman of This Century." Rev. of Hannah Arendt: For Love of the World, by Elizabeth Young Bruehl. New York Times Book Review 25 Apr. 1982: 1, 20-21.

A Signed, Untitled Review

Harrison, John F. C. Rev. of The Age of Capital, 1848-1875, by E. J. Hobsbawm. Victorian Studies 20 (1977): 423-25.

An Unsigned, Untitled Review

Rev. of The French Lieutenant's Woman, by John Fowles. Times Literary Supplement 12 June 1969: 629.

A Letter to the Editor

Flint, R. W. Letter. New Republic 18 Feb. 1957: 23.

A Response to a Letter or Letters

Lemann, Nicholas. Reply to letters of Roger Williams and Virginia K. Williams. Atlantic Dec. 1984: 14.

A Speech or Address for a Special Occasion Printed in a Periodical

Morrison, Toni. "Writers Together." Keynote speech. American Writers Congress. New York, 9 Oct. 1981. Nation 24 Oct. 1981: 396+.

An Article from Dissertation Abstracts or Dissertation Abstracts International

Webb, John Bryan. "Utopian Fantasy and Social Change, 1600-1660." DA 43 (1982): 8214250. State U of New York at Buffalo.

An Article from a Volume of Abstracts

Johnstone, John W. C. "Who Controls the News?" American Journal of Sociology 87 (1982): 1174-81. Abstract from America: History and Life 20. A (1983): no. 2120.

An Article from a Newsletter

Cliggott, Douglas. "Proposed Tax Reform Will Have Negative Effect
on Capital Investment." Business Executive Expectations Third
Quarter 1985: 2.

"Mathematics Credit for Computer Courses." NCTM News Bulletin 22.2
(1985): n. page.

"Report of Recent Events." American Studies International
Newsletter Aug. 1985: 1.

Note: Newsletters may not include volume and issue numbers, dates, or even pagination. Some, like the first item above, are only one sheet, so there is no need to indicate the absence of pagination as in the second citation. In cases where a publication does not employ the usual conventions needed for a citation, adapt what information you have to a form as close as possible to that of a conventional periodical citation, making sure that you provide enough information for readers to find the source. For example, the first citation uses "Third Quarter" to indicate the particular issue since there is no volume number or specific data given.

OTHER WRITTEN SOURCES

The Published Proceedings of a Conference

Conserving the Historical and Cultural Landscape. Proc. of the
Conference of the National Trust for Historic Preservation,
Western Region. 2-3 May 1975. Denver. Washington:
Preservation Press, 1975.

A Government Publication

Office of the Federal Register. United States Government Manual,
1980-81. Washington: GPO, 1980.

A Legal Reference

Brown v. Board of Education of Topeka. 347 US 483. US Supr. C.
1954.

A Pamphlet

Saltman, Jules. Teenagers and Alcohol: Patterns and Dangers. New
York: Public Affairs Comm., 1983.

Note: A pamphlet is treated like a book.

A Volume of Published Letters

Wilson, Elena, ed. <u>Edmund Wilson: Letters on Literature and Politics, 1912-1972</u>. New York: Farrar, 1977.

A Letter Printed in a Volume of Collected Letters

Wilson, Edmund. "To William Faulkner." 25 Sept. 1956. <u>Letters on Literature and Politics: 1912-1972</u>. Ed. Elena Wilson. New York: Farrar, 1977. 540.

An Unpublished Letter from a Collection

Stevenson, Adlai E. Letter to Ralph McGill. 11 May 1954. Ralph McGill Papers. Emory University, Atlanta.

Personal Letters

Paley, Grace. Letter to the author. 30 July 1981.

A Dissertation

Gray, Donald Joseph. "Victorian Verse Humor." Diss. Ohio State U, 1956.

A Document from an Information Service

Delker, Paul V. <u>Adult Education--1980 and Beyond</u>. Occasional Paper No. 59. Columbus: Ohio State U, 1979. ERIC ED 189 309.

A Manuscript or Typescript

Crane, Hart. <u>The Bridge</u>, ms. Hart Crane Collection. Columbia University, New York.

NON-PRINT SOURCES

A Lecture or Publicly Delivered Paper

Levine, George. "George Eliot's Scientific Ideal: The Hypothesis of Reality." English Institute. Cambridge, MA, 1 Sept. 1979.

A Radio or Television Program

<u>The Doomsayers</u>. Prod. Brian Capener. PBS Special. 8 Sept. 1982.
"Maya Angelou." Narr. Bill Moyers. <u>Creativity</u>. PBS Special. WPBA, Atlanta. 8 Jan. 1982.

Note: When you want to refer to a particular individual (producer, director, narrator, or actor), cite that person's name first:

```
Moyers, Bill, narr.  "Maya Angelou."  Creativity.  PBS Special.
     WPBA, Atlanta.  8 Jan. 1982.
```

A Performance of Music, Dance, or Drama

```
Puccini, Giacomo.  La Bohème.  Cond. James Levine.  With Teresa
     Stratas.  Metropolitan Opera.  Metropolitan Opera House, New
     York.  13 Jan. 1982.
```

Note: When you want to refer to a particular individual (conductor, director, choreographer), cite that person's name first:

```
Levine, James, cond.  La Bohème.  By Giacomo Puccini.  With Teresa
     Stratas.  Metropolitan Opera.  Metropolitan Opera House, New
     York.  13 Jan. 1982.
```

A Film

```
Vietnam: An American Journey.  Films Inc., 1979.
Rebel Without a Cause.  Dir. Nicholas Ray.  With James Dean, Sal
     Mineo, and Natalie Wood.  Warner Brothers, 1955.
```

Note: When you want to refer to a particular individual, cite that person's name first:

```
Ray, Nicholas, dir.  Rebel Without a Cause.  With James Dean, Sal
     Mineo, and Natalie Wood.  Warner Brothers, 1955.
```

A Face-to-Face Interview

```
Vitousek, Peter.  Professor of Biology, Stanford University.
     Personal interview.  21 Jan. 1993.
```

A Telephone Interview

```
King, Coretta Scott.  Telephone interview.  1 Nov. 1982.
```

A Work of Art

```
Cézanne, Paul.  A Modern Olympia.  Louvre, Paris.
```

A Work of Art with a Cited Illustration

Bonnard, Pierre. The Open Window. The Phillips Collection.
Washington. Illus. in Master Paintings from the Phillips
Collection. By Eleanor Green et al. New York: Penghurst
Books, 1981. 71.

A Musical Composition

Handel, George Frideric. Messiah. Ed. Watkins Shaw. Novello
Handel Edition. Sevenoaks, Eng.: Novello, n.d.

Note: Use n.d. (no date) for any undated material.

An Audio Recording

Hammer. Too Legit to Quit. Capitol Records, CA-98151, 1991.

A Song Referred to or Quoted from an Audio Recording

The Beatles. "Revolution." The Beatles/1967-1970. Capitol, SEBX-
11843, 1973.

An Audio Recording When the Work of the Performer or Performers Is Discussed

Horne, Marilyn. Orfeo ed Euridice. By Christoph Willibald Gluck.
Cond. George Solti. Orchestra and Chorus of the Royal Opera
House, Covent Garden. London, OSA1285, 1970.

A Videotape or Recording

The Nuclear Dilemma. Video Recording. BBC-TV. New York: Time-Life
Multimedia, 1974.

A Computer Program on Tape or Disk

Ward, Richard J. The Executive Game. Computer software. Bowling
Green State University. Hewlett-Packard. A880-2232A.

Note: Computer programs vary considerably. For this reason, you will
have to adapt a citation to the information you have. When possible, you
should include an author, title, place of production, company or organization producing the program, identifying number, and date.

```
"Salk, Jonas Edward."  American Men and Women of Science.  15th ed.
    Bowker, 1983.  Dialog file 236, item 0090936.
```

Note: Cite material from a computer service such as *Dialog* or *BRS* like printed material found in books and periodicals, but add a reference to the service at the end of the citation, giving the name of the service and the numbers identifying the database and the particular item from that base.

Special Cases

You will occasionally find sources that are different from any of the sample citations in this chapter. You may find, for example, a book with no date that has an author, an editor, and a translator. Privately printed material or books published in the seventeenth century may not include any publication information. To cite unusual or one-of-a-kind sources, you may have to devise your own citation, adapting the order suggested by the models above: author, title, editor, translator, place of publication, publisher, and date.

CITING MATERIAL FROM A SECONDARY SOURCE

There may be times when you will want to cite material from a book or an article that you have found in a secondary source rather than in the original. Generally, it is best to locate the original and to cite it directly; but in cases when the original is not available, you must cite the source you actually use.

For Citing the Source of Information Found in a Second Source

```
Squire, James R.  The Responses of Adolescents While Reading Four
    Short Stories.  Urbana: NCTE, 1964.  In David Bleich,
    Subjective Criticism.  Baltimore: Johns Hopkins UP, 1978.  101.
```

For Citing a Quotation from a Source Other Than the Original When You Want to Call Attention to the Original

```
Fish, Stanley E.  "Literature in the Reader:  Affective Stylistics."
    New Literary History 2 (1970): 140.  As quoted in David Bleich,
    Subjective Criticism.  Baltimore: Johns Hopkins UP, 1978.  122.
```

For Citing a Quotation or Paraphrase of a Quotation When You Have No Access to the Original

Branch, Taylor. <u>Parting the Waters: America in the King Years, 1954-63</u>. New York: Simon, 1988.

Note: Indicate the source of a quotation or paraphrase of a quotation in parentheses in your paper as follows:

(qtd. in Branch 922).

CITING TITLES WITHIN TITLES

When the title of one work is part of the title of another, you may be confused by what to underline and what to enclose in single or double quotation marks.

Any Titles Normally Underlined (Books, Plays, Films) That Are Part of the Titles of Articles Are Still Underlined

<u>The Duchess of Malfi</u>
"Sexual and Social Mobility in <u>The Duchess of Malfi</u>"

Omit Underlining of Titles That Would Normally Be Underlined but That Are Part of a Book Title

<u>Paradise Lost</u>
<u>Surprised by Sin: The Reader in</u> Paradise Lost

Underline the Titles of Books That Include Other Titles Normally Enclosed Within Quotation Marks

"Michael"
<u>Ten Interpretations of Wordsworth's "Michael"</u>

Use Single Quotation Marks for Titles Normally Enclosed in Quotation Marks That Are Part of the Title of an Article

"The Drowned Man of Esthwaite"
"The Illusion of Mastery: Wordsworth's Revisions of 'The Drowned Man of Esthwaite'"

A table or illustration should follow as closely as possible that part of the paper that it illustrates. Double-space before, after, and within tables, making ruled lines when necessary to clarify the material. Type any heading or caption at the top of the table or illustration flush with the left margin: Table 1; Fig. 1. Give the source at the bottom, also flush with the left margin:

```
Source: Harriet Kramer Linkin.  "The Current Canon in British
     Romantic Studies."  College English 53 (1991): 554.
```

Making an Annotated Bibliography

Occasionally an instructor will ask you to make an annotated bibliography. To do this, you simply add a brief descriptive note after the appropriate bibliographic entry. Consider the following examples:

```
Hareven, Tamara.  "Social and Political Apprenticeship, 1920-1933."
     Eleanor Roosevelt: An American Conscience.  Chicago:
     Quadrangle, 1968.  21-47.  This chapter is about Eleanor
     Roosevelt's initial work with social reform and labor groups.
     It outlines her development and increasing influence in
     politics and women's rights.  A good, concise overview of these
     years.
Lash, Joseph P.  Eleanor and Franklin.  New York: Norton, 1971.  A
     broad, reliable basis for further study, this book is a good
     place to begin a study of the Roosevelts.  Lash explores the
     environments in which they were raised and covers their lives
     up until Franklin's death.
Rice, Diana.  "Mrs. Roosevelt Takes on Another Task."  New York
     Times 2 Dec. 1928, sec. 5: 5.  This article is based on an
     interview with Eleanor Roosevelt in which she discusses her
     coming role as First Lady of New York State.  Her views on
     women in politics are particularly interesting and are reported
     in her own words.
```

Using and Interpreting Abbreviations

These designations are almost always indicated in abbreviated form:

AD (A.D.)	*anno Domini,* meaning "in the year of our Lord," as in AD 169
a.m.	*ante meridiem,* meaning "before noon"
BC (B.C.)	before Christ, as in 400 BC
BCE (B.C.E)	before Common Era
CE (C.E.)	Common Era
p.m.	*post meridiem,* meaning "after noon"

STATES

Spell out in the text of a research paper, but for documentation use the two-letter abbreviations recommended by the postal service.

AL	Alabama	MI	Michigan
AK	Alaska	MN	Minnesota
AZ	Arizona	MS	Mississippi
AR	Arkansas	MO	Missouri
CA	California	MT	Montana
CO	Colorado	NB	Nebraska
CT	Connecticut	NV	Nevada
DE	Delaware	NH	New Hampshire
DC	District of Columbia	NJ	New Jersey
FL	Florida	NM	New Mexico
GA	Georgia	NY	New York
GU	Guam	NC	North Carolina
HI	Hawaii	ND	North Dakota
ID	Idaho	OH	Ohio
IL	Illinois	OK	Oklahoma
IN	Indiana	OR	Oregon
IA	Iowa	PA	Pennsylvania
KS	Kansas	PR	Puerto Rico
KY	Kentucky	RI	Rhode Island
LA	Louisiana	SC	South Carolina
ME	Maine	SD	South Dakota
MD	Maryland	TN	Tennessee
MA	Massachusetts	TX	Texas

UT	Utah	WA	Washington
VT	Vermont	VI	Virgin Islands
WI	Wisconsin	WV	West Virginia
VA	Virginia	WY	Wyoming

DAYS AND MONTHS

Sun.	Jan.	July
Mon.	Feb.	Aug.
Tues.	Mar.	Sept.
Wed.	Apr.	Oct.
Thurs.	May	Nov.
Fri.	June	Dec.
Sat.		

PUBLISHERS' NAMES

The MLA recommends that in documentation you indicate publishers' names with appropriate abbreviations. Use the following samples as models:

Farrar	Farrar, Straus & Giroux
Knopf	Alfred A. Knopf, Inc.
MIT P	The MIT Press
MLA	Modern Language Association of America
NAL	New American Library, Inc.
Norton	W. W. Norton and Co., Inc.
Oxford UP	Oxford University Press, Inc.
Pocket	Pocket Books
Random	Random House, Inc.
U of Chicago P	University of Chicago Press
UP of Florida	University Presses of Florida
Viking	Viking Press, Inc.

THE BIBLE

Old Testament (OT)

Gen.	Genesis
Exod.	Exodus
Lev.	Leviticus

Num.	Numbers
Deut.	Deuteronomy
Josh.	Joshua
Judg.	Judges
Ruth	Ruth
1 Sam.	1 Samuel
2 Sam.	2 Samuel
1 Kings	1 Kings
2 Kings	2 Kings
1 Chron.	1 Chronicles
2 Chron.	2 Chronicles
Ezra	Ezra
Neh.	Nehemiah
Esth.	Esther
Job	Job
Ps.	Psalms
Prov.	Proverbs
Eccles.	Ecclesiastes
Song Sol.	Song of Solomon
(also Cant.)	(also Canticles)
Isa.	Isaiah
Jer.	Jeremiah
Lam.	Lamentations
Ezek.	Ezekiel
Dan.	Daniel
Hos.	Hosea
Joel	Joel
Amos	Amos
Obad.	Obadiah
Jon.	Jonah
Mic.	Micah
Nah.	Nahum
Hab.	Habakkuk
Zeph.	Zephaniah
Hag.	Haggai
Zech.	Zechariah
Mal.	Malachi

New Testament (NT)

Matt.	Matthew
Mark	Mark

Luke	Luke
John	John
Acts	Acts
Rom.	Romans
1 Cor.	1 Corinthians
2 Cor.	2 Corinthians
Gal.	Galatians
Eph.	Ephesians
Phil.	Philippians
Col.	Colossians
1 Thess.	1 Thessalonians
2 Thess.	2 Thessalonians
1 Tim.	1 Timothy
2 Tim.	2 Timothy
Tit.	Titus
Philem.	Philemon
Heb.	Hebrews
Jas.	James
1 Pet.	1 Peter
2 Pet.	2 Peter
1 John	1 John
2 John	2 John
3 John	3 John
Jude	Jude
Rev. (also Apoc.)	Revelation (also Apocalypse)

GENERAL

Some of the following abbreviations are occasionally used in writing using the new streamlined MLA style; you may encounter others in your reading. It is best to refer first to the sample citations in this chapter to document your own work and to use this list for clarification and for interpreting your sources. In general, use appropriate abbreviations in documentation and brief qualifying parenthetical asides (i.e., cf., etc.). Spell out most words in the text of your paper.

abbr.	abbreviation, abbreviated
abr.	abridged, abridgment
adapt.	adapted by, adaptation
anon.	anonymous

app.	appendix
assn.	association
assoc.	associate, associated
attrib.	attributed to
b.	born
bibliog.	bibliography, bibliographer, bibliographic
biog.	biography, biographer, biographical
bk.	book
bull.	bulletin
c. (ca.)	*circa,* meaning "about" (commonly used to indicate approximate dates, as c. 1840)
cf.	*confer,* meaning "compare"
ch., chs. (chap., chaps.)	chapter, chapters
col.	column
colloq.	colloquial (indicates informal speech)
comp.	compiled by, compiler
cond.	conducted by, conductor
cont.	contents, continued
(contd.)	continued
d.	died
dept.	department
dev.	developed by, development
dir.	directed by, director
diss.	dissertation
distr.	distributed by, distributor
div.	division
doc.	document
ed.	edited by, editor, edition
educ.	education, educational
e.g.	*exempli gratia,* meaning "for example"
esp.	especially
et al.	*et alii,* meaning "and others" (used in citing works with more than three authors)
etc.	*et cetera,* meaning "and so forth" (Avoid using this and most other abbreviations in the text of a paper.)
ex.	example
fac.	faculty
fig.	figure
fl.	*floruit,* meaning "flourished" (commonly used to indicate the approximate time that a person

	lived—usually the period of highest achievement—when birth and death dates are unknown)
fwd.	foreward, forward by
govt.	government
hist.	history, historian, historical
ibid.	*ibidem,* meaning "in the same place" (Though no longer recommended by the MLA or the APA style, this abbreviation was once commonly used in endnotes to indicate that a source is the same as the preceding one.)
i.e.	*id est,* meaning "that is" (Like "e.g." and "etc.," this abbreviation should be confined to parenthetical references and notes and avoided in the running text.)
illus.	illustrated by, illustrator, illustration
inst.	institute, institution
intl.	international
introd.	introduced by, introduction
jour.	journal
l., ll.	line, lines
lang.	language
legis.	legislation, legislative, legislature, legislator
mag.	magazine
misc.	miscellaneous
ms., mss.	manuscript, manuscripts
narr.	narrated by, narrator
natl.	national
n.d.	no date (of publication)
no.	number
n.p.	no place (of publication), no publisher
obs.	obsolete
P	Press (Note UP in documentation to refer to University Press, as Oxford UP.)
p., pp.	page, pages
pref.	preface, preface by
proc.	proceedings
prod.	produced by, producer
pseud.	pseudonym
pt.	part
pub. (publ.)	published by, publisher, publication
qtd.	quoted

rev.	revised by, revision; or review
rpt.	reprinted, by reprint
sc.	scene (used in citing passages from plays, omitted when scene and act are cited together: *Hamlet* 2.1)
sec. (sect.)	section
ser.	series
sic	"thus, so" (used in brackets within a quotation, or in parentheses following a quotation to indicate that an error in spelling, punctuation, grammar, logic, or fact is reproduced faithfully from the original)
soc.	society
st.	stanza
supp.	supplement
trans. (tr.)	translated by, translator, translation
U	University (Note UP in documentation to indicate University Press, as Oxford UP.)
UP	University Press, in documentation, as Oxford UP.
v., vv.	verse, verses (vs. and vss. also used)
viz.	*videlicet,* meaning "that is" or "namely"
vol., vols.	volume, volumes
vs. (v.)	versus or against (In titles of legal cases, v. is commonly used.)

Content Notes

Occasionally you may want to use a note to give information that would be distracting if you included it in the text of your paper. Michael Gold, for example, notes that new technology may well change the approach of future papers on his subject.

A content note is also useful to point the reader to several sources—perhaps not included in the bibliography—where he or she can find a full discussion of a topic. Whether it occurs at the foot of a page or the end of a paper, chapter, or book, a content note is simply a note that gives information or makes a comment instead of or in addition to a normal source citation. *Warning:* Content notes should only give significant information; avoid the temptation to include interesting but irrelevant facts in notes.

Activities

A. Using as a guide the MLA style represented by the examples in this chapter, write bibliographic citation for the sources below:

1. A book by Elizabeth Fox-Genovese entitled *Within the Plantation Household: Black and White Women of the Old South,* published in 1988 by the University of North Carolina Press in Chapel Hill, North Carolina.

2. An article by Richard Corliss in the 23 December 1991 *Time* entitled "Who Killed J.F.K.?" and running continually from pages 66 to 69.

3. A book by Adrian Forsyth and Ken Miyata entitled *Tropical Nature,* published in 1984 by Charles Scribner's Sons in New York.

4. A poem by Adrienne Rich entitled "Darklight," on pages 55–56 of her book *An Atlas of the Difficult World,* published in 1991 by W. W. Norton & Company in New York.

5. An essay by Gregory S. Jay entitled "The End of 'American' Literature: Toward a Multicultural Practice," published on pages 264–79 of the third number of volume 53 of the journal *College English* (March 1991). The pages of this journal are numbered continuously through each volume.

6. A video recording entitled *Shakespeare of Stratford and London,* produced in 1978 by the National Geographic Society in Washington, D.C.

7. An article by Malcolm W. Browne in the *New York Times* of 21 January 1992 entitled "Galapagos Mystery Solved: Fauna Evolved on Vanished Islands." The article begins on page 5 of section B and is continued on page 8.

8. A book entitled *The Second Sex,* written by Simone de Beauvoir, originally published in 1949, translated by H. M. Parshley, and published in 1975 by Alfred A. Knopf in New York.

9. An article called "Waste Disposal, Chemical" in the 1990 edition of the *Random House Encyclopedia* published by Random House in New York.

10. An article entitled "Ishmael Reed" by Henry Louis Gates in volume 33 of the multivolume *Dictionary of Literary Biography.* Published in Ann Arbor by Gale Research Company in 1984, volume 33, entitled *Afro-American Fiction Writers After 1955.* Entries are alphabetical. This volume is edited by Thadious M. Davis and Trudier Harris. There are 134 volumes in the series.

B. Write a bibliographic citation according to the APA style for the following:

   1. A book by Marjorie Shostak entitled *Nisa: The Life and Words of a !Kung Woman* published in Cambridge, MA, by Harvard University Press in 1981.

   2. A book by Joseph M. Hawes and N. Ray Hiner called *Children in Historical and Comparative Perspective: An International Handbook and Research Guide* published in 1991 by Greenwood Press in New York.

   3. An article on pages 8 & 10 of the November 1989 periodical *Natural History*. The author is Michael Fobes Brown, and the title is "Dark Side of the Shaman: The Traditional Healer's Art Has Its Perils."

   4. An article by C. A. Taube, B. J. Burns, and L. Kessler entitled "Patients of Psychiatrists and Psychologists in Office-based Practice: 1980." The article is on pages 1435–47 of volume 39 of *American Psychologist* published in 1984.

   5. An article by L. J. Weitzman and three other authors entitled "Sex-Role Socialization in Picture Books for Preschool Children," published on pages 1125–50 of volume 77 of *American Journal of Sociology* in 1972. The other authors are D. Eifler, E. Hokada, and C. Ross.

C. Write bibliographic citations for the following based on the CBE style in chapter 13:

   1. "Man as an Agent in the Spread of Organisms," a paper by Marston Bates presented at a symposium held from June 16 to 22 in 1955 at Princeton and published on pages 788–804 of a volume with the other papers presented at the symposium by the University of Chicago Press in 1956. Entitled *Man's Role in Changing the Face of the Earth* with the subtitle, *An International Symposium,* the volume is edited by William L. Thomas, Jr.

   2. An book with 192 pages by R. E. Schultes and A. Hofmann entitled *Plants of the Gods: Origins of Hallucinogenic Use* published in 1979 by McGraw-Hill in New York.

   3. An article entitled "Plant Reproductive Characteristics During Secondary Succession in Neotropical Lowland Forest Ecosystems," by P. A. Opler, H. G. Baker, and G. W. Frankie, published in 1980 on pages 40–46 of volume 12 of *Biotropica*. This journal is paginated continuously throughout the volume.

PRODUCING THE FINAL PAPER

10

Your final paper should be as neat and accurate as you can make it. A paper that is correct and readable is more effective than one with noticeable errors and will help persuade your reader that you have been correct and diligent in your research. After you have worked so hard, you will want your final paper to display the time and care that have gone into your entire project.

Before turning in your paper, you should complete the following steps:

Proofreading and Polishing: A Checklist

1. Proofread the revised draft carefully and make the final changes. Correct any errors in grammar, spelling, and punctuation.
2. Make sure that the list of sources, the notes, and the parenthetical documentation are typed according to a single style— the MLA, the APA, or the citation-sequence (number) system.
3. Produce a neat typed copy that conforms to a standard format. Study the guidelines in this chapter before you begin.
4. Proofread the final copy carefully, correcting all errors. Make a copy for yourself. Finally, submit the paper according to the instructor's directions.

Proofreading the Revised Draft

This is your last chance to make stylistic changes—to substitute a familiar word for an obscure one, to change a sentence from passive to active voice, to strike through unnecessary words. If you read your paper out loud, you may discover awkward sentences. Consult a standard handbook—there will be one in the reference room—for questions of grammar or usage. If you have any doubt about the spelling of a word, look it up in a dictionary.

Proofreading Symbols

Many instructors use the symbols below for correcting papers, but they're also useful for clearly marking changes in a draft before printing out—or retyping—the final version of your paper. Below the symbols is a portion of a draft with corrections marked.

- ⌄ Apostrophe or single quotation mark
- ⌒ Close up (basket ball)
- ⌄ Comma
- ℓ Delete
- ⌃ Insert
- ¶ Begin a new paragraph
- No ¶ Do not begin a new paragraph
- ⊙ Period
- ⌄" ⌄" Double quotation marks
- # Space
- ∿ Transpose elements, usually with *tr* in margin (thier)

    The fear that children experience is an appropriate and

perhaps inevitable response to the danger posed by nuclear

weapons, but it may have serious consequences for some.

Beardsley and Mack (1982) noted their strongest finding to be

"a general unquiet or uneasiness about the future and about

tr the present nature of nuclear weapons and nuclear power. There is a particular uncertainty about nuclear war or the limiting

of such a war should it occur and the possibilities of survival

(p. 89) One of the consequences results of this uncertainty

about the future for some youth is a sense of futurelessness.

The fact that so many young people are generally pessimistic

about whether there will be a future . . .

Note: Use these correction symbols only if you'll be reprinting or retyping a final version of your paper. If you catch a typographical or other error before you hand in the paper, use white correction fluid and black ink for your change.

PROOFREADING AND CORRECTING USING A WORD PROCESSOR

If your paper is stored on a computer file, then you will be able to make final revisions and correct mechanical errors with ease. If your word-processing program has a feature to correct your spelling, use it as soon as you have finished revising for style and organization (though you should *never* rely solely on computer spell checkers). After correcting any spelling errors, you may want to print out a working draft to use for making final corrections. Then carefully proof and correct your printed paper, checking for punctuation, consistency of tenses, agreement of subjects and verbs, and finally the accuracy of your documentation. At this point, you are ready to enter changes into the computer file and to print the final copy. You may want to print a second copy to retain for your own files.

Checking Punctuation

Before you check for punctuation errors, keep the following rules in mind; they cover the questions that most students have about punctuating research papers.

- Use a period to mark the end of straightforward sentences and to mark the end of some abbreviations: 2:00 a.m., Ms. Check the dictionary when you are in doubt about punctuating abbreviations.
- In quotations, place the period inside quotation marks: I think I know what Lewis Thomas meant when he said, "There is really no such creature as a single individual." When a quotation is followed by parentheses, however, place the period after the parentheses: "A director shows the way. He does not manipulate his actors" (Dalton 232).
- Use a period after indirect questions: Eleanor Roosevelt's friends often asked how she was able to accomplish so much.
- Double-space after a period at the end of a sentence.
- Single-space after personal initials: J. I. M. Stewart.
- Do not space after the period within an abbreviation: Ph.D.
- Do not space before commas or other punctuation that follows an abbreviation: Sherwyn M. Woods, M.D., Ph.D.
- Place periods after numbers and letters used to itemize:

1. Exercise vigorously at least three times a week.
2. Eat a diet high in carbohydrates and low in fat.
3. Sleep between six and eight hours a night.
4. Avoid nicotine and excessive amounts of caffeine and alcohol.

THE QUESTION MARK

- Place a question mark at the end of direct questions: What does it mean to be an adult?
- Place the question mark outside quotation marks if the quoted part of the sentence is not a question. Have you read a short story by William Faulkner called "The Old People"?
- Place the question mark inside the quotation marks if the quoted part of a sentence is a question, even when the sentence itself is not: Robert Lindner was in town to give a lecture entitled "Must We Conform?"
- Put a question mark inside the quotation marks if both the quotation and the sentence are questions: He turned and asked, "Have you read a novel by Horace McCoy called *They Shoot Horses, Don't They?*"
- Double space between a question mark—or the quotation mark after a question mark—and the first letter of the next word.

- Exclamation points are usually not effective in research reporting. If you have used one, try to find another way to stress the importance of your statement. For example, instead of "Eleanor Roosevelt was a great lady!" it would be more effective simply to write "Eleanor Roosevelt was one of the most important women of this century."
- The rules for placing exclamation points inside or outside quotation marks are the same as those for question marks (see above).

THE COMMA

- Use a comma after lengthy introductory phrases or clauses: Since he won the Nobel Prize, García Márquez has become increasingly popular in the United States.
- Use commas to set off modifying clauses that give extra (nonessential) information: Doris Lessing, who has written a number of powerful realistic novels, has recently written a series of novels that she calls space fiction.
- Do not use commas when such a clause is essential to the meaning of the sentence: The work of Lessing's that I find most intriguing is *The Golden Notebook.*
- Use a comma before a conjunction (and, but, so, etc.) that joins two independent clauses (complete sentences): I wanted him to write about the contemporary novel, but he chose to write about poetry instead.
- Use a comma to separate items in a series: Her computer components include two disk drives, a monitor, a keyboard, a high-speed printer, and the main computer chassis itself.
- Use a comma to set off other words or phrases that rename, contrast with, or qualify other words or phrases that are not essential to the meaning of the main clause:

  1. An appositive or parenthetical phrase: Norman Cousins, the long-time editor of the *Saturday Review,* believes that if people can understand a problem, they can solve it.
  2. A phrase of contrast: Swimming, not jogging, is the best sport for overall fitness.
  3. Qualifying words placed in the middle of a sentence: Many people became disillusioned, seriously disillusioned, in the sixties. Ralph

Nader, however, proved that an individual can influence public policy.

- Single-space after a comma, except before closing quotation marks: "Dave," he said, "what is the matter with you?"
- Place a comma inside quotation marks except when the quotation is followed by parentheses: He wanted to make a film shot through with "conflict" (Thomson 15), and he achieved that through the conflicts of real people.

THE SEMICOLON

- Use a semicolon to join closely related independent clauses: Most young people in the fifties conformed to society's expectations; most of their counterparts in the sixties rebelled.
- Use a semicolon between two independent clauses that are joined together by conjunctive adverbs like *however, nevertheless,* and *therefore:* Successful students keep up with their assignments; however, they also make time for recreation.
- Use a semicolon between items in a series when at least one includes commas: The participants in the 1982 Writers Congress included Toni Morrison, who stirred her audience by urging them to stay "at the barricades"; Meridel Le Sueur, who is as old as the century; and Kurt Vonnegut, whose novels are widely read by young and old.
- Single-space after a semicolon and place it outside closing quotation marks, as in the example above.

THE COLON

- Use a colon to introduce a list or an example, when it is not preceded by a preposition or a form of the verb *to be:* Each student should write a report on one of these artists: Mary Cassatt, Auguste Renoir, Henri Matisse, or Pablo Picasso. *Or:* Imagine a typical early painting by Picasso: large sculptural nudes, primitive African motifs, distorted faces, flattened forms. *Or:* Three kinds of music were popular among college students in the fifties: rhythm and blues, jazz, and rock and roll.
- Colons or commas may be used to introduce quotations, but colons are usually best when the introductory material is longer than a few words and when the quotation itself is fairly long, as here: The

president of the senior class concluded the graduation address with the following words: "Students today face many challenges. The question is not what will the world do for us, but how can we prepare ourselves to meet the needs of a complex and demanding society."

- Use a colon to introduce a second clause that amplifies the first: Many students have unusual jobs: One of my classmates is an animal trainer and another a lace maker.
- Single-space after a colon and put it outside quotation marks.

QUOTATION MARKS

- Put quotation marks around quotations of three lines or less of verse or four lines or less of prose when they are incorporated into the text of your paper (see p. 166).
- Set off longer quotations by indenting ten spaces from the left margin. Do not use quotation marks (see p. 167).
- Enclose quotations within quotations with single quotation marks: According to one critic, "George Eliot's favorite poem was Wordsworth's 'Ode to Duty.' "
- Use quotation marks around the titles of short works: essays, poems, short stories, or songs. Quotation marks are also placed around the titles of parts of books: chapters, introductions, and afterwords.

THE APOSTROPHE

- Use an apostrophe to form the possessive as follows: Morrison's novels; an actor's life; Keats's poetry (a single-syllable word ending in "s"); Dos Passos' early work (a word of more than one syllable that ends in an "s" sound); Dumas's plays (a word of more than one syllable that ends in a silent "s"); Terence's comedies (a word ending in an "s" sound and a final "e").

THE HYPHEN

- Use a hyphen to divide a word at the end of the line. Always break the word between syllables as designated in a standard dictionary, and avoid divisions that leave only one or two letters on a line: adjust-ment, *not* ad-justment. Divide compound words between the two words: type-writer. Divide hyphenated words only at the hyphen: computer-generated, *not* computer-gen-erated.

- Use a dash to add information that interrupts the flow of a sentence: The growing agitation for a nuclear freeze—which seemed to go beyond mere party politics—resulted in widespread demonstrations in the fall of 1982.
- Use a dash to add extra information that is itself divided by commas: Some environmental problems—global warming, ozone depletion, deforestation—threaten the entire planet.
- Use a dash to set off a word or group of words that summarizes what comes before: Among Michael's friends were drummers, pianists, vocalists, guitarists—all kinds of musicians.
- To type a dash, use two hyphens. Do not space before or after.

PARENTHESES

- Use parentheses for the same purposes that you use a dash, reserving parentheses for more radical interruptions of a sentence: Big business entered the sports world with the baseball players strike of 1981 (though financial considerations affected professional sports from their beginnings) and played havoc with football the next year.
- Do not space between a beginning parenthesis and the first letter or between the last character and the closing parenthesis: Many young people in this culture (most of them in fact) earn some of their spending money.
- When you include a complete sentence within parentheses as part of another sentence, it is not necessary to capitalize the first letter or to put a period at the end: Young people in the nineties face many serious problems (AIDS is one of the most frightening) that were unheard of by their counterparts in the sixties.
- Other punctuation follows parentheses: In the nineteenth century, mothers tranquilized their hungry babies with opium (a widely used legal drug at the time). After a long, set-off quotation, however, parenthetical documentation is placed after final punctuation (see p. 180).
- A period is included within the parentheses only when the parenthetical statement is completely independent: Historians are only now beginning to try to make sense of the turbulent events of the 1960s. (An early work that tried to interpret some of the ideas and values of the youth culture in the 1960s was Theodore Roszak's *The Making of a Counter Culture.*)

BRACKETS

- Use brackets to insert an editorial comment or explanatory name or word within a quotation: One biographer has concluded that ''even though he suffered from a prolonged illness, he [D. H. Lawrence] never lost his love of life.''
- If you change the capitalization of a letter in a quotation, place brackets around the letter to indicate the change: Steffi Sidney has said of Nicholas Ray that ''[h]e wanted the movie to come from *us,* rather than from his direction.''

ELLIPSIS DOTS

- Use ellipsis dots within a quoted passage to indicate that part of the quotation has been omitted: On April 8, 1928, the *New York Times* quoted Eleanor Roosevelt as saying that if women ''expect equal political preferment . . . they must study history, economics and political methods, and they must mix with their fellow human beings.''
- If the omission comes at the end of the sentence, add a period before the ellipsis dots: Eleanor Roosevelt argued that women interested in becoming involved in politics ''must study history, economics and political methods. . . .''
- Use ellipsis dots at the beginning of a sentence only if it is not clear that something has been left out.
- Space before, between, and after the individual ellipsis dots.

UNDERLINING

- Use underlining where italics would be used in a printed text. Underline titles of complete works—books, films, radio and television programs, plays, operas, and long poems published as books. Underline titles of periodicals (newspapers, magazines, and journals) and works of art (paintings and sculptures) as well as the names of ships, aircraft, and spacecraft. If you use a computer and printer that allow you to italicize, you may want to check with your professors to see which they prefer.

SPACING OF PUNCTUATION

- The following lists summarize standard rules on the spacing of punctuation.

1. After a period within most abbreviations
2. After a quotation mark at the beginning of a quotation or before a quotation mark at the end of a quotation
3. Before punctuation used to divide or end a sentence
4. Before or after hyphens
5. Before, between, and after hyphens used to make a dash
6. After a beginning parenthesis (or bracket) or before a closing one

1. After the period following personal initials
2. After commas, semicolons, and colons
3. Before, between, and after ellipsis dots
4. Before a beginning parenthesis within a sentence
5. After a closing parenthesis within a sentence unless the parenthesis is followed by another punctuation mark

1. After a period, question mark, or exclamation point at the end of a sentence except when it is followed by quotation marks
2. After quotation marks that follow a period, question mark, or exclamation point
3. After a closing parenthesis that encloses an independent sentence and the end punctuation

Printing the Final Copy

If you have composed your paper on a word processor, then preparing a clean copy will be easy if your printer is working properly. You may want to make your final corrections on a printed (hard copy) draft before entering them into the computer. Once this is accomplished, make sure you have the following:

1. A printer compatible with the computer you are using
2. Appropriate paper for the printer
3. A working ribbon or ink cartridge

Typing the Final Copy

ASSEMBLING TYPING MATERIALS

Before you begin typing, have the following materials on hand:

1. A clean black typing ribbon and a typewriter with a plain standard typeface. Avoid colored typing ribbons and unusual typefaces such as italic or script.
2. Adequate correction tape, film, or liquid—whichever is appropriate for your typewriter.
3. A supply of white 8½-by-11-inch, twenty-pound-weight typing paper. Do not use onionskin or erasable paper.

MAKING CORRECTIONS

Make as many corrections as possible on the typewriter before you remove each sheet. Once a page is removed, it is more difficult to make typed corrections. Some errors (such as minor spelling and typographical errors or two words reversed) can be corrected by covering the mistake with liquid paper or correction tape and then writing over it in black ink. But if a page contains several errors that will be difficult for you to correct, you ought to retype it.

COPYING THE PAPER

It is always a good idea to make a copy of your paper and to keep the copy separate from the original. A photocopy can be even neater than the original since it often does not show corrections made with tape and liquid paper.

Specifications

MARGINS

For the main text of the paper, use one-inch margins at the top, the bottom, and on the left side of the page. The margin on the right should be as close to an inch as possible, though it is better to have it wider than an inch than narrower. Use a hyphen to divide words that would otherwise extend beyond the margin. For the first page of notes, list of sources, and other pages with a separate title, use a one-inch margin at the top.

The page number should be one inch from the right edge of the paper and a half-inch from the top.

SPACING AND INDENTATION

Double-space between the title and the first paragraph. Double-space the entire text, including quotations, notes, and bibliography.

Indent the first line of each paragraph five spaces and all lines of long quotations ten spaces. Quotations may be typed flush with the right margin.

TITLE PAGE

The standard MLA format for indicating the title and author of a research paper as well as the course for which the paper has been written and the date of the paper's completion is as follows:

On the first page of the paper, place the author, instructor, course, and date in the upper left corner one inch from the top, and the page number in the upper right. Double-space, center the title, and double-space before the beginning of the paper (see pp. 178, 237).

ARRANGEMENT OF PAGES

You should begin typing each item on the list below on a separate page. Arrange the parts of your paper in the following order, whether a paper has all or some of the items. Your instructor will tell you which of these to include:

1. Title page
2. Outline
3. Text of paper
4. Appendix
5. Endnotes
6. List of sources (bibliography or works cited)
7. Blank sheet for instructor's comments

This is a complete list. Some papers will simply have a title and author page or section for this information on the first page, the main text, and the list of sources.

NUMBERING PAGES

Always count the first page of the text, and number consecutively through the list of sources. Some instructors may ask you to omit the number on the first page. Others may ask you to place a number on all pages including the first. The pages of an outline inserted after the title page and before the text of the paper should be numbered with lowercase Roman numerals.

LABELING PAGES

As a courtesy to your instructor, place your last name immediately before the page number. Then if the pages of your paper are mixed in with those of another paper, it will be easy to reassemble the individual papers.

APPENDICES

Tables, illustrations, photographs, and charts are often placed at the end of a paper before notes and/or the list of sources. If you think such material is important but will distract the reader if included in the main text, place it in an appendix. For each item of supplementary material, make a separate appendix. A set of drawings might constitute "Appendix I," a chart "Appendix II." Place the title of an appendix one inch from the top of the page and double-space before beginning the text.

The Finished Paper

PROOFREADING

Working on a word processor will make it easy for you to proofread and correct your work up to the last minute. Once you have printed what you think is a final copy, you may choose to make corrections using liquid paper and black ink. For more than a few corrections, go back to your computer to make changes and then print the paper again.

If you are typing your paper, proofread every page before you remove it from the typewriter. When you have finished typing, proofread it again. It is sometimes easier to find errors if you read a paper out loud including marks of punctuation.

If your instructor allows you to get help with proofreading, you may want to ask a patient friend to give your paper a look. If you place a light pencil mark at the end of each line that contains an error, you can evaluate the whole paper and decide how to make corrections.

BINDING

Most instructors prefer students to bind their papers together with a large paper clip in the upper left corner. A slip of paper placed under the clip will protect your paper from being damaged by the clip.

Activity

The following paragraph is from an early rough draft of Carla Medina's paper on *The Color Purple*. Carla later dropped this paragraph from her paper since it does not really contribute to her discussion of the novel's voices. Had she used this paragraph, however, she could have improved it by cutting out unnecessary words, varying the choice of words, and correcting errors in punctuation, typing, and documentation. Read the passage carefully, correct the errors, and improve it in any other way you can.

When Alice Walker published The Color Purple in the spring of 1982, some
ten years ago, she was a respected, but no particularly well known
novelist, poet, and essayist. However within a few weeks after this
controversial novel was published, it became a bestseller and Alice
Walker became well known to people who keep up with popular novels.
Awarded the American Book Award and the Pulitzer Prize for literature in
1983, it has been the subject of much controversy. Even more
controversial, however, is the Stephen Spielberg film based on the novel
released in 1985. Pauline Kael, the critic who reviewed the movie for
the December 30 edition of the New Yorker, condemns both the book and
the film, though she indirectly praises the novel for its "earthy folk
style". (Kael, p. 69).

Project Activity

If you are working on a word processor, print double-spaced copies of your paper at least twice before you prepare the final paper—after the first draft and the next to the last draft. Use these printouts or your own hand-written or typed drafts and revise as follows:

1. After reading through your first draft, evaluate the organization and mark passages that you want to move.
2. Check your paragraphs. Have you introduced the subject of each paragraph effectively? Are they too long or too short? Would it be better to break up some paragraphs into more than one or move parts of one paragraph elsewhere?
3. Check your sentences. Have you used varied sentence structures? Which sentences are too wordy and can be improved by cutting out unnecessary words.
4. Check your words. Take out any that do not contribute to what you want to say. Notice any words that are unnecessarily obscure and replace them with others that are more easily understood. If you are using a computer, enter all changes into your file. If not, you may need to cut and paste pieces of your paper to reorganize it.
5. Using the guidelines in this chapter, check to make sure your sentences are properly punctuated. If you are using a word-processing system that will check your spelling, do that now; if not, circle any words that you have doubts about and look them up.
6. After making the appropriate changes on the computer or on the original draft, reread your improved paper and check once again to make sure that it flows smoothly from one part to another.
7. Prepare the final copy, proofread it carefully, and make final corrections in black ink.

WRITING RESEARCH PAPERS IN THE HUMANITIES

11

Approaches to Research in the Humanities

The humanities include those academic disciplines that explore human beings and their cultures: art, history, literature, music, and philosophy. Each of these disciplines is subdivided into a number of categories; the visual arts, for example, include motion pictures, graphics, painting, photography, and sculpture. There is some overlap between the humanities and the social sciences: in recent years some historians have applied the methods of social science to historical topics by doing very detailed quantitative studies with the help of computers, while some literary texts are examined as sociological documents. There are many kinds of investigations that students can pursue in the humanities involving both primary and secondary materials. Doing primary research in literature, history, or philosophy involves examining original documents in these fields: in literature, for example, studying the text of a novel, letters written to and by the author, manuscripts or facsimiles of manuscripts of the literary text, or other writings by the author referring to the text. Secondary research related to the same novel would include the study of critical essays, book reviews, or other materials about the text or author written by others.

Since production of visual art predates written history, students have a vast array of material to explore spanning many centuries, ranging from the cave drawings at Lascaux in southwestern France to the subway graffiti of the 1980s. To do primary research in the visual arts you would study works themselves, usually in museums. To do secondary research, you would examine reproductions of the art (printed photographs or slides), as well as books and articles written about artists and their work. You might research the career of an individual artist—Velasquez, Vermeer, Van Gogh; the influence of an artist on others—Caravaggio on Ribera and Rembrandt; the relationship of an artist to a patron—Goya to Charles IV; an artist's treatment of a particular subject—Mary Cassatt's paintings and drawings of children; or even a single painting—Picasso's *Guernica*.

History, in some ways the broadest of disciplines since it comments on all others—the history of science, of economics, of art, literature, and ideas—involves using a great variety of resources to reconstruct the past of human experience. There are three different kinds of materials available to professional historians and student researchers: primary sources generated by events themselves—letters, government reports, newspaper accounts, video or audio tapes of events; secondary sources—books and articles produced by historians who have studied the primary materials; and tertiary sources—encyclopedia articles, textbooks, or popular histories based on the secondary sources.

Ideas about what constitutes literature are changing to include much more than poetry, drama, and fiction written by established writers. Literary scholars now do serious research that involves examining essays, memoirs, diaries, and letters, as well as popular novels, film scripts, and even television scripts. Although writing about literature in some courses may simply involve examining and analyzing a novel, poem, or play without reference to any other sources, you may have an opportunity to do some original research. Teachers of literature who assign research projects, like instructors of other disciplines, usually are very specific about the kind of research they want students to pursue. Possibilities include synthesizing various interpretations of a work by reading and evaluating critical essays about it, researching the critical reception of a book by reading the original reviews published in periodicals and newspapers, studying published letters to discover an author's intentions in writing a work, or reading a biography to find out how a particular work relates to the author's life. In some cases, you may be asked to research some aspect of the social context in which a work was written. In a course on Victorian literature, for example, you might be asked to research child labor practices in the period and to show how particular writers—Elizabeth Barrett Browning and Charles Dickens—used their works to protest those practices.

There are many interesting research projects for students to pursue in the area of music, ranging from the life and works of one of the great classical composers to the role of music in a first-grade classroom. In a course in music theory, for example, you might study the ideas of the classical theorists and perhaps compare Plato's and Aristotle's theories of the relationship between musical tones and emotional states. In a course that relates music criticism to composition, you might research the relationship of the critical writings of Robert Schumann to the music produced in the mid-nineteenth century, focusing perhaps on the work of Johannes Brahms. In another context, you might examine the historical and critical issues surrounding Mozart's *Requiem* and its place in the development of church music. If you are studying popular culture and contemporary music, you might want to explore the public demand for censorship of lyrics of rock and roll songs.

There is enormous variety among the works of philosophers who reflect on and discuss the nature and meaning of human existence. As a student of philosophy, you might be asked to research the historical foundations of a school of thought—the development of utilitarianism; to research perennial themes such as perception and reality, the nature of the moral life, or the interplay between justice and freedom; or to examine the influence of a particular philosopher on some aspect of a culture, perhaps the influence of Kant on German education or Simone de Beauvoir on American feminism.

A Sample Paper in the Humanities

MICHAEL GOLD

When Michael's freshman English teacher asked the class to choose a topic and write a research paper in one of the disciplines within the humanities, he chose film studies since he has always been interested in movies. His paper on *Rebel Without a Cause* draws on a variety of sources, including contemporary reviews, the book that originally inspired the film, books about the director and the actors, articles in popular magazines, and critical essays in film journals. The paper is documented with parenthetical references in the text and a list of sources at the end, the style recommended by the Modern Language Association, which is the style most commonly used in college courses in the humanities.

STEPS LEADING TO MICHAEL'S PAPER

1. Develops an existing interest and focuses his subject (p. 23)
   - Is surprised to discover academic courses in film
   - Goes to the library and reads an *Encyclopedia Americana* article on the history of motion pictures
   - Concludes that the best way to approach the subject is to break it down into different types of movies
   - Visits a bookstore and studies textbooks used in film courses
   - Talks to a film student about cult movies
   - Jots down ideas and consolidates his list
   - Chooses to study *Rebel Without a Cause*

2. Identifies his sources (p. 34)
   - Talks with the reference librarian
   - Consults appropriate indexes in the library and collects relevant articles and books
3. Plans his strategy (p. 75)
4. Writes a letter to the film's distributor asking how often *Rebel* is shown (p. 101)
5. Takes notes—quoting, paraphrasing (p. 125), and interpreting (p. 128) his sources
6. Sorts and classifies his note cards (p. 141)
7. Writes out a preliminary thesis statement (p. 144)
8. Writes a thesis statement setting up his argument (p. 144)
9. Outlines, drafts, and revises his paper (p. 152)
10. Prepares a list of works cited, checks spelling and punctuation, and prints out the finished version of his paper

Introductory paragraphs catch reader's attention and lead to thesis statement.

Gold 1

Michael Gold
Professor Levine
English 102
13 March 1992

Conflict and Cooperation:
The Making of Rebel Without a Cause

In the 1950s movies were very different from what
they are today. The most popular were musicals,
Westerns, and comedies; and most were intended for
family entertainment. Only a few were produced
primarily for a teenage audience. Young people referred
to them as movies, adults as picture shows and hardly
anyone thought of going to a film--which is what movies
or picture shows are called when they are taken
seriously. Occasionally a film was made in those days
that influenced future films and that affected the way
people behaved. Such a film was Rebel Without a Cause.

Most people who remember Rebel associate it with
one person, James Dean--his life, his death, and the
cult that developed among some of his more ardent fans.
A few may recall that Rebel was also the film that made
Sal Mineo and Natalie Wood famous. Perhaps because of
the premature deaths of all three of its stars, Rebel
feeds a kind of nostalgia among people who first saw it
in their teens, and it continues to attract young
audiences in colleges across the country (Lusk). The
association of Rebel with the sudden death of young
people began when James Dean was killed--clearly because
of his own recklessness--in an automobile accident

Source indicated in parentheses; details given in bibliography.

No comma between source and page number.

before the film was released in 1955. It continued in 1976 when Sal Mineo was stabbed by an unknown assailant and again in 1981 when Natalie Wood drowned under somewhat mysterious circumstances.

Immediately after James Dean's death, a large number of young people became obsessed with keeping his memory alive, their efforts soon reaching the intensity of hysteria. For some, grief developed into a kind of death cult. According to Life magazine, thousands of fans wrote letters to Dean every month in which they insisted either that he was not dead or that he was immortal (Goodman 75). In 1957, Sam Astrachan reported in the New Republic that a whole generation of young people had adopted the jacket, gestures, and expressions that were part of Dean's image in Rebel (17). The Dean mania became a profitable business: some fans were willing to pay up to two hundred dollars for poorly done oil paintings of Dean (Mitgang 114); others purchased life-sized casts of Dean's head, records of ballads about his death, and pieces of old Porsche aluminum purported to be part of his car (Goodman 78). What Life magazine referred to as the "Delirium over Dead Star" lasted a long time. As late as 1969, a reporter for the New Yorker interviewed fifty-seven-year-old Mrs. Therese J. Brandes, the founder of the James Dean Memory Club. Mrs. Brandes, who had been in her mid-forties when Dean died, explained that while teenagers may have had a romantic attachment to Dean, she and her contemporaries "loved him as a son." Mrs. Brandes showed the reporter

Brief quoted phrase integrated into sentence.

Several sources are used in this paragraph; each requires separate citation.

Gold 3

two closets full of recent letters as evidence of Dean's
continuing popularity ("Fan" 22).

The Dean mania has subsided somewhat, but the film
remains a favorite. It periodically plays in commercial
theaters that book classic or cult films. According to
Jack Lusk, who distributes the film to colleges,
churches, and other nonprofit institutions, Rebel "is a
perennially popular title" with a "steady booking
pattern." It is "one of the few cult films, like
Casablanca, that people see over and over again" (Lusk).

It is of course impossible to know what our
perceptions of Rebel Without a Cause would be if it were
not for James Dean's untimely death, but it is obvious
that the Dean mania has obscured the real story of how
Rebel Without a Cause came to be. James Dean made an
important contribution to Rebel, but he was only one of
many people who helped to make this film memorable.
Rebel was really the product of the imagination, the
creative energy, and the plain hard work of a group of
people--the producer, director, writers, actors, and
technical experts--who compose the community of a film.
More than any other work of art, a film is a
collaborative effort requiring cooperation and
compromise. Some films--and Rebel is one--grow not only
from the minds of the collaborators but also out of
existing social concerns and the demands of the movie-
going public. Once films are released, they go back
into society, influencing the feelings, behavior, and
ideas of their audiences. And finally they become

Thesis statement or controlling idea

Gold 4

subjects for interpretation, for critics and historians who try to understand what films mean.

The story of <u>Rebel Without a Cause</u> began in 1944 when a young psychologist named Robert Lindner published a book entitled <u>Rebel Without a Cause . . . The Hypnoanalysis of a Criminal Psychopath</u>, which was widely read. George Mayberry, writing in the <u>New Republic</u>, referred to it as a "deeply and tragically human" story (108); and Edwin J. Lukas, in the <u>Annals of the American Academy of Political and Social Science</u>, hailed it as essential reading for professionals concerned with the criminal personality (216). In 1947, Warner Brothers purchased the right to make a movie based on Lindner's book and signed the young Marlon Brando to star; when Brando's contract expired, the project was temporarily abandoned. Juvenile delinquency, however, was a serious social concern, spurring Columbia Pictures to make a successful film on the subject, <u>The Wild Ones</u>, starring --a popular choice for the role of delinquent--Marlon Brando. When Nicholas Ray became a director for Warner Brothers in 1954, he too wanted to make a film about juvenile delinquency, and as a consequence the <u>Rebel</u> project was revived (Kreidl 91). But the film Ray wanted to do had little in common with the content of Robert Lindner's professional case history.

Some of Lindner's material was used in the film, from the title--which would catch the imagination of a generation of teenagers--to the suggestion that problems within a family are the cause of antisocial

Michael's own conclusions—no citation needed.

behavior among the young. Lindner's study reveals how family conflicts lead young Harold to chronic criminal behavior; in the film unhappy homes provoke Jim, Judy, and Plato to pranks and illegal acts that have serious consequences. But the details are very different. Lindner's sullen Harold, based on an actual case history, is from an immigrant-laborer home with few material comforts. He engages in criminal behavior from the age of twelve, drops out of school, is periodically arrested, put on probation, sentenced to jail, and finally committed to a penitentiary. Jim Stark (James Dean) is one of a group of indulged but unhappy, privileged but rebellious teenagers who argue with their parents, drink, and sometimes steal cars. Their escapades end in the deaths of Buzz (Corey Allen) in a car accident and of Plato (Sal Mineo) in a shootout with the police, who mistakenly assume that he is armed. For Jim Stark, however, the day ends positively, as he gets the pretty girl (Natalie Wood) and is reconciled with his parents.

When Nicholas Ray's proposal to make a film about affluent suburban kids was merged with the studio's plan to make a movie called Rebel Without a Cause, there was no script and no real vision of how the differences between the original book and Ray's intentions could be resolved. In fact, the seeds that would flower in the final film were scattered in the minds of many different people. Nicholas Ray brought them together. He chose Dave Weisbart for the producer because Weisbart had two

Movie titles underlined.

teenage children, and Ray thought that he would have a special sympathy with the project (Ray 70). Leonard Rosenman, the musical director, was a good choice because he had already worked with Dean in _East of Eden_ (Kreidl 94).

Finding a screenwriter was more difficult. According to Ray, there is often animosity between a writer and a director, since each is dependent on the other and yet each wants to make final decisions. Famous writers present additional problems, since they often want to follow their own ideas, while the studio requires that they cooperate with the needs of a production. Sometimes a studio will insist that a director use a writer who is already under contract to the studio, even though the writer is not suited to the project (Ray 71-72).

Ray originally approached Clifford Odets, a friend, to do the script; but Warner Brothers had other ideas since Leon Uris, a best-selling author and successful scriptwriter, was already under contract to them (Dalton 225). Ray agreed to Uris's joining the project since he was interested in the subject, had experience working with teenage boys, and was willing to do research. But when Uris produced a sketch of a small town plagued by juvenile delinquency, Nicholas Ray did not like it, and Uris had to be replaced. Ray's account of his experience with Uris suggests that studying and finally rejecting Uris's work allowed Ray to refine and clarify his own intentions. By seeing what he did not want, he

Source is noted at the end when all information in a paragraph is from a single source.

perhaps came closer to knowing what he did want (Ray 73).

The next writer to work with the Rebel crew was Irving Shulman, a novelist and scriptwriter who had been a high school teacher and who loved sports cars, something that Ray hoped would provide a bond with the moody James Dean. Although an affinity with Dean never developed and his vision of the film proved incompatible with that of Nicholas Ray, Irving Shulman was directly responsible for significant features of the film. His discovery of a newspaper article about a teenage boy who plunged to his death off the Pacific Palisades when he failed to jump free in a "chickie run" became the famous scene in which Buzz accidentally drives his car off a cliff because his sleeve is caught and he cannot open the car door to escape. Shulman also helped develop the character of Plato; Plato's luxurious house, self-indulgent mother, and absent father were all his ideas. It was finally a disagreement about the character of Plato, however, that led to Ray's decision that he needed still another writer (Ray 73).

Leonard Rosenman, the musical director of Rebel, suggested the thirty-one-year-old Stewart Stern, who worked with Ray until the film was finished, bringing together the ideas of previous writers with his own (Kreidl 93). But even Stern did not produce a final, definitive screenplay. Although he wrote at least three different versions, none reflects completely the dialogue and the action of the final film. Once the

Gold 8

actors went to work, the script continued to evolve,
with James Dean, in particular, creating as he acted
(Kreidl 86).

"Please let me do something here. Let me play with
it. Just roll it." When Dean asked to be allowed to
play a scene his way, Ray said yes (Dalton 236). It is
difficult to know what subtle character traits
contribute to a successful collaboration between an
actor and a director, but we do know that Nicholas Ray
trusted James Dean's instincts. From the beginning, Ray
followed the advice of Elia Kazan, who insisted that a
good director never tries to direct a natural actor.
Ray's version of Kazan's rule was this: "A director
shows the way. He does not manipulate his actors"
(Dalton 232). Two of the more famous scenes in the
film--the opening scene with Dean lying drunk in the
street playing with a toy monkey and the scene after the
fatal car accident with Dean taking a bottle of milk and
slowly pressing it to his face--were the actor's
spontaneous performances (Dalton 236, 253). The milk
bottle scene was planned one night at Ray's house with
Dean thinking through the situation and Ray playing the
father (Houston and Gillett 184).

Nicholas Ray encouraged the other young actors to
develop their own parts. Looking back on the
experience, Natalie Wood observed: "Nick gave me a
career . . . with Rebel. . . . Because he regarded me as
an actress with a meaningful contribution to make, I
felt better of myself and better of my work. . . . I

Ellipsis dots are used to indicate words
omitted.

think he did that for a lot of people" (Kreidl 208).
Steffi Sidney, who played one of the gang members, has
also testified to Nicholas Ray's freeing his actors to
develop the character of a gang: "He wanted the movie to
come from us, rather than from his direction." When Ray
felt that they were still acting as individuals rather
than as a gang, he urged them to go out together and to
do things as a group--to go to the beach and prowl
around deserted buildings at night (Dalton 230).

The evidence is abundant: from the very beginning,
Nicholas Ray recognized that the kind of film he wanted
to make would be a community effort requiring the
cooperation of many people. He wanted to make a film
shot through with "conflict" (Thomson 15), and he
achieved that through the conflict of real people--the
producer, the director, the writers, the actors, and
others. The conflicts among young people trying to grow
up, between the young and their baffled parents, and
between the young and the forces of authority--all are
portrayed convincingly. Ray brought together the
fragments of many people's experiences: Uris's talks
with juvenile authorities and delinquents (Kreidl 77),
the newspaper article about a chicken run, Shulman's
work as a high school teacher (Ray 74), Sal Mineo's
actual idolizing of Dean (Kreidl 82), and the ganglike,
semidelinquent behavior of many of the young actors
(Dalton 227). Perhaps Ray achieved a kind of
authenticity and unity because he was able to fuse the
experiences of so many real people struggling to say

something about the eternal conflicts between the young
and the old.

Although there are probably very few people who
would insist today that James Dean lives, Rebel Without
a Cause is still alive in the minds of people who study
the history of film. In recent years, scholars have
tried to judge the film as a whole, rather than as a
showcase for the magic that Dean created. They are
studying its values, its art, and its place in American
film history. Peter Biskind, writing in Film Quarterly,
sees Rebel as a reflection of the conservative values of
mid-fifties America. He argues that the young
characters condemn their parents' weaknesses, but that
in the end the film affirms traditional family values
and remains "a profoundly conservative film" (37).
David Cook, on the other hand, in his History of
Narrative Film, sees the film as "a definitive statement
of the spiritual and emotional ills that beset America
during the period" (500). Douglas McVay considers Rebel
to be Nicholas Ray's masterpiece and one of the four
best films of the fifties (24). David Thomson, who
thinks of Rebel as the work of a director who was both a
serious social critic and a "great romantic" producing
great art (15), warns of the difficulty of ever
recreating that initial response:

Note how Michael uses the names of
authors he quotes; he then does not need
to repeat name in the parenthetical
citation.

Long quotation is indented ten spaces;
double-spaced before, throughout, and
after quotation.

> So Rebel is vibrant with yearning aspirations,
> and Ray's beautiful and brave venturing with
> space, decor, and faces lost in a night
> wilderness of screen. We can never regain the
> view we had of the film in 1955, when its
> rueful passion swept so many of us away. (16)

Even though almost thirty years have passed since
audiences first settled down to watch Rebel Without a
Cause, evaluating its place both in film history and in
American society is still not easy. A profoundly
conservative film, a tragedy in the classical sense, a
high romance, or scathing social comment--which is the
appropriate category for this still controversial film?
When we consider the many different people who
contributed to its creation, we may conclude that it is
all of these. It is certainly not surprising to
discover that the film that has what Kreidl calls "a
disparate smattering of different vocabularies from
different sources" should evoke such varied responses
(86).

Rebel Without a Cause was generated through
conflict; it was finally realized when the community of
people who wanted to bring it about discovered ways to
compromise and cooperate. But the conflict that created
Rebel is still alive in the minds of people who
interpret it. A film more than a book exists in the
minds of its viewers. Although some may have a
videotape of the film, which they can study at their
leisure, most people must rely on memory.[1] The

Concluding paragraph echoes thesis
statement: note repeated ideas *community,
compromise, cooperate.*

community of interpreters--those who remember, study, and talk and write about <u>Rebel</u>--will probably always be fraught with conflict both because memories are highly personal and because the struggle between generations that <u>Rebel</u> explores is constantly being renewed.

Note

[1]The availability of videotape for purchase or rental makes it possible to study films the way scholars study written works of literature. Future responses to <u>Rebel</u> may be based more on careful critical analysis than on emotional response.

Content note offers a thought of Michael's that is interesting and relevant but that would distract from the main point if included in the text of his paper.

Items in bibliography are alphabetized by
last name of author.

When there is no author, item is
alphabetized by first word of title
(excluding *a, an,* or *the*).

Works Cited

Astrachan, Sam.   "The New Lost Generation."   <u>New
     Republic</u> 4 Feb. 1957: 17-18.

Biskind, Peter.   "Rebel Without a Cause: Nicholas Ray in
     the Fifties."   <u>Film Quarterly</u> 28.5 (1974): 32-38.

Cook, David A.   <u>A History of Narrative Film</u>.   2nd ed.
     New York: Norton, 1991.

"Correspondence."   <u>The New Republic</u> 18 Feb. 1957: 22-23.

Dalton, David.   <u>James Dean: The Mutant King</u>.   San
     Francisco: Straight Arrow, 1974.

"Fan."   "The Talk of the Town."   <u>New Yorker</u> 2 Aug. 1969:
     21-23.

Goodman, Ezra.   "Delirium over Dead Star."   <u>Life</u> 24
     Sept. 1956: 75-76.

Houston, Penelope, and John Gillett.   "Conversations
     with Nicholas Ray and Joseph Losey."   <u>Sight and
     Sound</u> 3 (1961): 182-87.

Kreidl, John Francis.   <u>Nicholas Ray</u>.   Twayne's
     Theatrical Arts Series.   Boston: Twayne, 1977.

Lindner, Robert M.   <u>Rebel Without a Cause . . . The
     Hypnoanalysis of a Criminal Psychopath</u>.   New York:
     Grune, 1944.

Lukas, Edwin J.   Rev. of <u>Rebel Without a Cause . . . The
     Hypnoanalysis of a Criminal Psychopath,</u> by Robert
     M. Lindner.   <u>The Annals of the American Academy of
     Political and Social Science</u> 236 (1944): 215-16.

Lusk, Jack.   Swank Motion Pictures, Inc.   Letter to the
     author.   28 Feb. 1992.

Indent second and subsequent lines of
bibliographic citations five spaces from left
margin.

Mayberry, George. "Alternatives to the Novel." <u>New Republic</u> 24 July 1944: 108.

McVay, Douglas. "Rebel Without a Cause." <u>Films and Filming</u> 23.2 (1979): 16-24.

Mitgang, Herbert. "The Strange James Dean Death Cult." <u>Coronet</u> Nov. 1956: 110-15.

Ray, Nicholas. "Story into Script." <u>Sight and Sound</u> 26 (1956): 70-74.

Thomson, David. "Rebel Without a Cause." <u>Take One</u> Mar. 1979: 15-16.

WRITING RESEARCH PAPERS IN THE SOCIAL SCIENCES

12

Approaches to Research in the Social Sciences

The social sciences are primarily concerned with how human beings, and sometimes other animals, relate to each other. There is no absolute agreement about what constitutes a social science, but generally included in the area are anthropology, economics, political science, psychology, and sociology. In some institutions, however, history might be considered one of the social sciences, while certain psychologists consider their work to be part of the biological sciences. There is some overlap in the various social sciences, and some research may be conducted by teams of researchers from various disciplines. There are many topics in the social sciences that are appropriate for college students to research, but most projects that are suitable for the time limitations of an academic term and for the resources of beginning students will involve studying and synthesizing secondary materials. Beginning students in the social sciences mainly work with the written reports of other investigators who are experts in a field they are studying and who have conducted surveys, administered questionnaires, observed behavior, and arrived at conclusions based on studies that may have extended over a period of years.

Students of anthropology tend to specialize in one of two very different areas: physical anthropology, which studies humans as a biological species, and cultural anthropology, which grows from the study of single cultural groups. Each of these two disciplines is subdivided into numerous specialties. In an undergraduate course in physical anthropology, you might want to research the techniques used to examine human fossil remains to determine the diet of primitive peoples or whether they were warlike. As a student of cultural anthropology, you would study the written accounts of anthropologists who have done fieldwork by leaving their own societies behind and immersing themselves in the cultures of relatively simple peoples. You might, for example, want to focus on the work that has been done on a particular group of people, such as the Kung San hunter-gatherers of the Kalahari Desert in southern Africa. Other fields that are sometimes considered part of anthropology are linguistics and archeology.

The field of economics offers many possibilities for student research: in a course on the history of economic thought, the influence of a particular classical economist—John Stuart Mill, David Ricardo, or Adam Smith; in the study of macroeconomics, one aspect of the complex workings of the Federal Reserve Bank in the contemporary United States; in a course on industrial organization, an analysis of the internal structure of a specific American industry; or in the area of economic development, the strategies for industrialization (or for food distribution) in a less-developed country—Chad, Bolivia, or Turkey.

Since the systematic and therefore scientific study of governments and politics dates back to classical Greece, students studying governments and political processes have a vast historical background to explore. If you are taking a course in ancient political theory, you might want to examine how questions of justice or social responsibility are treated by certain classical authors—Aristotle and Plato, perhaps. Students taking a course in contemporary comparative governments might conduct studies of the role of government in education in two different countries, while those studying international relations could explore some aspect of international law (the battle for an international copyright law), of diplomacy (the establishment of diplomatic relations between the United States and China), or international organizations (Eleanor Roosevelt's role in the United Nations).

There are many possibilities for pursuing interesting research in the field of sociology. You might explore an historical topic, such as the work of the great social reformers of the nineteenth century, people like Robert Owen, who formed a model industrial community in Scotland and later established a Utopian agricultural community in New Harmony, Indiana, or Charles Fourier, the French social philosopher, whose dreams of social harmony resulted in the establishment of a number of colonies in the United States, including the famous Brook Farm. You might want to investigate the early history of sociology as an academic discipline as reflected in the *American Journal of Sociology,* the first academic journal to publish articles on sociological topics. In a course on that aspect of sociology called social psychology, you might study some aspect of human communication, such as the speech habits of street gangs or some other social unit. Your research in this area might lead you to studies conducted by sociologists, psychologists, and linguists. You may want to focus on some aspect of group life within a single community—an ethnic enclave, a small town, or a hospital for the mentally ill.

Like the other social sciences, psychology is rapidly expanding and becoming increasingly complex. Undergraduate students in psychology usually survey the field, taking courses in several areas, such as experimental, developmental, physiological, and abnormal psychology. Students doing research in these areas might study the process by which early investigators—Pavlov and Skinner—discovered the function of rewards in conditioning behavior (experimental), the controversy about attaching psychiatric labels to children (developmental), the role of neural mechanisms in aggressive behavior (physiological), or the theories of the genesis of schizophrenia (abnormal).

As you develop some expertise in a field, you will have more opportunity to do basic or primary research. If you take a course in experimental psychology, for example, you might conduct your own experiment, perhaps using animal subjects like mice or pigeons to investigate the effects of behavior modification techniques. As you advance in a field, you could participate in ongoing research conducted by a team of investigators. Undergraduate students could conceivably conduct primary research by doing one of the following: joining a summer expedition doing fieldwork in cultural anthropology; interviewing people to find out about their political beliefs, voting behavior, or perception of government officials; administering questionnaires to find out about people's drinking habits, sexual behavior, or marriage plans; studying programs conducted in nursing homes, mental health clinics, or birth control clinics and then trying to find out how people value the services they receive; observing children at play in a nursery school or adolescents interacting in a drug rehabilitation center.

Making a Reference List for Papers in the Social Sciences

Most undergraduate students doing research projects in the social sciences will find adequate guidance here for making a reference list. Those who need to cite types of material not noted here should consult the *Publication Manual of the American Psychological Association* [APA] (1983). All examples and rules in this chapter are based on the style established by the APA manual.

Typing References Using APA Style: A Checklist

1. Type the first line of each reference flush with the left margin, and indent the following lines three spaces.
2. Space once after commas, semicolons, and the colon following the location of the publisher. (APA requires two spaces after a colon in sentences.)
3. Use a solid underline with no break between words for titles.

BOOKS

A Book with One Author

Coles, R. (1986). <u>The moral life of children</u>. Boston: Atlantic Monthly Press.

A Book with Two Authors

Colarusso, C. A., & Nemiroff, R. A. (1981). <u>Adult development</u>. New York: Plenum Press.

A Book with a Corporate Author

American Psychological Association. (1983). <u>Publication manual of the American Psychological Association</u> (3rd ed.). Washington, DC: Author.

Note: In this citation, the author and publisher are the same.

A Book with No Author or Editor

<u>Writers' and artists' yearbook</u>. (1980). London: Adam and Charles Black.

A Translation

Piaget, J. (1980). <u>Experiments in contradiction</u> (D. Coltman, Trans.). Chicago: University of Chicago Press. (Original work published 1974)

A Book with an Editor

Erikson, E. H. (Ed.) (1978). <u>Adulthood</u>. New York: Norton.

Note: The name of the editor appears first when the whole text is cited rather than a single essay or chapter.

A Revised Edition

Selye, H. (1978). <u>The stress of life</u> (rev. ed.). New York: McGraw-Hill.

Note: Abbreviate the edition as it is noted on the title page: 2nd ed. for second edition, 3rd ed. for third edition, and rev. ed. for revised edition.

An Article or Chapter in an Edited Book

Rohlen, T. P. (1978). The promise of adulthood in Japan. In E. H. Erikson (Ed.), <u>Adulthood</u> (pp. 129-140). New York: Norton.

PERIODICALS

A Journal Article with One Author

Rogers, C. R. (1964). Toward a modern approach to values. <u>Journal of Abnormal and Social Psychology, 68</u>, 160-167.

A Journal Article with Two Authors

Feather, N. T., & Barber, J. G. (1983). Depressive reactions and unemployment. <u>Journal of Abnormal Psychology, 92</u>, 185-195.

A Journal Article with More Than Two Authors

Kerr, B., Davidson, J., Nelson, J., & Haley, S. (1982). Stimulus and response contributions to the children's reaction-time repetition effect. <u>Journal of Experimental Child Psychology, 34</u>, 526-541.

Note: Cite all authors in the list of references, but in the parenthetical reference in the text, when there are six or more authors, cite the last name of the first author followed by "et al.": (Rogers, et al.)

An Article from a Journal Numbering Pages Continually Throughout a Volume

Weeks, S. G. (1973). Youth and the transition to adult status: Uganda. Journal of Youth and Adolescence, 2, 259-270.

An Article from a Journal Numbering Pages Separately for Each Issue

Braddock, J. H. (1985). School desegregation and black assimilation. Journal of Social Issues, 41(3), 9-22.

An Article Written in a Language Other Than English

Delgorgue, M., & Engelhart, D. Style graphique chez l'enfant: Deux recherches sur la discrimination entre dessin d'enfant "normal" et dessin d'enfant "pathologique" [Graphic style among children: Two studies of differences between the drawings of "normal" and "pathological" children]. Bulletin de Psychologie, 38, 303-321.

Note: If the source used is an English translation, cite only the English title, and do not use brackets.

An Article Condensed or Reprinted in a Journal Other Than Its Original Source

Coleman, J. S. (1973). How do the young become adults? The Education Digest, 38, 49-52. (Condensed from Review of Educational Research, 1972, 42, 431-439)

A Work Cited in a Secondary Source

Tizard, B. (1984). Problematic aspects of nuclear education. Harvard Educational Review, 54, 271-281.

Note: Cite the secondary source in the reference list, but cite both the original and secondary sources in the text. For example, Tizard refers to the results of an unpublished paper given at a conference in 1984. Cite that study in the text as follows: A study conducted in Sweden by Holmberg and Bergstrom in 1984 . . . (cited in Tizard, 1984, pp. 273–274).

The Entire Issue of a Journal

VandenBos, G. R. (Ed.). (1986). Psychotherapy research [Special issue]. <u>American Psychologist, 41</u>(2).

Note: If there is no editor for the special issue, cite the title first, alphabetizing it by the first significant word in the title.

An Abstract

Harding, C., & Kristiansen, C. M. (1984). Statistically sophisticated subjects' perceptions of the health risks of smoking. <u>Journal of Social Psychology, 124</u>(2), 263-264. (From <u>Psychological Abstracts</u>, 1986, <u>73</u>, Abstract No. 3651)

An Article in a Periodical Published Annually.

Kessler, R. C., Price, R. H., & Wortman, C. B. (1985). Social factors in psychopathology: Stress, social support, and coping processes. <u>Annual Review of Psychology, 36</u>, 531-572.

A Magazine Article

Bettelheim, B. (1982, March 1). Reflections: Freud and the soul. <u>New Yorker</u>, pp. 52-93.

Note: APA uses "p." and "pp." to indicate pages of magazines, newspapers, and books, but not for journals.

A Signed Newspaper Article

Anderson, J. (1983, July 25). Finding loving homes for hard-to-place children. <u>Christian Science Monitor</u>, p. 16.

An Unsigned Newspaper Article

Women and gun ownership. (1986, February 24). <u>New York Times</u>, p. 18.

A Newspaper Article with Discontinuous Pages

Pear, R. (1986, February 24). Stiffer rules for nursing homes proposed. <u>New York Times</u>, pp. 1, 9.

An Article from a Newsletter

Staff. (1986, February 17). Effects of cocaine abuse on the unborn. *Behavior Today*, p. 3.

OTHER WRITTEN SOURCES

A Report from the Government Printing Office

National Institute on Alcohol Abuse and Alcoholism. (1980). *Facts about alcohol and alcoholism* (DHHS Publication No. ADM 80-31). Washington, DC: U.S. Government Printing Office.

A Report from an Information or Document Deposit Service

Meyer, J. A. (Ed.). (1982). *Meeting human needs, toward a new public philosophy* (Report No. ISBN-0-8447-1358-9). Washington, DC: American Enterprise Institute for Public Policy Research. (ERIC Document Reproduction Service No. ED 223 327)

A Report of a Congressional Hearing

Hearing before the House of Representatives Select Committee on Children, Youth, and Families. (1983). *Children's fear of war*. Washington, DC: U.S. Government Printing Office.

NON-PRINT SOURCES

A Video Recording

National Institute of Mental Health. (1980). *Drug abuse* [Videotape]. Bethesda: Author.

A Cassette Recording

Shapiro, H. (Speaker). (1971). *Future of evolution* (Cassette Recording No. 010-13492). Center for Cassette Studies.

A Film

Frenzini, L. R. (Producer). (1973). *Neurotic behavior* [Film]. Del Mar, CA: CRM Educational Films.

Note: For films with both director and producer, cite as follows: _____. (Producer), & _____. (Director).

The citations of references within the text of David Harris's paper provide models for the most common kinds of references. The following rules will help you cite other references in the text of your paper:

1. Separate references with more than two authors by commas and an ampersand (&) before the last: _____, _____, _____, & _____.
2. List all the names of authors for sources in the reference list. For parenthetical references of sources with six or more authors, use the name of the first author and "et al."
3. Omit initials in textual citations except when there are two authors with the same last name.
4. Include all references cited in the text in a list of references at the end of the paper, except personal communications (letters or conversations) that cannot be retrieved by the reader.
5. Write out the full name of corporate authors for the first citation. You may, however, choose to abbreviate for citations after the first: American Psychological Association (APA).
6. Cite references that have no author by a shortened version of the title, usually the first two or three words, using quotation marks for articles or parts of books and a solid underline for titles of books.

A Sample Paper in the Social Sciences

DAVID HARRIS

David wrote the sample paper in this chapter in a course in developmental psychology that focused on children and adolescents. He argues convincingly that the nuclear threat causes serious problems for some children and that responsible adults must take appropriate action to deal with these problems.

David's paper, written in the mid-eighties, illustrates that research is an ongoing process. His argument—that children need help in dealing with their fears of a nuclear disaster—is still valid, but the context for that position has changed. A student in the nineties doing research on the subject of the psychological effects of the nuclear threat is not likely to find that American children fear Russians or vice versa. Such a student might, however, explore how the end of the cold war and the changes in the former Soviet Union have affected young people's perceptions of the nuclear threat. David's paper illustrates the writing style and documentation method appropriate for a paper in the social sciences, following the guidelines of the American Psychological Association (1983).

STEPS LEADING TO DAVID'S PAPER

1. Adapts his assigned topic (p. 27)
   - Studies the table of contents and index of a textbook on child psychology
   - Discovers that his younger brother suffers from nightmares about nuclear war
2. Finds out more about one of the authors he is reading (p. 66)
3. Identifies other sources (p. 77)
   - Searches the card catalog and bound volumes of *Psychological Abstracts* with little success
   - Makes an appointment with a reference librarian to discuss how to find information on his topic
   - Schedules and participates in a computer search
   - Orders an off-line printout of sources found in the search
4. Writes a thesis statement setting up his argument (p. 145)
5. Writes a carefully constructed sentence outline (p. 155)
6. Drafts and revises his paper
7. Documents his findings, checks spelling and punctuation, and prepares the final paper

The Need for Education to Combat the Psychological
Effects of the Nuclear Threat on Children
David Harris
Psychology 325

Running head: EFFECTS OF NUCLEAR THREAT

The running head (at the top right of every
page) is a short version of the paper's title.

An abstract is a concise summary of the
contents of the paper.

Abstract

A significant number of children experience serious
worry about nuclear weapons. The fear that they may not
have a future may have harmful consequences for some,
including living for the moment, engaging in self-
destructive behavior, and leading a double life. These
children need help from adults to deal with their fears
and to regain a sense of hope; the first step in meeting
these needs is for responsible adults to educate
themselves about the problem and then to share
appropriate knowledge with the young.

Effects of Nuclear Threat

3

The Need for Education to Combat the Psychological
Effects of the Nuclear Threat on Children

A bright flash and a terrible noise followed by a
sense of dreadful loneliness in an empty, desolate
plain--then a child wakes crying and afraid from a
nightmare that is all too common among children. Child
psychiatrists, pediatricians, educators, and legislators
are becoming increasingly aware that the nuclear threat
is affecting the psychological welfare of the world's
children, and many have concluded that they must do
something and encourage others to respond to the
problem. Although there is much to learn about how to
deal with children's fears of nuclear disaster, those
responsible for the welfare of children must act now to
educate themselves and to provide children with the
information and reassurance they need to grow up in the
nuclear age.

That significant numbers of children suffer from
fears of a nuclear catastrophe has been known for some
time. In the wake of the threats to use nuclear weapons
at the time of the Berlin crisis in 1961 and the Cuban
missile crisis in 1962, two researchers, Escalona (1965)
and Schwebel (1965), independently undertook studies in
U.S. high schools to discover how young people are
affected by living in the nuclear age. Both concluded
that the majority of high school students are seriously
worried about the danger of nuclear war. At the time
that these studies were published, there was little

public response to the problems they exposed, and it was
not until the late 1970s that researchers resumed
investigation into the psychological effects of the
nuclear threat on children. Inspired in part by the
accident at the Three Mile Island nuclear reactor plant
and further spurred by recent findings that a nuclear
war would create a "nuclear winter" with devastating
effects on plant and animal life (Turco, Toon, Ackerman,
Pollack, & Sagan, 1983), increasing numbers of
researchers in psychiatry, the social sciences, and
education, as well as legislators, have undertaken
investigations to discover what children know and think
about the issue and how their perceptions may affect
their lives.

A number of studies conducted in the first half of
the eighties reveal that significant numbers of children
are profoundly concerned about nuclear weapons. As part
of a report published by the American Psychiatric
Association, Beardsley and Mack (1982) prepared an
article entitled "The Impact on Children and Adolescents
of Nuclear Developments," in which they reported the
results of a study based on 1,151 questionnaires
administered to three diverse groups--one made up of
grammar school students, two of high school age youth--
in three U.S. cities. This study revealed that a
sizable number from all groups were "deeply disturbed
about the threats of nuclear war and the risks of
nuclear power" (p. 88). When asked what the word

This paragraph presents data and builds
the argument.

For more than two authors but fewer than
six, use names of all authors for first
citation.

Effects of Nuclear Threat

5

"nuclear" brings to their minds, the respondents came up
with largely negative images: "Dead wildlife and humans
. . . cancer . . . people dying, buildings ruined,
society demolished . . . stars, planets, space, darkness
. . . the world's final demise" (pp. 75-76). In a study
based on lengthy interviews with thirty-one high school
students, Goodman, Mack, Beardsley, and Snow (1983)
found that "although some try not to dwell on it, while
others claim that they worry constantly, all 31 of the
adolescents assert that the existence of nuclear weapons
impinges upon their lives on a daily basis" (p. 510).
There is also evidence that the number of young people
who worry about this issue is increasing. Bachman
(1983) studied the attitudes toward the military of
graduating high schools seniors every spring from 1976
to 1982 and found that the percentage who said that they
often worried about the nuclear threat rose steadily
from 7.2 percent in 1976 to 31.2 in 1982.

Most of the studies reveal that a significant
number of youth are seriously worried, and they also
suggest that a substantial number are not troubled by
nuclear fears, a fact that leads some researchers to
question which children are concerned and why. Studies
suggest that age and socioeconomic status affect
children's level of awareness and concern. In his book
The Moral Life of Children (1986) Robert Coles reports
the results of research conducted over a period of some
six years during which he interviewed and observed small

David uses name of the author earlier in the paragraph; he then does not need to repeat name in the parenthetical citations.

groups of children around the country, coming back to talk to some of the children more than once and over a period of years. Coles concludes that young children are incapable of comprehending certain laws of physics and chemistry, and as a consequence some have little or no knowledge of the nature of the nuclear threat. He talked to several children who "thought that nuclear bombs have more 'dynamite' than other bombs" (p. 259). Others, like a black child from Mississippi who worries what would happen "if the Klan ever got that bomb" (p. 257), incorporate nuclear anxieties within more absorbing fears.

Before the age of twelve many children may have very distorted notions about what nuclear bombs are, but once they are old enough to comprehend the nature of nuclear weapons, the degree of children's concern seems to be affected by parental attitudes and social class. Poor children are preoccupied with much more immediate fears of hunger, parental unemployment, and violence (Coles). Among the large number of children of lower-middle-class families, where having enough money to maintain a certain standard of living is a primary concern, the "end of the world" is likely to mean always having "a bill collector at the door" (Coles, p. 278). In more affluent families, on the other hand, children are likely "to worry long and hard about nuclear accidents or wars" if their parents do, and yet these are the same children who seem to be able to adapt to the nuclear world, to express their fears and to go on enjoying their privileged lives (p. 279).

Children in countries with nuclear weapons and those from non-nuclear countries seem to have comparable levels of concern. A study by Chivian and Mack (1983) comparing attitudes of U.S. and Soviet children found that although more children from this country thought that a nuclear war was likely to occur in their lifetimes, more Soviet children thought that if such a war should occur, they would not survive. Children in neutral countries that do not have nuclear weapons are anxious about the same issues. A study conducted in Sweden (Holmberg and Bergstrom, 1984) revealed that Swedish children are equally concerned, though the fears they emphasize fall halfway between those of the Soviet and U.S. children (cited in Tizard, 1984). Another study, in Finland, also found widespread anxiety about nuclear issues (cited in Tizard, 1984).

The fear that children experience is an appropriate and perhaps inevitable response to the danger posed by nuclear weapons, but it may have serious consequences for some. Beardsley and Mack (1982) noted their strongest finding to be

> a general unquiet or uneasiness about the future
> and about the present nature of nuclear weapons and
> nuclear power. There is a particular uncertainty
> about nuclear war or the limiting of such a war

Set off a quotation of more than forty words in a block indented five spaces.

Indicate in parentheses that a source is cited in a secondary source.

After first citation of a source with more
than two authors, give first author's name
followed by "et al."

should it occur, and the possibilities of survival.
(p. 89)
One of the consequences of this uncertainty about the
future for some youth is a sense of futurelessness.

The fact that so many young people are generally
pessimistic about whether there will be a future "might
make some adolescents disillusioned and highly present-
oriented rather than being willing to accept delay of
gratification or to plan for the future" (Beardsley and
Mack, 1983, p. 82). Goodman et al. (1983) found that
some of the adolescents they interviewed say they "live
for the day" and "don't hold back," behavior that they
blame on their fear of a nuclear catastrophe (p. 526).
Although these investigators warn that the nuclear
threat is probably only one of many factors contributing
to "impulsivity and immediacy in personal relationships
and behavior," it does seem to make a significant
contribution to that behavior (p. 526).

A number of researchers associate the lack of hope
in the future with self-destructive behavior. A sense
of futurelessness resulting from the nuclear threat may
be the cause of drug and alcohol abuse for some young
people and suicide for others. Goodman et al. (1983)
had several respondents claim that the nuclear threat is
responsible for excessive drug use. One sixteen-year-
old made the connection explicit: "When I was doing
drugs though, I was scared of nuclear [arms]" (p. 512).
Carl Rogers (1984), who believes that "the prospect of

Use brackets around any material added to
a quotation.

nuclear war" has a serious detrimental effect on the
young, quotes one young alcoholic who drinks "to get
wasted" because then "nothing seems to matter" (p. 11).
Some psychologists attribute the alarming increase in
the suicide rate among young people to a growing sense
of hopelessness about the future, and Rogers (1984)
insists that there can be no doubt that "the possibility
of a nuclear war plays a part in that hopelessness"
(p. 11). Others, however, warn of the misconceptions
that could come from taking children's fear of nuclear
war out of context of their other fears (Tizard).
Elkind (1983), testifying before the House Select
Committee on Children, Youth, and Families, argued that
the recent increases in suicide, substance abuse, and
crime among the young are attributable to all the
stresses that they encounter, the nuclear threat being
only one (Hearing, p. 54).

If fear of nuclear annihilation leads some young
people to live for the moment, sometimes engaging in
self-destructive behavior, others learn to cope by
leading what Robert Lifton (1982) has called "a double
life" (p. 627). Goodman et al. (1983) note that some
adolescents who "fear that nuclear war is inevitable"
live on two levels, fearing that there will be no future
and yet planning for it. Coles (1986) tells about the
teenage girl from an affluent family who answered a
questionnaire in which she "quite truthfully proclaimed
her horror of a nuclear war," and then that very evening

Page number is needed here for particular
part of report.

This paragraph shifts from a presentation
of the problem to the need for a solution.

attended an elegant party and had a wonderful time
(p. 279). Lifton (1983) explains that living such a
double life has detrimental effects, and that "children
experience it with particular intensity because they
lack the psychological defenses and rationalizations
that adults are so skillful at constructing." He adds
that it "complicates young people's already difficult
task of coming to terms with death which, in turn,
impairs their psychological capacity to live" (Hearing,
p. 71).

Children need help from responsible adults in
dealing with their fears of the nuclear threat.
Salguero (1983), a child psychiatrist at Yale
University, argues that since all children need to feel
protected by their parents from serious external threats
as well as from everyday dangers, parents must recognize
that many children are afraid and that their fears are
affecting their psychological well-being. Salguero
explains that what often happens is that in order to
cope themselves, adults engage in "massive denial," and
that some children who appear to deny the nuclear threat
are actually "waiting for a signal" that it is all right
to talk about their fears. In order to help youth "to
change fear into hope," adults need to "communicate
their true feelings and their own views and perceptions"
(p. 95). Lifton, who has studied a form of denial that
he calls "psychic numbing" (1982), explains that
adolescents have problems when they suppress fears in

childhood because the denial of fears does not last forever. The images suppressed in childhood come back to haunt them in adolescence.

Some children hold adults responsible for what they consider to be an absurd situation. Interpreting the work of Carey, who has studied the effects of bomb shelter drills on children during the 1950s, Lifton (1982) explains that children who were told that they could protect themselves from a nuclear blast by diving under a desk and covering their heads with paper knew that what they were doing was ridiculous. Testifying before the House Select Committee on Children, Youth, and Families, Lifton explained that children sense that their parents doubt their ability to see them safely into adulthood and they "associate it with an overall inability on the part of the adult world to guarantee the safety of the young" (p. 68). Some researchers speculate that young people's perception of the absurdity of "duck-and-cover drills" may have contributed in the sixties to the breakdown of confidence in their elders, who some young people felt were "unreliable, perhaps even insane" (Gittelson, 1982, p. 145). Mack (1982) found that teenagers' attitudes toward the nuclear threat include "a protest at the arrogance of adults who have put them in this situation" (p. 593). Salguero (1983) goes a step further, arguing that unless parents talk to their children and take steps with them to cope with the nuclear threat,

Note two different ways author's name and date and page number of reference are incorporated into the text.

Type a dash as two hyphens, with no
space before or after.

"adolescents will view adults' denial as numbness and
folly, responsible for the world's destruction" (p. 96).

Children and adolescents need to have solutions,
hope for the future, and a first step in creating that
hope is for adults to work to rebuild confidence between
themselves and youth. According to Escalona (1982), the
way adults respond to "ultimate danger" is to children
"the ultimate test of the trustworthiness of adult
society" (p. 607). To be hopeful about the future,
young people "need to know that there are adults
struggling to see that reason prevails in human affairs
--strong adults, whom they can depend upon" (Schwebel,
1982, p. 613). They need to be engaged in dialogues in
which they can "see adults confronting the danger and
acting responsibly" (Goodman et al., p. 529).

There is no single solution to the nuclear threat
or to the problems it creates for children and
adolescents, but one significant aspect of any set of
solutions must be education. Although some people argue
that youth should be shielded from the horrible facts of
the nuclear threat (Hearings, Voth, 1983, p. 11), most
people realize that it is impossible to protect even
very small children from knowledge of the nuclear
danger. They already know, and they want to know more.
Goodman et al. found that when questioned about the
issue, young people repeatedly insisted that they wanted
information about nuclear weapons in order to "overcome
an overwhelming sense of frustration and helplessness"

Ellipsis dots are used to indicate words
omitted.

(p. 528). Among the teenagers interviewed for Goodman's
study, many said that they want to learn more about
nuclear issues. One girl expressed a desire to "know
more," though she did not know where to go for
information. Another insisted that "the public . . .
has to be educated," while still another saw the only
chance for change to be in "people being more aware."
One seventeen-year-old who had taken a course in nuclear
weapons felt that the fear of the unknown was much
greater than the known: "Before, I just didn't
understand it. It was just this huge fear, like a black
hole" (p. 521). After reviewing the literature on
children's understanding of nuclear war, Tizard (1984)
concludes that significant numbers of young people are
anxious about the nuclear threat, that their level of
understanding of the issue is low, and that they want to
be "better informed" (p. 280).

Education, then, seems to be the logical first step
in dealing with the psychological problems caused by the
nuclear threat, but to begin that process, adults must
deal with what Mack (1984) calls "resistance to knowing"
(p. 263). Educators and other responsible adults must
end their own denial of the problem and learn more about
the effects that living in the nuclear age is having on
today's youth. The mechanisms by which people draw back
from the contemplation of intense horror are often used
to avoid confronting the reality of nuclear
annihilation. Even people who have an adequate

intellectual understanding of the nuclear dilemma need
to reduce what Mack calls "the margin between
intellectual and emotional knowing" (p. 264) in order to
become effective educators.

Researchers may not know very much about how to
help young people deal with their fears, but most agree
with Lifton that they can begin with "the sharing of
knowledge" (Hearing, 1983, p. 73). Goodman et al.
(1983) note that when young people are educated to the
realities of the threat, "they can overcome at least
that aspect of fear that stems from ignorance and that
leaves them powerless" (p. 528). Goldenring (1983)
urges that adults must find a forum to discuss the
nuclear threat with children "in churches, in schools,
in communities, and in families throughout the US and
indeed throughout the world" (Hearing, p. 63), while
Mack (1983) notes the need for educational programs in
the schools and for opportunities for young people to
talk about the issue (Hearing, p. 46).

There are significant numbers of children and
adolescents in the United States and other countries who
are affected by the nuclear threat, and for some, fears
of a nuclear disaster may be causing serious
psychological problems, ranging from drug abuse to the
consequences of psychic numbing. Responsible adults--
psychologists, educators, legislators, and parents--must
help troubled youth cope with their fears first by
confronting their own fears and by demonstrating to

Concluding paragraph summarizes main
points of paper and notes conclusions
drawn.

Even though some lines appear short, try
not to hyphenate words at the ends of
lines.

young people that there are concerned people struggling
to prevent a catastrophe. The next step is to work to
devise means to educate young people in a way that will
help them have or gain a sense of control over an issue
that troubles so many. There is a need for more
research both on the impact of the nuclear threat on
youth and, since there is considerable controversy about
how to provide children and adolescents with information
appropriate to their age and level of development, on
the kinds of educational experiences that will be most
helpful. Adults must not wait until there is a
consensus about the best course of action, however.
They must do the best they can with the information they
have to talk to children, to teach them, and to provide
them with an opportunity to express their fears.
Children are having nightmares now.

First line of each entry begins at the left
margin; subsequent lines are indented
three spaces.

References

Bachman, J. G. (1983). American high school seniors view
   the military: 1976-1982. Armed Forces and Society,
   10, 86-104.

Beardsley, W., & Mack, J. E. (1982). The impact on
   children and adolescents of nuclear development. In
   Psychological Aspects of Nuclear Developments, Task
   Force Report #20. Washington, DC: American
   Psychiatric Association.

Beardsley, W., and Mack, J. E. (1983). Adolescents and
   the threat of nuclear war: The evolution of a
   perspective. Yale Journal of Biology and Medicine,
   56, 79-91.

Coles, R. (1986). The moral life of children. Boston:
   Atlantic Monthly Press.

Escalona, S. K. (1965). Children and the threat of
   nuclear war. In M. Schwebel (Ed.), Behavioral science
   and human survival (pp. 201-209). Palo Alto, CA:
   Science and Behavior Books.

Escalona, S. K. (1982). Growing up with the threat of
   nuclear war: Some indirect effects on personality
   development. American Journal of Orthopsychiatry, 52,
   600-607.

Gittelson, N. (1982, May). The fear that haunts
   children. McCalls, pp. 77-146.

Use "pp." to indicate page numbers in
books, magazines, and newspapers, but
not for journal articles.

Capitalize only the first word of title and
subtitle for books and articles.

Goodman, L., Mack, J., Beardsley, W., & Snow, R. (1983).
The threat of nuclear war and the nuclear arms race:
Adolescent experience and perceptions. Political
Psychology, 4(3), 501-514.

Hearing before the House of Representatives Select
Committee on Children, Youth, and Families. (1983).
Children's Fear of War. Washington, DC: U.S.
Government Printing Office.

Lifton, R. J. (1982). Beyond psychic numbing: A call to
awareness. American Journal of Orthopsychiatry, 52,
619-629.

Mack, J. E. (1984). Resistances to knowing in the
nuclear age. Harvard Educational Review, 54, 260-270.

Rogers, C. R. (1982). A psychologist looks at nuclear
war: Its threat, its possible prevention. Journal of
Humanistic Psychology, 22(4), 9-20.

Salguero, C. (1983). Children and the nuclear threat: A
child psychiatrist's personal reflections. Yale
Journal of Biology and Medicine, 56, 93-96.

Schwebel, M. (1965). In M. Schwebel (Ed.), Behavioral
science and human survival (pp. 210-223). Palo Alto,
CA: Science and Behavior Books.

Schwebel, M. (1984). Effects of the nuclear war threat
on children and teenagers: Implications for
professionals. American Journal of Orthopsychiatry,
52, 608-617.

Tizard, B. (1984). Problematic aspects of nuclear
education. Harvard Educational Review, 54, 271-281.

Turco, R. P., Toon, O. B., Ackerman, T. P., Pollack,
J. B., & Sagan, C. (1983). Nuclear winter: Global
consequences of multiple nuclear explosions. <u>Science</u>,
<u>222</u>, 1283-1292.

WRITING

13

RESEARCH PAPERS IN

THE NATURAL AND

APPLIED SCIENCES

Approaches to Research in the Natural and Applied Sciences

The natural sciences are divided into three groups: physical sciences—chemistry, physics, and astronomy; the earth sciences—geology, paleontology, oceanography, and meteorology; and the life sciences—biology and medicine. Each of the individual disciplines is divided into different branches, and a student who does research in one of the sciences would focus on a very narrow aspect of one of the subdisciplines, such as a single chemical reaction.

Students who do research in the sciences might write papers based on one of the following: their own original research projects; a review of the literature in scholarly journals on a particular topic; a study of review articles; or an examination of articles in popular science journals such as *Scientific American.*

In chemistry, senior-level students might do research to develop a method for a particular chemical analysis—toxic wastes, for example—and then write a paper based on the research. Such a paper is divided into three parts. The first is a review of the history of the problem to be studied; the second is a discussion of the methods used, the results obtained, and an interpretation of the results; and the third section is a detailed description of the methods.

Undergraduate students of chemistry may also write research papers based strictly on what other people have done. In a class requiring a research paper, one student might review the literature published in scholarly journals on a topic like the absorption of light by inorganic compounds, bioluminescence (why fireflies light up), or the conversion of coal to oil. Another student might read review articles on a single topic like the

---

Topic: The Rain Forest

Scientists who specialize in tropical biology might spend their entire professional lives exploring and researching the earth's tropical rain forests and still understand only a small fraction of what there is to know. These vast areas of largely unexplored life are found on either side of the equator in Central and South America, Africa, Asia, Malaysia, Indonesia, Northern Australia, and numerous islands in between the larger land masses. While there is general understanding in the scientific community about the possible location of tropical forests, these storehouses of life are being destroyed so rapidly that no one has reliable data about how much remains, which forests are in immediate peril, and what and how much damage has been done to forests that have been partially depleted.

Within specific geographical areas—the small country of Costa Rica, for example—there are different types of tropical forests, ranging from the lowland forests to the montane, or cloud forests, at higher altitudes. Within these two general categories are numerous subcategories determined by variations in rainfall, altitude, drainage, location and condition of rivers, and proximity to the sea. The alteration of even one of these features might affect the lives of numerous organisms, and ultimately the entire ecosystem of a forest.

While people around the globe have in various degrees begun to learn about the wonders of these forests and the dangers involved in their destruction, and while a significant number have taken action to protect these forests, a much smaller number of scientists continue to pursue painstaking research aimed at understanding the complex biological and chemical processes that form the basis of these fragile environments that may well be necessary for the sur-

---

vival of many living things, including human beings. Some of those who study tropical forests may spend years of their lives tromping through the rain and mud of a lowland rain forest observing the feeding habits of particular primates; others may pass many days a year suspended in harnesses high in the tops of the trees of the canopy collecting leaf litter from bromeliads or observing the habits of colorful birds that are rarely seen on the ground; still others may work in laboratories analyzing some of the many chemical compounds that plants and animals use to protect themselves from predators.

Whether they are looking up from the muddy floor of a forest, down from the third tier of trees, or into a microscope, tropical scientists share a commitment to understanding how the rain forests work. They ask questions—about the evolution of the forests; about the way animals disperse seeds and what conditions are necessary for seeds to germinate; about how plants defend themselves against herbivores and animals against carnivores; about feeding habits, pollination, and distribution of species; and about the complex interdependencies of life forms. Others breed wild plants with traditional agricultural crops to produce more productive strains and seek ways to preserve the genetic material that is being lost with continuing destruction of the forests.

While some researchers are looking to the rain forests for solutions to particular human needs—new agricultural food plants or drugs that might be effective against cancer or AIDS, for example—others seek the most basic knowledge about how life sustains itself, evolves, and adapts to change. They might discover how plant species adapt to available light, develop protective coloration that repels predators, attract pollinators, and lure seed dispersers.

In recent decades, perhaps beginning with the publication of Rachel Carson's *Silent Spring* in 1963, it has become increasingly apparent that human welfare is inexorably linked to biological processes that have been going on for many thousands of years with little or no interaction with humans. While in very recent years there has been considerable publicity about human destruction of the forests, few people even in the scientific community understand very much about the forces that sustain and regenerate tropical forests— such as how the seed of a huge canopy tree would ever find the conditions necessary to germinate, grow, and eventually tower over smaller trees and shrubs.

synthesis of a chemical compound, while yet another might consult a number of articles in popular science periodicals to write a paper on pheromones or DNA chemistry.

Undergraduate students majoring in biology will probably write research papers that review the literature on a topic studied in conjunction with a lab project or, as in other sciences, they might review the literature and write a paper on topics that are being discussed in class. The topics that students might research in order to write a review paper range from the effects of acid rain on the growth and development of spruces, firs, and pines to how cell membranes function.

Students of physics, geology, and the remaining natural sciences might write research papers to accompany a laboratory or field project, review the literature on a topic considered in class, or explore the practical application of a natural phenomenon.

The applied sciences include the traditional fields of engineering—mechanical, civil, electrical, architectural, chemical, aeronautical—as well as the rapidly expanding fields of technology related to computer science. Students might research new synthetic building materials, explore the use of computers in diagnosing heart disease, or study and evaluate the achievement of a particularly influential architect.

Making a Reference List for Papers in the Sciences

If you are writing a paper for a science class, your teacher may suggest a particular form to follow. Researchers in the natural sciences typically use either a citation-sequence (number) system or a name/year system similar to the APA style used in chapter 12. This chapter explains how to document a paper using the citation-sequence, or number, system. The examples of bibliographic references listed below and those used at the end of Lisa Lee's paper are consistent with the recommendations of the new style manual published by the Council of Biology Editors (1993), commonly known as the *CBE Style Manual*. This manual generally follows the recommendations of the *National Library of Medicine Recommended Formats for Bibliographic Citation* (1991). The CBE manual is designed to be tailored to particular situations as it has detailed, comprehensive instructions for documenting papers using both the citation-sequence (number) system and the name-year system. Scientists adapt the recommendations of the Council of Biology Editors to meet the requirements of specific journals.

Whether you are preparing a paper for a science class or for a composition class, the citation-sequence (number) system of documentation is

Lisa uses the citation-sequence system recommended by the Council of Biology Editors. Working on a word processor, she first lists her sources alphabetically by author. After composing her paper, indicating sources in parentheses after each use, she then goes back through her paper, numbering the sources in the order they appear in her paper, and then assigning the appropriate number to each reference on her list. She then deletes the parenthetical identification of sources and rearranges the items of her list in numerical order.

appropriate and easy to adapt to a class assignment. References are listed in the sequence in which they appear in the paper. Each reference is given a number based on when it is first cited in the text. The first reference is number 1, the second number 2, and so on. Each time information from a source is used, the writer places its number in superscript at the appropriate place in the text.

Typing References Using CBE Style: A Checklist

1. Use periods to separate elements of a reference, such as between author and title.
2. Use commas to separate equivalent items within an element, such as author names, or to add information such as editor or translator.
3. Use a semicolon after the year of publication of a journal or an article.
4. Use a colon before subordinate information such as a subtitle or page numbers following a volume number.
5. Space as follows: one space between surname and initials of author; separate names of multiple authors with a comma and one space; one space after the title of a journal before the year, but no space thereafter, except after commas separating groupings of discontinuous pages.
6. Capitalize only the first word of titles and proper names.
7. Number the citation at the end in a "List of References." Follow the number with a period and one space.

Students who wish more details for citing unusual sources may consult the *National Library of Medicine Recommended Formats for Bibliographic Citation* (1991) or the style manual of the Council of Biology Editors (1993). The following sample references will be sufficient for the needs of most undergraduate students who choose to use the CBE citation-sequence style.

BOOKS

Note that the format for books is the same as that for booklets or pamphlets.

Book with One Author

1. Perry D. Above the jungle floor. New York: Simon and Schuster; 1986. 170 p.

Note: If the whole book is cited, the total number of pages is indicated at the end. It is also appropriate to call attention to particular pages as in citation number 6 of Lisa Lee's paper on page 301.

Book with Two Authors

2. Forsyth A, Miyata K. Tropical nature: life and death in the rain forests of Central and South America. New York: Charles Scribner's Sons; 1984. 242 p.

Book with Three or More Authors

3. Brown LR and others. State of the world 1991: a Worldwatch Institute report on progress toward a sustainable society. New York: W. W. Norton; 1991. 254 p.

Book with Editor or Editors

4. Head S; Heinzman R, editors. Lessons of the rainforest. San Francisco: Sierra Club Books; 1990. 275 p.

Book with Organization as Author

5. Living Earth Foundation. The rainforests: a celebration. San Francisco: Chronicle Books; 1990. 223 p.

Book with a Separate Title That Is One of Two or More Volumes of a Single Work

6. Fa JE; Southwick CH, editors. Ecology and behavior of food-enhanced primate groups. Vol. 11, Monographs in primatology. New York: Alan R. Liss; 1988. 355 p.

PARTS OF BOOKS

Chapter or Part with a Separate Title

7. Konner M. Why the reckless survive. New York: Viking; 1990. Minding the pain; p. 263-74.

Part with a Different Author and Title

8. Boucher DH. Coffee. In: Janzen DH, editor. Costa Rican Natural History. Chicago: University of Chicago Press; 1983. p. 86-88.

JOURNALS

Article in Journal Paginated Continually Through the Volume

1. Idani G. Seed dispersal by pygmy chimpanzees (Pan paniscus): a preliminary report. Primates 1986;27:441-48.

Article in a Journal Paginated by the Issue

2. Jewell JL and others. Microlasers. Scientific American 1991;265(5):86-94.
3. Freeth S. Incident at Lake Nyos: Tracking the source of a deadly cloud of gas. The Sciences 1992;May/June:30-36.

Article on Discontinuous Pages

4. Davis G. The stormy future of weather forecasting. Popular Science 1991;237(3):78-83, 94, 98.

Article in a Supplement to an Issue

5. Fleming TH, Heithaus ER. Frugivorous bats, seed shadows, and the structure of tropical forests. Biotropica Reproductive Botany 1981;13(Suppl.):45-53.

6. Browne MW. New animal vaccines spread like diseases. New York
   Times 1991 Nov 26;Sect.B:5(col. 5).

Note: The format for newspaper articles is the same as that for journals
with the addition of section, page, and column.

OTHER REFERENCES

Paper Published as Part of a Volume of Conference Proceedings

1. Russell R. Environmental changes through forces independent of
   man. In: Thomas WL, editor. Man's role in changing the face of the
   earth. Proceedings of an International Symposium; 1955 June 16-22;
   Princeton, NJ. Chicago: University of Chicago Press; 1956. p. 453-
   70.

Audio and Audiovisual Publications and Materials

To write a citation for a non-print source like an audiocassette or
videocassette, adapt the information you have to the following general
format: Title [medium]. Authors, editors, narrators, directors, or produ-
cers, as appropriate. Producer, if other than publisher. Place of publication: publisher; date of publication. Description of item, indicating number of tapes, format, whether there is sound, color. Accompanying
materials, etc.

2. Audobon society's videoguide to birds of North America: II
   songbirds [videocassette]. Godfrey M, author, director, narrator.
   Audobon Society, producer. New York: MasterVision; 1988. 1
   videocassette: 80 min., sound, color, 1/2 in.

Electronic Publications

In general electronic publications will be cited in the same format as their
counterparts in print form. For non-print publications indicate the form
you use in brackets after the title of the publications indicate the form you
use in brackets after the title of the publication (such as title of encyclopedia, journal, or newspaper). For more details on citing electronically retrieved information, consult the *National Library of Medicine Recommended
Formats for Bibliographic Citation.*

A Sample Paper in the Natural and Applied Sciences

LISA LEE

Lisa's English teacher allowed her to fulfill her research assignment by writing a paper on a scientific topic. As a biology major who intends to study environmental studies or forestry in graduate school, Lisa Lee began her project by reading general works on tropical rain forests. She then consulted her biology teacher for guidance in focusing her topic on some aspect of the ways plants and animals interact. After narrowing her topic again to "the role of animals in seed dispersal in certain tropical forests," she then limited her paper to factors that determine effective seed dispersal. She organizes her paper into parts commonly used in scientific writing. Her headings include an abstract, an introduction, methods, discussion of three main points, and a conclusion.

STEPS LEADING TO LISA'S PAPER

1. Develops an existing interest (p. 11)
   - Attends a lecture on rain forests
   - Reads *Tropical Nature*
2. Breaks down a large subject (the environment) using a branching diagram (p. 16)
3. Narrows her topic further by making a list of questions she'd like answered (p. 18)
3. Brainstorms on the subject of rain forests (p. 20)
4. Focuses her subject (pp. 25–26)
   - Gets approval from her instructor to do research on tropical forests
   - Checks out books and begins reading
   - Makes an appointment with her biology teacher, who helps her brainstorm
   - Arrives at a tentative topic
5. Reads an encyclopedia article on the subject of rain forests (p. 35)

6. Identifies other sources (p. 55)
   - Searches the on-line computer catalog by subject and identifies several books
   - Using a more specific subheading, locates additional sources
7. Writes a letter to Professor Vitousek requesting an interview when he visits her campus (p. 102)
8. Interviews Professor Vitousek (p. 108)
   - Prepares a list of questions for her interview on a computer file
   - Conducts the interview, takes notes, and records answers on a computer file
9. Is careful while writing her paper not to plagiarize inadvertently (p. 136)
10. Discovers that her implied hypothesis is inaccurate and develops a new working hypothesis (p. 142)
11. Writes a thesis statement setting up her argument (p. 145)
12. Organizes her material and constructs an outline on the computer (p. 154)
13. Sorts out unnecessary material in a separate file labeled "Sources not used" (p. 168)
14. Lists her sources alphabetically by author, composes her paper, and numbers her sources (p. 283)
15. Organizes her final paper into parts commonly used in scientific writing (p. 287)

Lisa's title is brief and basic, and clearly
indicates the focus of her paper.

The Fate of Seeds in Tropical Forests:
Determining Factors

Lisa Lee

English 102

University of California, Santa Cruz

February 12, 1993

This abstract indicates the three main
points of the paper.

ABSTRACT

Whether a seed will have a chance to grow to a mature
tree in a tropical forest depends on features of its
parent tree, such as the rate at which it ripens fruit,
the size of its fruit crop, and the seasonal timing of
its fruiting. The fate of seeds is also determined by
the treatment they receive by the digestive processes of
animals that ingest them and by the way such animals
handle them. Seeds that are favorably treated by
primary dispersers and that escape being eaten by seed
predators must also have the space and light necessary
for germination and growth.

INTRODUCTION

Countless species of trees in tropical rain forests
depend on the activities of animals for survival.
Animals carry pollen, eat insects that prey on leaves
and bark, and transport seeds to locations in the forest
where they may have a chance to germinate. Some will
grow into saplings; and a few, maybe only one from a
solitary tree, will find the space and light necessary
to mature and rise to the high canopy of the forest.
D. H. Janzen, an eminent scientist committed to
understanding the workings of tropical forests, explains
that "the progression from adult tree to seed to another
adult tree involves many complex interactions with
animals"[1].

   In the last two decades, tropical scientists have
steadily published the results of their investigations
into how animals and plants interact in tropical

1

References are numbered in sequence as
they are cited.

forests. Some researchers concentrate on the animals'
use of plants, emphasizing the biological basis of an
animal's selection of usable foods that will supply its
nutritional needs[2]. In 1984, most studies of fruit-
eating (frugivorous) primates had focused on feeding
behavior for its own sake rather than its role in seed
dispersal[3]. Other investigators consider the strategies
that plants use to maximize the use of fruit by animals,
thus resulting in maximum scattering of seeds[4].
Increasing numbers of recent studies that focus on
animal feeding behavior from the perspective of plant
survival suggest that most tropical plants would not
survive without the help of animals[5].

   While the seeds of some plants high in the canopy
are transported by the wind and others have explosive
pods that eject seeds many meters, a significant number
produce succulent fruits that attract animals to
disperse the seeds[6]. Among the creatures known to be
responsible for scattering seeds throughout a forest are
birds, rodents, crabs, insects, bats, large mammals, and
primates. Frugivores disperse seeds by carrying the
fruit some distance and discarding the seeds,
regurgitating the seeds after the fruit pulp has been
removed, or more commonly by ingesting the seeds and
defecating them elsewhere in the forest. Seed
predators, those that diet on seeds rather than fruits,
often remove the seeds from the dung piles of the
dispersers and either eat them or horde them for later.

2

This is Lisa's description of the research process.

METHODS

Based on a selective review of the recent literature on seed dispersal in tropical forests, this study surveys and in the following discussion explains the current scientific understanding of the ways that plants facilitate seed dispersal, the role of animals in that process, and other factors that affect the possibility of germination. Significant published results in this field were identified by searching through Biological Abstracts, both the available CD-ROM as well as bound volumes of the index, using the heading "seed" and the subheading "dispersal." The list of references at the end of key essays identified in this search, such as Colin Chapman's "Primate Seed Dispersal"[7] and Fleming and Williams's "Phenology, Seed Dispersal, and Recruitment"[8], provided other important sources.

D. McKey's "The Ecology of Coevolved Seed Dispersal Systems"[9], given as a paper in 1973 and published in 1975, evaluates the field of seed dispersal studies and offers hypotheses to be tested by future research. A study of selected papers published in Frugivores and Seed Dispersal[10] reveals the progress that has been made since then in understanding how the interaction of plants and animals determines how a forest works. The studies cited in this paper are based on research conducted in tropical forests of Costa Rica, Mexico, Panama, and Peru. New world tropical forests are commonly referred to as neotropical forests.

3

Headings for separate parts of paper are capitalized.

HOW PLANTS FACILITATE DISPERSAL

Four features of a plant's fruiting behavior determine how animals are attracted to eat its fruit and disperse its seeds:

1. Schedule of ripening
2. Influence of disperser's feeding behavior on ripening
3. Size of fruit crops
4. Availability during periods of scarcity

The amount of available ripe fruit determines the amount of time dispersers stay in a particular tree and ultimately affects the likelihood that seeds will travel to a location where germination and survival are even possible. In a study of spider monkeys, one researcher observed that the animals spent much of a day in the same part of the forest feeding from trees with abundant ripe fruit. Since the first seeds from a meal pass through the spider monkey's gut in about four hours, most of the seeds would be passed near the parent tree, where they would have no chance of ultimate survival. When the same monkeys eat from trees that ripen only a few fruits at a time, they typically eat and move on to another part of the forest, thus increasing the opportunity for some seeds to have a chance to become mature trees[11].

Though very little is known about the effect that feeding animals have on a host plant, at least one plant is known to encourage dispersers by ripening fruit more rapidly when dispersers are abundant. The Hamelia

4

Lisa lists her main points at the beginning of each of the three parts.

patens tree will ripen remaining fruit faster when
almost ripe fruits are removed. By this process the
tree makes its fruit more available to highly seasonal,
migratory dispersers[12].

While some plants seem to regulate their fruit
production and ripening schedules to attract occasional
dispersers, others beat the odds by playing all out for
a short period of time. By producing a copious crop of
fruits that are consumed by numerous dispersers, some
trees succeed in the reproductive game by increasing the
probability that a few, or even just one, will end up in
an opportune spot[13].

Though it may seem that a tree's reproductive
future would be insured simply by providing succulent,
nutritious fruit that is attractive to a number of
dispersers, some trees seem to hedge their bets by
fruiting during the dry season when other fruits are
scarce. One researcher, who has studied extensively the
feeding behavior of five neotropical primates, has
determined that during the annual period of scarcity,
these animals feed on a mere dozen plant species[14]. Of
these "keystone" plants, those with seeds to be
dispersed would seem to have a much better chance of
success during the dry season than during a time of
plenty when the competition for animal attention is
fierce.
FACTORS DETERMINING A DISPERSER'S EFFECTIVENESS
Four factors in an animal's physiology and behavior
determine its reliability as a disperser of seeds:

·   5

Lisa uses a word taken from the article just
cited.

1. The degree to which digested seeds survive
and/or are made more viable by the digestive process

2. The rate of passage through the gut of the
animal that is adequate to allow the animal to move a
sufficient distance from the parent tree to occasionally
deposit seeds in favorable locations

3. The way the animal handles seeds in the process
of eating fruit

4. The frequency with which the animal fails to
retrieve seeds that have been hoarded for later use

What happens to a seed once an animal takes it into
its mouth varies considerably from seed to seed and
animal to animal. Seeds may be destroyed by an animal's
teeth or damaged by digestive juices. Still others
might be rendered more likely to germinate by mechanical
scarring of their hard outer shells or by chemical
action that encourages sprouting. Some seeds seem to
fare better if they are actually changed somehow by the
animal, while others survive to grow into seedlings
apparently unaltered by their journey[9].

Studies of the fruit-eating and dispersing habits
of howler monkeys have demonstrated that, for several
plant species, seeds that pass through a monkey's
digestive track are more likely to germinate than seeds
that do not[3]. The results of this study, however, do
not apply to primates in general. Other researchers
report a failure to germinate seeds passed through
spider monkeys15[(cited in 8)].

Scientists attempting to determine which animals

6

Citation in parentheses (8) is the source of
information.

Reference is to an article already referred
to earlier in the paper.

deposit seeds in locations appropriate for germination
have reached some tentative conclusions. In general,
birds and bats pass seeds rapidly, sometimes in less
than thirty minutes. Birds, however, are more likely
than bats to defecate seeds under a tree where there
would be next to no chance of their germinating and
growing to maturity; bats may deposit seeds as they
return some distance to their roosts. Since seeds pass
much slower through monkeys than through birds and bats,
monkeys have more time to move away from the parent tree
before depositing a seed[8]. But then, if some monkeys
fail to pass viable seeds, it hardly matters that they
are deposited in a favorable spot. For some trees in
specific habitats, bats may be the most effective
dispersers, with birds following, and monkeys having
little or no effect.

Also of significance are the variable ways that
animals handle fruit and seed. While some birds pass
most seeds in just a few minutes under or near their
source, others handle different seeds in different ways,
and thus become better dispersers for some trees than
others. Some birds spit or regurgitate seeds under the
parent tree, while others defecate seeds at least some
of the time away from their source. Horses that feed on
fruit from tropical trees will spit some seeds and
ingest and pass others in a viable state[16].

Seeds that are too large to be passed unharmed
through an animal's digestive system are usually
dispersed by animals that hoard food for times of

7

Lisa defines new words or terms *when she introduces them.*

scarcity. Agoutis, large rodents common in low-lying neotropical forests, are dispersers of large seeds. Typically they carry fruit some distance from the parent tree to an open spot, eat the edible material surrounding the seeds, and then bury the remaining seeds. Since agoutis seem to remember the kind of environment where they hide seeds, rather than the exact location, they presumably leave some seeds to germinate and mature[17]. Some agoutis would themselves become victims of predators, an ocelot perhaps, and never have a chance to retrieve their seeds[18].

OTHER FACTORS THAT AFFECT THE FATE OF A SEED
1. Presence of seed predators
2. Number of seeds in dung pile
3. Adequate light and space: treefalls

The fact that a seed survives the activities of its disperser and is successfully placed in a place favorable for germination does not insure that it will even sprout, let alone grow to a sapling. Seeds defecated on the forest floor become an attractive meal to animals that feed on seeds. In his work on the fate of guanacaste seeds deposited on the forest floor by horses, D. H. Janzen observed spiney pocket mice foraging at night in horse dung searching for seeds which they store in their underground burrows. Generally the mice eat up to 99 percent of these stored seeds[1]. Chapman found that most of the seeds that primates disperse are eventually destroyed as they are eaten by seed predators, or moved by secondary

8

dispersers, perhaps buried by hoarding rodents.
Following the fate of a particular seed once it is
traveling in the pouch of a second animal is not easy,
and researchers recognize the need for more knowledge
about what happens when secondary dispersers move in on
a seed[7].

How the number of seeds deposited in a dung pile
affects the prospect of one seed growing to maturity is
a complicated and poorly understood matter. In cases
where there are many effective seed predators preying on
a particular pile, the likelihood of a seed surviving
would seem greater if there are many seeds. But Janzen
has observed that piles with many seeds are more
thoroughly mined than are those with just a few, which
may be ignored by predators seeking abundance[1]. When
there are no seed predators, a large number of seeds in
a pile reduces the possibility of any single seed's
success since there is such fierce competition for
nutrients and space.

Suppose all goes well for a seed: it survives the
eating habits and digestive processes of its disperser
and is deposited in a spot favorable to germination
where it avoids destruction by seed predators. With
little competition from neighboring seeds, it sprouts
and becomes a seemingly healthy seedling. Unless the
overall habitat is amenable to growth, it will
ultimately languish and die before fulfilling its
potential. The space, light, and nutrients required for
a seedling to mature usually are provided by the death

9

Multiple citation numbers are separated by commas and have no space between them.

of another tree. Treefalls create gaps in otherwise dense, dark forests, and it is in these gaps that young trees flourish.

A lucky seed may be the one that is deposited at random in a very recently formed gap, one that has yet to be filled in by masses of striving plants; perhaps even more fortunate are those that manage to survive in a part of the forest which is opened up later by a treefall, so that its growth is stimulated by the added light and nutrients[18]. The most promising spot of all for a seed to germinate may be on the periphery of a gap since trees on these borders are often unstable and likely to fall, opening up new space, widening the gap, and allowing new seedlings a chance to grow[4,13].

CONCLUSIONS

Though a number of significant scientists are engaged in studying the mechanisms of seed dispersal, much remains to be explored. Study after study concludes by warning that there is much we do not know and that only a small number of fruiting trees and animals have been studied and those for inadequate periods of time. John Terborgh suggests that keystone plant species may determine how groups of animals evolve over time, but he urges that this possibility "be regarded as wide-eyed speculation"[14]. Many scientists would agree with Peter Vitousek that in order to reach effective generalizations, we need "more specific examples of how animals interact with plants"[18].

As scientists continue to explore the interactions

10

within the lower ranges of tropical forests and in the
canopy, which Norman Myers has referred to as "the last,
great unexplored frontier of life on Earth"[19], some
questions are answered. But with each new answer
additional questions are raised.

11

Use only initials (without space or punctuation between them) for first and middle names of authors.

LIST OF REFERENCES

1. Janzen DH. Removal of seeds from horse dung by tropical rodents: influence of habitat and amount of dung. Ecology 1982;63:1887-1900.

2. Rodman PS, Cant JG, editors. Adaptions for foraging in nonhuman primates: contributions to an organismal biology of prosimians, monkeys, and apes. New York: Columbia University Press; 1984. 351 p.

3. Estrada A, Coates-Estrada R. Fruit eating and seed dispersal by howling monkeys (Alouatta palliata) in the tropical rain forest of Los Tuxtlas, Mexico. American Journal of Primatology 1984;6:77-91.

4. Levey DJ. Tropical wet forest treefall gaps and distributions of understory birds and plants. Ecology 1988;69:1076-89.

5. [Anonymous]. Fruit and seed eaters. In Collins M, editor. The last rainforests: a world conservation atlas. New York: Oxford University Press; 1990. p. 76-79.

6. Longman KA, Jenik J. Tropical forest and its environment. 2nd ed. Essex (England): Longman; 1987. p. 98-99.

7. Chapman C. Primate seed dispersal: The fate of dispersed seeds. Biotropica 1989;21:148-54.

8. Fleming TH, Williams CF. Phenology, seed dispersal, and recruitment in Cecropia Peltate (Moraceae) in Costa Rican tropical dry forest. Journal of Tropical Ecology 1990;6:163-78.

12

Capitalize only the first word of title and subtitle.

9. McKey D. The ecology of coevolved seed dispersal systems. In: Gilbert LE, Raven PH, editors. Coevolution of animals and plants. Austin: University of Texas Press; 1975. p. 159-91.

10. Estrada A, Fleming TH, editors. Frugivores and seed dispersal. Dordrecht (Netherlands): Dr. W. Junk; 1986. 392 p.

11. White F. Census and preliminary observations on the ecology of the black-faced spider monkey. American Journal of Primatology 1986;11:125-32.

12. Levey DJ. Facultative ripening in Hamelia patens (Rubiaceae): effects of fruit removal and rotting. Oecologia 1987;74:203-8.

13. Howe HF. Monkey dispersal and waste of a neotropical fruit. Ecology 1980;61:944-59.

14. Terborgh J. Community aspects of frugivory in tropical forests. In: Estrada A, Fleming TH, editors. Frugivores and seed dispersal. Dordrecht (Netherlands): Dr. W. Junk; 1986. p. 371-84.

15. Vasquez-Yanes C, Orozco-Segovia A. Dispersal of seeds by animals. Effect of light controlled dormancy in Cecropia obtusifolia. In: Estrada A, Fleming TH, editors. Frugivores and seed dispersal. Dordrecht (Netherlands): Dr. W. Junk; 1986. p. 71-77.

16. Janzen DH. Guanacaste tree seed-swallowing by Costa Rican range horses. Ecology 1981;62:587-92.

13

Name of periodical, date, volume number, and pages of article.

Note style for interview with Professor
Vitousek.

17. Smythe N. Relationships between fruiting seasons and
    seed dispersal methods in a neotropical forest.
    American Naturalist 1970;104:25-35.
18. Vitousek P. Interview with: Lisa Lee. 1993 Jan 21.
19. Myers N. The primary source: tropical forests and
    our future. Exp. ed. New York: W. W. Norton; 1992.
    p. 60.

14

WRITING RESEARCH PAPERS ABOUT LITERATURE

14

Kinds of Research

Research about literature may involve study, analysis, or interpretations of individual poems, stories, plays, and novels. Once you become interested in a particular work, you may want to investigate the method of composition, its reception by reviewers and the general public, or wider issues such as its place in the author's work as a whole or in its cultural or social setting. Among the topics that students might want to investigate are the following:

1. How the work was written
2. How the work was received by the public (reviews, letters, private journals)
3. How critics have interpreted the work (professional journals and books)
4. How the critical reception/interpretation of the work has changed through the years
5. How the work relates to time and place of publication, for example the geographical, historical, or cultural context
6. How a work relates to other literary works published at the same time

7. How a work relates to the literary tradition
8. How a work relates to others by the same author
9. How a work relates to philosophical, political, religious, or social values
10. How a work relates to events of the author's life
11. How a work relates to author's character or psychological makeup
12. How the work is illuminated by particular critical methods, such as formalism, reader response, or the new historicism

The first step in studying a literary work is always to read the text carefully and to identify the other works it reminds you of, questions it raises about background, or other areas you would like to know more about. Particular works of literature raise certain kinds of questions that might lead to meaningful research. For example, a student reading Ernest Hemingway's *For Whom the Bell Tolls* may find out about the Spanish Civil War, while someone studying Willa Cather's *My Antonia* may want to investigate the history of the railroad or pioneer life in Nebraska. Works by writers using myth or folklore in unconventional ways (William Butler Yeats, William Blake, Toni Morrison) may attract students to explore the sources of such works; those by authors with large public reputations (William Faulkner, Tennessee Williams, or Lillian Hellman) encourage detailed studies of the authors' lives. The list below gives examples of kinds of research that may illuminate works of literature:

1. Charlotte Brontë's *Jane Eyre* and the role of the governess in the nineteenth century
2. Joseph Conrad's *Heart of Darkness* and colonialism and racism in the nineteenth century
3. Charles Dickens's *Tale of Two Cities* and the French Revolution
4. F. Scott Fitzgerald's *The Great Gatsby* and the 1919 World Series
5. Bobbie Anne Mason's *In Country* and the Vietnam veterans
6. Herman Melville's *Billy Budd* and the U.S. Navy
7. Toni Morrison's *Beloved* and the Underground Railway
8. Tim O'Brien's *Going After Cacciato* and the Vietnam War
9. William Shakespeare's *Othello* and Africans in Renaissance Europe; *The Merchant of Venice* and antisemitism.
10. Leslie Marmon Silko's *Ceremony* and problems of retaining Native American traditions
11. Kurt Vonnegut's *Slaughterhouse-Five* and the bombing of Dresden
12. Virginia Woolf's *Orlando* and Vita Sackville-West

You may be asked to research some aspect of an author's general concerns. The following list suggests broad topics that need to be narrowed and focused. For example, a paper on Faulkner's use of the grotesque might focus on humor and pathos in "Spotted Horses."

1. Jorge Luis Borges: narrative techniques, the story within the story
2. Willa Cather: the American Midwest
3. George Eliot: marriage
4. William Faulkner: the grotesque
5. Gabriel García Márquez: magical realism
6. Nadine Gordimer: apartheid in South Africa
7. Nathaniel Hawthorne: Puritanism
8. Zora Neale Hurston: African folk tales
9. Maxine Hong Kingston: Chinese traditions
10. Wole Soyinka: Yoruba ritual and religion
11. Harriet Beecher Stowe: the abolitionist movement
12. Tennessee Williams: the southern aristocracy
13. Richard Wright: the Communist Party
14. William Butler Yeats: the Irish independence movement

Sample Papers in Literature

CARLA MEDINA

Carla decided to write her paper on Alice Walker's *The Color Purple* in order to fulfill one part of her class assignment to research two controversial literary works. After discovering that secondary material on the work concentrated largely on the character Celie's voice, she chose to focus her subject on the voices of *The Color Purple*.

STEPS LEADING TO CARLA'S PAPER

1. Instructor assigns two research papers on controversial literary works, and she chooses to write her first on *The Color Purple* (p. 27)

2. Identifies her sources (p. 49)
   - Makes an appointment with the reference librarian
   - Performs a computer search in two indices, the *MLA International Bibliography* and *InfoTrac*
   - Consults the *Book Review Index* and the *New York Times Index* for more references
   - Locates the articles in her library
   - Reads through several articles, photocopying three and taking notes from others
3. Focuses her topic on the voices of the novel, and makes source cards for articles that treat this issue (pp. 86, 116)
4. Calls professor and interviews her over the phone (p. 103)
5. Organizes her paper, writes a first draft, and prepares a list of references (p. 169)
6. Prepares her final paper

Carla's main idea or thesis statement

Medina 1

Carla Medina
Professor Walker
English 110
28 February 1992

The Voices of The Color Purple

Alice Walker's The Color Purple, winner of the American Book Award and the Pulitzer Prize for literature, was a best-seller in 1982. It has received considerable attention both in the popular press and in scholarly publications. The novel's success is in part due to the voice of its ignorant, poor, but appealing heroine, Celie, and the lively group of characters to whom she gives a voice. Equally compelling is the novel's vision of people as constantly in flux and therefore capable of being transformed for the better. Such change takes place through human interaction as the characters speak and listen to each other.

An epistolary novel, The Color Purple consists of letters: from Celie to God; from Celie to her sister, Nettie, a missionary in Africa; and from Nettie to Celie. Celie writes about being raped, about having her children taken from her, and eventually about being transformed from a woman who passively accepts her lot to one who sets the terms of her own life. The more educated Nettie tells of her harsh life among the Olinka, an African tribe devastated by British rubber planters; of the conflicts she and the other two missionaries have with the Africans; and of her own disappointment over their failure to help the Olinka.

A description of the novel to help readers unfamiliar with it

Medina 2

Though Nettie too gives voice to others, this paper will focus on the more lively and immediate voices of Celie's letters to God and to Nettie.

In an article that came out just as the novel was published in 1982, Gloria Steinem calls Alice Walker a "necessary" and "major" writer (35); and she praises the novel for its "storytelling style," particularly Celie's voice as she "writes her heart out" in letters first to God and then to her sister, using the powerful rhythms of her own "black folk English" (89). Steinem also admires Nettie's letters to Celie for their "blow-by-blow" accounts of the devastating consequences of British colonialism, which say more about that subject "in a few pages than do many academic tomes" (90). But most reviewers of the novel either ignore or criticize Nettie's letters and single out Celie's language for praise. The New Yorker reviewer feels that Celie's letters "burst with a kind of poetry," and Dinitia Smith in the Nation commends the novel's "vivid figures of speech" and its "black folk idiom" (182). Similarly, Mel Watkins, writing for the New York Times, applauds the "lyrical cadence" of Celie's "intensely subjective voice" (7). Trudier Harris, who has serious reservations about the novel's merit, considers Celie's voice to be "powerful, subtly humorous" and "perfectly suited to the character" (156).

Some of the more memorable passages of the novel are those in which Celie recounts in letters to God private experiences that she has never told to anyone

Name of author used to introduce quotation.

Medina 3

else. In the early parts of the novel, she often
compares herself and others to trees or inanimate
objects rather than to other people. When her husband
beats her, Celie writes that she talks to herself: "I
say to myself, Celie, you a tree. That's how I come to
know trees fear men" (30). She feels so little for her
stepchildren that patting them is like patting a piece
of wood: "Not a living tree, but a table" (37). And
when she first sees Shug Avery, Celie projects her
response onto the trees: "The trees all round the house
draw themself up tall for a better look" (50).

The power of the novel lies not just in Celie's
account of her own subjective experiences, but in the
way she consumes and then recounts the stories of
others. Henry Louis Gates, Jr., points out that Celie's
growth "in self-awareness" is revealed as she finds her
voice in part by giving voice to other characters,
including her sister, Nettie (250). Nettie lives not
just in her own speaking, but in Celie's accounts of
her. Celie lives--and grows and develops--as she
absorbs the voices of Nettie and others. Celie's unique
character is the consequence of the particular voices
she absorbs. She grows by the discovery not of her true
inner self, but of an evolving self, a self constantly
recreated by the voices she encounters.

There are four distinct ways that Celie gives voice
to others: she relates the speech of others and calls
attention to her own silence; she recounts a dialogue
between herself and one other person; she relates a

conversation between two or more other characters; and she recounts a discussion she has had with someone about what someone else has told her. Though toward the end of the novel Celie conveys the transformed voice of the once abusive Albert, most of the strong voices are those of women. Mae Henderson proposes that Walker signs the novel at the end "A.W., author and medium" to suggest that her intention has been "to give voice and representation to these same women who have been silenced and confined in life as well as literature" (14). While Celie herself has been silenced by abuse, fear, and ignorance, she learns to speak by listening to and reporting the words of those who have not.

At first Celie is even silent about how she perceives the world. When they are growing up, the man they know as "Pa" tells Celie that she is "dumb" and that Nettie is "the clever one" (19). Being told by an adult that she is not smart seems to have more power over Celie than anything her sister does to counter it. Though Nettie attempts to help her with her lessons, Celie does not learn:

> I feel bad sometime Nettie done pass me in learnin. But look like nothing she say can git in my brain and stay. She try to tell me something bout the ground not being flat. I just say, Yeah, like I know it. I never tell her how flat it look to me. (20)

Celie's world at this point is flat, and she cannot see beyond what is immediately in front of her.

Note short quotation integrated into paraphrase.

When she is first married to Albert, whom she calls Mr. _____, Celie cannot imagine a life for herself except one of mistreatment, deprivation, and loneliness. It is not until other people enter her world--and talk to her--that the possibility of a better life even occurs to her. Kate, her husband's sister, chides her brother for letting Celie wear rags and takes her to be fitted for a new dress. Celie is so moved that she stutters trying to explain what it means to her to "be the first one in my own dress." By first listening to Kate, a woman who stands up for other women, and then giving voice to Kate's position, Celie grows. When Kate tells her that she deserves "more than this," Celie seems to hear: "Maybe so. I think" (28). That silent, but nevertheless thought and recorded, "maybe so" is a first step in discovering new possibilities for herself.

At other times Celie writes about conversations she has listened to and then rejected. When her brother-in-law argues that certain views of women are hard to "prove to the world," Celie silently disagrees: "What the world got to do with anything, I think" (61). Because she remains in an isolated, private world, it will be a long time before Celie grows in her understanding of what the world has to do with things. It will also be a long time before she speaks out and gives voice in the world to her own thoughts. Typically, her letters to God relate how people from Celie's world gather together to have fun, to fight, to argue, or to solve problems. An example is the scene in

References that are clearly from the book
don't require the author's name.

which Sophia's friends and family sit down after supper
to discuss how they might get Sophia out of jail. Celie
reports the conversation with so much detail that it is
clear she is listening carefully, but she also points
out that she "don't say nothing" (90).

Eventually Celie becomes a full participant in such
gatherings, and her voice becomes strong and persuasive.
Two events seem to lead Celie to discover her voice.
First, Shug Avery encourages her to talk about her early
sexual experiences, and for the first time, Celie tells
another human being about the horrible details of the
repeated rapes she endured as an adolescent. The second
event is the discovery of Nettie's letters, which her
husband has been hiding from her for years. Shug gives
Celie the support she needs to talk about her pain;
Nettie's letters provide her with the information she
needs to confront those who have abused her.

In one of her early letters, Nettie explains to her
sister that even though she knows Celie is not receiving
the letters, writing them keeps her from feeling "locked
up in myself and choking on my own heart" (122).
Nettie's letters give Celie the courage to speak out.
One of her first acts after reading the long-hidden
letters is to visit the man who raped her and to let him
know that she knows he is not her father but her step-
father. Shortly afterward, the long-silent Celie
confronts Albert, tells him she is leaving, and warns
him that she will kill him if he tries to stop her: "You
a lowdown dog is what's wrong, I say. It's time to

leave you and enter into the Creation. And your dead body just the welcome mat I need" (181).

In her letters to Nettie, unlike the earlier ones to God, Celie increasingly plays a dominant role in the conversations she reports. Rather than silently agreeing or disagreeing with what others say, she often sets the terms of the dialogue, challenging what others say and letting her voice be heard. When Celie curses her husband, he attempts to dismiss her: "You can't curse nobody. Look at you. You black, you pore, you ugly, you a woman. Goddam, he say, you nothing at all" (187). But Celie gets the last word: "I'm pore, I'm black, I may be ugly and can't cook, a voice say to everything listening. But I'm here" (187). What is new about the way Celie reports this conversation is that she recognizes her voice as powerful and she perceives that others are listening. Celie has heard her own voice.

With the help of Shug Avery, Celie soon turns her life around, and the talk about being poor, black, and ugly is transformed in the opening words of a letter to Nettie: "I am so happy. I got love. I got work. I got money, friends, and time" (193). When Shug temporarily abandons her, Celie is sad and loses some of her confidence. But in her longest letter to Nettie (229-41), Celie reveals that she now has many resources to get her through a hard time: the conversations of her friends, a letter from Shug, and a letter from Nettie. Celie even assumes the role of teacher, and she writes to Nettie about how she is teaching Albert about African customs and beliefs, information which of course she received in a letter from Nettie.

By the end of the novel, Celie has become an accomplished storyteller, who not only recounts her own personal experience but takes the stories of others and remakes them, giving them voice and new functions in the lives of others. Albert knows Nettie because Celie recreated her voice. If Nettie were to receive that letter, she would know Albert through Celie's recapitulation of the conversation she had with him about the letter Nettie wrote to her. The many voices of The Color Purple live not just in the moment that they speak (or write), but as others hear them, respond to them, and in the process transform their lives.

Celie even finds the words to speak of the transformation of her relationship with Albert:

> Then the old devil put his arms around me and
> just stood there on the porch with me real
> quiet. Way after while I bent my stiff neck
> onto his shoulder. Here us is, I thought, two
> old fools left over from love, keeping each
> other company under the stars. (238)

The man that Celie describes here is quite different from the one readers meet in the opening passages of the novel.

In an essay entitled "Writing The Color Purple," Walker recounts the process of creating this enormously popular book. In quiet moments in the country, in

Quotations longer than four lines are indented ten spaces and double-spaced before, throughout, and after.

California, where she was living, "Celie, Shug, Albert,
Sophia, or Harpo would come for a visit" (359). By
listening to the characters as individuals, Walker was
able to recreate them in Celie's letters, giving them
the authority of voices that she has listened to and
heard. In an interview published in <u>Newsweek</u>, Walker
refers to the characters as real people and expresses
her concern whether readers will be able to hear what
they have to say: "Let's hope people can hear Celie's
voice. There are so many people like Celie who make it,
who come out of nothing. People who triumph"
("Characters in Search of a Book"). At the time that
Walker expressed this hope, it was still not clear how
important <u>The Color Purple</u> would become. Today we know
Celie and her friends have been heard.

Use shortened title in parentheses when
there is more than one source by the same
author. (No page number is needed here
since the article is only one page.)

If a review is neither titled nor signed,
begin entry with ''Rev. of'' and
alphabetize under title of work reviewed.

Works Cited

Rev. of <u>The Color Purple</u>, by Alice Walker. <u>New Yorker</u> 6
    Sept. 1982: 106.

Gates, Henry Louis, Jr. <u>The Signifying Monkey: A Theory</u>
    <u>of Afro-American Literary Criticism</u>. New York:
    Oxford UP, 1988.

Harris, Trudier. "On <u>The Color Purple</u>, Stereotypes, and
    Silence." <u>Black American Literature Forum</u> 18
    (1984): 155-61.

Henderson, Mae G. "<u>The Color Purple</u>: Revisions and
    Redefinitions." <u>SAGE: A Scholarly Journal on Black</u>
    <u>Women</u> 2 (1985): 14-18.

Smith, Dinitia. "Celie, You a Tree." Rev. of <u>The Color</u>
    <u>Purple</u>, by Alice Walker. <u>The Nation</u> 4 Sept. 1982:
    181-83.

Steinem, Gloria. "Do You Know This Woman?" <u>Ms.</u> June
    1982: 35+.

Walker, Alice. "Characters in Search of a Book."
    Interview with Ray Anello and Pamela Abramson.
    <u>Newsweek</u> 21 June 1982: 67.

---. <u>The Color Purple</u>. New York: Harcourt, 1982.

---. "Writing <u>The Color Purple</u>." <u>In Search of Our</u>
    <u>Mothers' Gardens</u>. New York: Harcourt, 1983. 355-
    60.

Watkins, Mel. "Some Letters Went to God." Rev. of <u>The</u>
    <u>Color Purple</u>, by Alice Walker. <u>New York Times</u> 25
    July 1982: 7.

Use three hyphens followed by a period for
additional books by the same author.

While Carla is researching the paper on *The Color Purple,* she finds an article by Leland Krauth comparing Walker's novel to Mark Twain's *Adventures of Huckleberry Finn.* Though she does not use Krauth's essay, reading it gives her the idea of doing her major research paper on Twain's most famous novel. When Carla takes the novel home with her for the weekend, her mother explains that *Huck Finn* was banned in her high school in the 1960s mainly because Huck uses racist language. Browsing through the essays at the end of the edition she is reading, Carla learns that there were people who objected to this novel from the time it was first published, and so she decides to investigate the controversy that has led to censorship, bannings, and much argument.

SEARCH STRATEGY

To do research on one of the most popular novels of all times can involve overwhelming amounts of material. Carla makes another appointment with the same reference librarian who helped her before and who explains that to research a topic about a book that is more than a century old will be more complicated than researching one published just over a decade ago. She recommends that Carla look for articles by searching the following:

1. *MLA International Bibliography*
2. Appropriate databases in *InfoTrac*
3. *ERIC*
4. *New York Times Index*

Carla is able to search the first three indexes very rapidly by using the CD-ROM disc loaded into a computer, but she finds that she must experiment somewhat to locate what she needs. This is how Carla finds her first sources:

1. After loading the MLA compact disc into the computer, using the "browse" mode, Carla keys in "Samuel Clemens" and finds 771 articles under that heading. To narrow the search to a more manageable number, she uses the "Wilsearch" mode and requests articles

that are about both Samuel Clemens and *Adventures of Huckleberry Finn*. This time she finds only 51 articles. After scanning these, she identifies 9 that seem relevant. When Carla asks for *Adventures of Huckleberry Finn* and ''censorship,'' she finds 6 articles. All seem relevant.

2. To search *Infotrac,* or the *General Periodicals Index,* Carla finds that the appropriate heading is ''Twain,'' rather than ''Clemens,'' and that subheadings appear under this. This index produces a number of different articles under the subheading ''Criticism and interpretation.''

3. To search the *ERIC* CD-ROM, Carla uses the headings *''Huckleberry Finn''* and ''censorship'' to locate 11 more articles. Because the *ERIC* index includes brief summaries (abstracts) of the articles, she is able to identify 3 to add to her list of sources.

4. To search the *New York Times Index* for accounts of bannings, Carla uses the bound volumes. To find news articles about the on-going controversy, Carla discovers that ''Samuel Clemens'' is the appropriate heading, which directs her to another heading, ''books and literature.'' In less than an hour she is able to find some 13 articles about the censorship of *Huck Finn* published in the *Times* since 1957.

5. To find books that deal with the subject, Carla begins with the library's on-line catalog and identifies several books that seem to be about *Huck* or about Twain and *Huck.* After getting the call numbers (Carla's library's computerized catalog prints out the bibliographic information of each book), she goes directly to the stacks to look for books that seem relevant to her topic. Carla finds several books, but others are not on the shelf. Browsing through the many books about Twain and his work, she selects a couple of others that interest her.

6. Carla's next step is to check out the books she has found and to recall the relevant books that have been checked out. She also requests from interlibrary loan those articles that her library does not have. With the help of electronic indexes, Carla is able to complete this part of her search in an afternoon.

COLLECTING SOURCES

After browsing through the books and carefully studying the bibliographies in search of more material, Carla goes back to the library to begin collecting sources. She plans to stay long enough to determine which articles are worthwhile. Some journal articles she reads and discards as not useful, and others she photocopies to consult later. She reads newspaper articles on microfilm readers and photocopies several.

SCHEDULING AND CONDUCTING THE COMPUTER SEARCH

Before leaving the library, Carla shows what she has found to the reference librarian, who suggests that Carla has narrowed her topic enough to do a computer search on *Dialog,* a database that contains several hundred indexes that extend over a longer period of time than the CD-ROM disc available to Carla. For example, the MLA CD-ROM includes citations from 1981–91, while the *MLA Bibliography* available through a computer search goes back to 1963.

Carla sets up an appointment with a librarian, fills out a form explaining what she wants to find, and meets with the librarian during the search so that she can answer questions.

RESULTS AND COST OF THE SEARCH

Surprisingly, very little is found searching the *MLA Bibliography.* The librarian then suggests they search the on-line index of *America: History and Life.* Using *"Huckleberry Finn,"* "controversy," "censorship," "race," and "racism" as descriptors, they find several relevant sources.

The cost of computer searches varies from one library to another and among the databases. Because Carla has limited funds, she finds out that her college pays for the first fifteen minutes of a computer search, and so she and the librarian plan carefully to limit the search to that time. The librarian warns Carla that searches that are not carefully planned can be quite expensive. For example, if she had asked simply for articles about Mark Twain, the cost would have been much higher, as she would have found many more articles than the few that she identified by carefully narrowing the search.

ALTERNATIVE SEARCH STRATEGIES

Students using libraries that do not have the CD-ROM indexes or on-line computers that Carla uses may find the same sources by

using the bound volumes of the *MLA Bibliography, ERIC,* the *Readers'
Guide to Periodical Literature,* and *America: History and Life.* Other relevant material may be found in the bound volumes of the *New York
Times Index,* which Carla uses, and in *Essay and General Literature
Index.* For books others may use a card catalog rather than the on-line
catalog.

GETTING STARTED

After two more sessions in the library collecting, reading, taking
notes from, and photocopying materials, Carla is ready to plan her
paper. Because Carla has photocopied so many articles, she is able to
sort her sources into two categories: those that deal with the opposition to *Huck Finn* and those concerned with its defense. She decides
to trace the two main parts of the controversy, with each organized
chronologically from the time of the book's publication to recent
episodes in the battle between those who attack and those who
champion the novel.

By the time Carla is ready to write her paper she has many
notecards, books, and photocopies of articles—more than she can
handle on a small desk. She then divides them into three categories:
those she intends to use, those she might use, and those that are
irrelevant. Using her bed as well as her desktop, she sorts the ones
she intends to use into two groups: those dealing with the controversy during Twain's time and those concerned with the more recent
controversy. After subdividing her sources within the two groups,
Carla is able to make a rough plan for her paper:

```
    I.   Introduction: the Huck Finn debate
         A. History's interpretation
         B. The novel's provocation
    II.  The prepublication uproar
         A. The obscene drawing
         B. The Century magazine excerpts
            1. Deletions
            2. Debates about race
    III. Reactions to publication
         A. Reviews and commentary
         B. Concord library ban
         C. Twain's rebuttal
```

COMPOSING AND TAKING A POSITION

Using this plan, Carla composes this paper directly on the computer. As she is drafting her introduction, she becomes clear about what position she intends to take: that the terms of the debate about the novel are determined by moral and social values of a given time, but that the debate itself is inherent in the provocative nature of the story. As she continues drafting her paper, she often stops to reread parts of books and articles, discovering as she goes more and more evidence of the ways the issues of the *Huck Finn* controversy are both provoked by the novel and dictated by their times.

As she writes her paper, Carla enters her references into the bibliography, following the MLA parenthetical style of documentation.

Introduction to long quotation (note name
of author).

Medina 1

Carla Medina
Professor Walker
English 210
9 April 1992

   Always Trouble: <u>Huck Finn</u> and American Social Values

      Students of Mark Twain's <u>Adventures of Huckleberry</u>
<u>Finn</u> who want to find out how the book has been
reviewed, interpreted, and criticized will find an
enormous number of books, essays, and newspaper articles
that discuss this most talked-about and written-about
American novel. Fifty years ago there was already so
much written about this novel that Kenneth Burke
described it as a complex cultural conversation:

          Imagine that you enter a parlor. You come
          late. When you arrive, others have long
          preceded you, and they are engaged in a heated
          discussion, a discussion too heated for them
          to pause and tell you exactly what it is
          about. . . . You listen for a while, until
          you decide that you have caught the tenor of
          the argument; then you put in your oar.
          Someone answers; you answer him; another comes
          to your defense; another aligns himself
          against you, to either the embarrassment or
          gratification of your opponent, depending upon
          the quality of your ally's assistance.
          However, the discussion is interminable. The
          hour grows late, you must depart. And you do
          depart, with the discussion still vigorously

Quotation of more than four lines is set off
and indented ten spaces.

in progress. (Mailloux 107)
Burke published these words in 1941, fifty-six years
after the novel came out. Another half century has
passed since then, and the "heated discussion" he
describes has gone on and on, growing louder and louder.
With the help of indexes, bibliographies, and even a
computer search, it is now possible to sort out some of
the major topics that the participants continue to
debate and the sides they take.

This paper will trace two currents within the
discussion about the ultimate value of <u>Huckleberry Finn</u>,
and it will demonstrate that the controversy is larger
than the book. The terms of the debate are dictated by
moral and political concerns of a particular time in
history, but the energy that fuels the battles comes
from the provocative nature of the novel. Readers will
never be neutral about this book in which a poor white
boy uses the most offensive racial epithets to refer to
a black man who risks his life to help him. The very
fact that the controversy rages as strong as ever
suggests that the book is capable of offending and
pleasing with equal intensity. Perhaps the greatest
value of the novel lies in its ability to create
controversy and discussion about larger social issues,
keeping those issues alive in the process. It is not so
much that one side is wrong and the other right, but
that each side is responding to aspects of the novel
that seem to reinforce or challenge its own values.

One side of the debate is concerned with what is

Carla sets up her argument.

Medina 3

wrong with the novel and why people, particularly young
people, should not read it. The other is about why <u>Huck
Finn</u> is one of our most important, if not <u>the</u> most
important, American novel. As in any debate, the
persistence of one side sustains the other.

Mark Twain's <u>Adventures of Huckleberry Finn</u> itself
aroused controversy before it was ever published as a
book. <u>Huck Finn</u>'s bad reputation may have begun with
pictures, rather than words. One of the illustrations
was altered at the printers, presumably as a joke, to
show Uncle Silas "in a flagrant act of indecent
exposure" (David 269). The obscene picture was
corrected, but a New York newspaper published the story,
creating undesirable publicity and perhaps starting the
idea that the book was improper and inappropriate for
children (Egan 9). Publication was delayed and the
Christmas season was missed (Blair 366-70).

When the editor of <u>Century</u> magazine published
extracts from the novel in December, January, and
February of 1884-85, he must have anticipated trouble
because he omitted some 18 percent of the passages he
selected. For example, he took out all references to
nakedness and deleted such expressions as "to be in a
sweat" (Rule 9). Even so, a school superintendent, who
objected even to the expurgated magazine excerpts, wrote
an angry letter complaining to the editor of <u>Century</u>
(Scott 356-58).

Though the deletions did not have to do with race,
<u>Huck</u> was from the beginning surrounded by discussions of

When an author's name is used or implied in sentence, it isn't necessary to use name in parenthetical citation.

racial issues. The January 1885 issue of <u>Century</u> magazine that contained excerpts from <u>Huck Finn</u> also ran an article by George Washington Cable, who challenged southern notions of white supremacy. Cable's arguments stimulated more controversy, and in April, two months after <u>Huck</u> appeared in book form, <u>Century</u> published an article by Henry Grady, the editor of the <u>Atlanta Constitution</u>, who countered Cable's position by arguing for separation of the races and for white supremacy. In a recent essay, Stephen Mailloux has pointed out that <u>Adventures of Huckleberry Finn</u> entered the world in the context of "this highly charged and polarized argument" (112). Furthermore, he notes that Twain and Cable had teamed up for a much-publicized reading tour, thus further associating Huck and Jim with the public conversation about race (110). According to Mailloux, Twain reinforced the connection by reading passages from the novel that made fun of white supremacy (112). But it would be more than seventy years before the race issue would become the focus of <u>Huck</u>'s detractors, and then not because Twain was critical of white racist attitudes, but because the book was perceived to be racist.

The publication of <u>Adventures of Huckleberry Finn</u> in February 1885 was greeted by a moderate number of reviews compared to the fifty-odd reviews received by earlier works, <u>The Innocents Abroad</u> and <u>The Gilded Age</u>. In a recent study of the way <u>Huck</u> was received in the months following publication, Victor Fisher found some

twenty reviews, but more than a hundred editorials and
articles that reported the goings-on following the
novel's appearance (2). The public argument was
launched in March 1885 when the Concord Free Public
Library in Massachusetts banned it from circulation, an
event that has been widely discussed in and out of
print, and the argument has gone on ever since. There
are a number of published articles and essays that
include an account of the story of this first of many
public bans of Huckleberry Finn (see Fischer 16-32;
Stanek 19-20; Gerson 1655-56), not just because it was
first, but because of the prestige of the people who
served on the committee. Ralph Waldo Emerson's son was
a member, having taken the place his father held until
his death three years before (Gerson 1656). But the
Concord ban was also important because of the enormous
public response that followed in its wake. Fisher's
article includes excerpts from many newspapers that took
a stand either for or against the censorship of Huck
Finn.

The Concord committee was clear that the novel was
"the veriest trash . . . more suited to the slums than
to intelligent, respectable people." At the same time,
Louisa May Alcott condemned the book and chided Twain,
suggesting that if he "cannot think of something better
to tell our pure-minded lads and lasses, he had better
stop writing for them" (Gerson 1656). These frequently
quoted scoldings reveal the primary concerns of those
who first disapproved of Huck. The boy was simply not

nice, he spoke poor English, he behaved badly, and he was in every way a poor role model for nice boys and girls. Twenty years later, when <u>Huckleberry Finn</u> was banned from the Brooklyn public library in 1905, Twain, fed up, responded with sarcasm, insisting that he never intended the book to be read by children:

> I wrote <u>Tom Sawyer</u> and <u>Huck Finn</u> for adults
> exclusively, and it always distresses me when
> I find that boys and girls have been allowed
> access to them. The mind that becomes soiled
> in youth can never again be washed clean. I
> know this by my own experience, and to this
> day I cherish unappeasable bitterness against
> the unfaithful guardians of my young life, who
> not only permitted but compelled me to read an
> unexpurgated Bible through before I was
> fifteen years old. (Rule 12)

In 1907 a librarian defended the book in terms that Twain himself might have used. In a tongue-in-cheek article published in <u>The Library Journal</u>, E. L. Pearson created a mock debate between himself and a prudish female librarian who expels Huck and Tom from her shelves on the grounds that they "glorify mischief." Pearson counters "that literature is nothing but a record of people doing the things they should not do" (313).

Though there was a relative lull in the <u>Huck Finn</u> disputes during the years following the Pearson article in 1907, a quarter of a century later, in 1931, Harper &

Journal title is not necessary; used here for emphasis.

Medina 7

Brothers published an expurgated edition of the novel
that was intended to be acceptable in the classroom
(Rule 13). Other new editions of the novel followed,
and by mid-century many students encountered Huck either
straight or diluted.

The specific battle over <u>Huckleberry Finn</u> as a book
suitable for classroom study began again in 1957 when
the New York City schools dropped it from their list of
approved books, largely because of protests about the
book's alleged racism. Some writers assume that the
race issue became important in the <u>Huck Finn</u>
conversation only after the Supreme Court decision of
<u>Brown v. Board of Education</u> on integration in the
schools made educators conscious of the possible harm
done to black students by demeaning racial stereotypes.
In fact Twain himself was very aware that the friendship
between Huck and Jim was a threat to widely accepted
ideas about race at the time the novel was published
(Mailloux 110-12). What changed in the more than
seventy years that intervened between the publication in
1884 and the New York ban in 1957 was the prevailing
attitude about race.

In 1957, however, the civil rights movement was
already beginning to bring an end to the legal
separation of the races, and critics of the novel
ignored Twain's attack on racism and focused instead on
the novel's racial slurs and stereotypes that would
embarrass black students in integrated classrooms and
perpetuate racial prejudice. The <u>New York Times</u> carried

Article title is used when no author is given; no need for page number for one-page article.

the story for some months. During the more than thirty years since the New York school board's action, there have been more banning incidents in schools. In 1963, the Board of Education of Philadelphia replaced Twain's <u>Huck</u> with an adapted version that softens the violence, simplifies the dialect, and removes all racist passages ("Schools in Philadelphia"). Serious protests about <u>Huck Finn</u> continued: in Washington, Florida, Texas, Pennsylvania, Iowa, and Illinois. A widely publicized case for censorship was made by an administrator at, ironically, the Mark Twain Intermediate School of Fairfax, Virginia, who argued that the novel was "the most grotesque example of racist trash ever written" (Rule 16).

And so the conversation continues. The Fairfax case was in 1982, and others have cropped up regularly. But the condemnations, indictments, and official bans that continue to plague <u>Huck</u> are only half of the story. From the earliest days to the present, <u>Adventures of Huckleberry Finn</u> has also been the object of extravagant praise. Among the early positive reviewers were Brander Mathews, who found in <u>Huck</u> no "waste word"; Thomas Perry, who described the vendetta episode as "a masterpiece"; and Andrew Lang, who declared the whole book "a masterpiece" (Inge 32, 34, 40). The word "masterpiece," once used, set the tone for others to praise <u>Huck</u> with superlatives. William Dean Howells, who as Twain's friend and adviser read the novel four times before publication (Blair 360), wrote in 1901

Page numbers are listed in order of reference.

Medina 9

about having "half a mind to give my whole heart to
Huckleberry Finn" (Simpson 3, 104). Others, however,
gave all, heart and mind. H. L. Mencken in 1913
declared it "one of the great Masterpieces of the world
. . . the full equal of Don Quixote" (Inge 69), and
V. S. Pritchett in 1941 called it "one of the funniest
books in all literature" and "a comic masterpiece" (Inge
76, 79).

    During the middle decades of the twentieth century,
Huck's status was rising even higher, as a number of
famous poets, novelists, and critics began to sing its
praises. For T. S. Eliot, the novel was "the only one
of Mark Twain's various books which can be called a
masterpiece," and it is Twain's use of the Mississippi
River that makes a boy's book "a great book" (Inge 111).
F. Scott Fitzgerald glorified the novel as the first
objective insider's view of America (Simpson 107).
Ernest Hemingway raised the stakes even higher by
claiming that "All American literature comes from one
book by Mark Twain called Huckleberry Finn . . . the
best book we've had" (Blair 7). Respected critics
joined the Huck Finn fan club in the middle of the
century: For the Englishman F. R. Leavis, it was
"supremely the American classic" (Simpson 109), and
Lionel Trilling called it "one of the world's great
books and one of the central documents of American
culture" (Inge 82). The importance of these men--and
not surprisingly most if not all champions of this
"boy's book" seem to be men--has resulted in their

Carla's own conclusions; no need for documentation.

opinions being often quoted and used by those who defend the book as great literature.

Recent scholars who have defended the novel against charges of racism have turned their attention to character and theme in efforts to prove that Jim is presented as a noble and admirable figure, that Huck's progress is one that leads him to understand the evils of slavery, and that the novel as a whole condemns racism. Far from submitting to Twain's warning that readers should avoid searching for a "motive" in the novel, this new generation of Huck Finn defenders have deliberately set out to do just that: to find evidence of what Twain intended to say about race.

In an essay published in 1984, Richard Barksdale argued that "Twain's literary intention" is to dramatize how "an authentic black-white friendship" could develop during pre-Civil War America only away from society, on a raft, perhaps, in the middle of a large river. That the partners of this friendship represent members of social groups that at the time the book was published had become "inveterate enemies"--poor whites and recently freed slaves--suggests that it is social values, not some kind of inborn racism, that keep people apart (19). Barksdale concluded then, that Twain's novel, "by motive and intention, is really an ironic appraisal of the American racial scene circa 1884" (20).

Like Barksdale, David L. Smith, also in 1984, defended Huck Finn on grounds that it is a "subtle attack on racism" (5). Countering those who denounce

the book because of its stereotyping of Jim, Smith
showed how Jim's behavior actually contradicts the
stereotype and how rather than acting like the gullible
clown that he seems to some, Jim behaves with
"forethought, creativity and shrewdness" (7). He is "in
most ways a better man than the men who regard him as
their inferior" (10).

Three years later, Stephen Railton, who conceded
that <u>Huck Finn</u> is "racist as well as about racism"
(393), argued that Twain ultimately chose to have it
both ways and that the book belongs in the classroom
precisely because of its contradictory attitudes toward
race. While there are passages that expose "the
terrible price people pay for prejudices," the novel
does not finally "overcome Huck's enslavement to his
culture's distorted values" (396-97). It is true that
Huck plays a childish trick; Jim's response is "as
authentically noble as any speech in Shakespeare" (398);
and to Railton, in the whole first two-thirds of the
novel, Huck remains a naive racist while Jim is "a
magnanimous figure" (399-400). In the ending chapters,
Twain shifts, perhaps to appeal to the racist prejudices
of his readers, and turns Jim into a "comic stereotype"
(407).

The <u>Huck Finn</u> controversy is far from limited to
librarians, scholars, and famous writers. From time to
time, sometimes in response to a particular banning
threat, sometimes for no apparent reason, newspapers
publish editorials taking a stand on this issue. In

Quotes in this paragraph come from
different pages of the same source.

August 1982, a writer for the <u>Nation</u> countered the
Fairfax County censoring by comparing Huck to Martin
Luther King, Jr., since both chose to break unjust laws
(Hearn 117). The lead editorial of the 1 January 1984
<u>New York Times</u> asked readers to think back to 1884
instead of 1984 and to think about the importance of the
freedom to read the documents of the past: "To blot out
1884 by purging or purifying Twain is to rob life, and
the passage of time, of all meaning" ("Think Back,
Too"). In the fall of 1990, John Head, a columnist for
the <u>Atlanta Journal and Constitution</u>, responding to a
campaign to ban <u>Huck</u> in Plano, Texas, concurred with
some of Twains's earliest defenders that the book is "a
masterpiece," and that good teachers can help students
understand the novel's context so that they can "learn
something valuable from a great writer's portrait of
racism's silly and downright ugly face."

The issues debated have altered through the years
in response to changing times, but the battles continue.
Explaining why they recommended that libraries initiate
discussions of censorship, Gerson and Stavely concluded
that librarians have a responsibility to create dialogue
about controversial books because "only through dialogue
will those books lined up on our stacks ever stir and
quicken and belong to all of us" (1658).

Whether the <u>Adventures of Huckleberry Finn</u> belongs
to all of us is debatable, but no one can deny that the
dialogue goes on, keeping the antics and language of
Huck and Jim alive in the minds of many. Surely Twain

Both authors of this article need to be
mentioned if introduced in body of paper.

himself intended to stir up such talk simply by
forbidding it:

> Persons attempting to find a motive in this
> narrative will be prosecuted; persons
> attempting to find a moral in it will be
> banished; persons attempting to find a plot in
> it will be shot. (Clemens 2)

This "notice" on the title page of the novel continues
to serve not as a warning, but as a provocation, as
students, scholars, and general readers argue about what
Twain intended, what moral principles are conveyed by
the story, and what harm or good might be done by those
who read it.

Far more important than a discussion about the
novel's literary worth is the debate over social and
cultural values that it incites. Since the values the
novel challenges have altered through the years, there
is reason to think that in a different time, The
Adventures of Huckleberry Finn will provoke debate about
still other social concerns.

Carla returns to the paper's thesis in her
conclusion.

Works Cited

Barksdale, Richard K. "History, Slavery, and Thematic
    Irony in Huckleberry Finn." Mark Twain Journal
    22.2 (1984): 17-20.

Blair, Walter. Mark Twain and Huck Finn. Berkeley: U
    of California P, 1960.

Clemens, Samuel Langhorne. Adventures of Huckleberry
    Finn. Ed. Sculley Bradley, Richmond Croom Beatty,
    E. Hudson Long, and Thomas Cooley. 2nd ed. New
    York: Norton, 1977.

David, Beverly R. "The Pictorial Huck Finn: Mark Twain
    and His Illustrator, E. W. Kemble." Huck Finn
    Among the Critics: A Centennial Selection. Ed. M.
    Thomas Inge. Frederick: University Publications of
    America, 1981. 269-91.

Egan, Michael. Mark Twain's Huckleberry Finn: Race,
    Class and Society. Sussex: Sussex UP, 1977.

Eliot, T. S. Introduction. Adventures of Huckleberry
    Finn. By Samuel Clemens. London: Cresset/New
    York: Chanticleer, 1950. Rpt. in Huck Finn Among
    the Critics: A Centennial Selection. Ed. M. Thomas
    Inge. Frederick: University Publications of
    America, 1981. 103-11.

Fisher, Victor. "Huck Finn Reviewed: The Reception of
    Huckleberry Finn in the United States, 1885-1897."
    Mark Twain Journal 16.1 (1983): 1-57.

For an essay in a collection of previously
published works, provide data for earlier
publication, followed by "Rpt. in," title of
collection, and publication data.

When a normally underlined title is part of
an underlined title, the incorporated title is
not underlined.

Fitzgerald, F. Scott. *Fitzgerald Newsletter* 8 (Winter
    1960). Rpt. as "Viewpoints: F. Scott Fitzgerald."
    Twentieth-Century Interpretations of Adventures of
    Huckleberry Finn. Ed. Claude M. Simpson.
    Englewood Cliffs: Prentice, 1968. 107.

Gerson, Lani, and Keith Stavely. "We Didn't Wait for
    the Censor: Intellectual Freedom at the Watertown
    Public Library." *Library Journal* 108 (1983): 1654-
    58.

Haight, Anne Lyon. *Banned Books: 387 B.C. to 1978 A.D.*
    Updated and enlarged by Chandler B. Grannis. New
    York: Bowker, 1978.

Head, John. "It's Absurd to Accuse Twain of Being
    Racist." *Atlanta Journal and Constitution* 26 Nov.
    1990, sec. A: 13.

Hearn, Michael Patrick. "Expelling Huck Finn." *The
    Nation* 7 Aug. 1982: 117.

Howells, William Dean. "Mark Twain: An Inquiry." *North
    American Review* 172 (1901): 311-15. Rpt. as
    "Viewpoints: William Dean Howells." *Twentieth-
    Century Interpretations of* Adventures of
    Huckleberry Finn. Ed. Claude M. Simpson.
    Englewood Cliffs: Prentice, 1968. 103-05.

Leavis, F. R. Introduction. *Pudd'nhead Wilson*. By
    Samuel Clemens. London: Chatto, 1955. Rpt. as
    "Viewpoints: F. R. Leavis." *Twentieth-Century
    Interpretations of* Adventures of Huckleberry Finn.
    Ed. Claude M. Simpson. Englewood Cliffs: Prentice,
    1968. 109-11.

Abbreviated publisher's name

Mailloux, Steven. "Reading Huckleberry Finn: The
    Rhetoric of Performed Ideology." New Essays on
    Adventures of Huckleberry Finn. Ed. Louis J. Budd.
    Cambridge: Cambridge UP, 1985. 107-33

Mathews, Brander. Rev. of Adventures of Huckleberry
    Finn, by Samuel Clemens. Saturday Review (London)
    31 Jan. 1885: 153-54. Rpt. in Huck Finn Among the
    Critics: A Centennial Selection. Ed. M. Thomas
    Inge. Frederick: University Publications of
    America, 1985. 27-32.

Pearson, E. L. "The Children's Librarian Versus
    Huckleberry Finn: A Brief for the Defense." The
    Library Journal 32 (1907): 312-13.

Perry, Thomas Sergeant. Rev. of Adventures of
    Huckleberry Finn, by Samuel Clemens. Century
    Magazine May 1885: 171-72. Rpt. in Huck Finn Among
    the Critics: A Centennial Selection. Ed. M. Thomas
    Inge. Frederick: University Publications of
    America, 1985. 33-35.

Pritchett, V. S. "America's First Truly Indigenous
    Masterpiece." New Statesman and Nation 2 Aug.
    1941: 113. Rpt. in Huck Finn Among the Critics: A
    Centennial Selection. Ed. M. Thomas Inge.
    Frederick: University Publications of America,
    1985. 75-79.

Railton, Stephen. "Jim and Mark Twain: What Do Dey
    Stan' For?" The Virginia Quarterly Review 63
    (1987): 393-408.

Rule, Henry B. "A Brief History of the Censorship of
the Adventures of Huckleberry Finn." Lamar Journal
of the Humanities 12.1 (1986): 9-18.

"Schools in Philadelphia Edit 'Huckleberry Finn.'" New
York Times 17 Apr. 1963, sec. 1: 44.

Scott, A. L. "The Century Magazine Edits Huckleberry
Finn, 1884-1885." American Literature 27 (1955):
356-62.

Smith, David L. "Huck, Jim, and American Racial
Discourse." Mark Twain Journal 22 (1984): 4-12.

Stanek, Lou Willett. "Huck Finn: 100 Years of Durn Fool
Problems." School Library Journal 31.6 (1985): 19-
22.

"Think Back, Too." Editorial. New York Times 1 Jan.
1984: E12.

Trilling, Lionel. "The Greatness of Huckleberry Finn."
The Liberal Imagination. New York: Scribner's,
1950. Rpt. in Huck Finn Among the Critics: A
Centennial Selection. Ed. M. Thomas Inge.
Frederick: University Publications of America,
1985. 81-92.

If the author's name is unknown, entry is
alphabetized by the first word in the title
other than a definite or indefinite article.

Appendix A

THE MLA ALTERNATIVE: DOCUMENTING WITH NOTES

Some instructors may request that you document your papers with both notes and a list of sources, though you may be asked to document a paper with endnotes or footnotes only. Since all the information needed to identify a source is included in a note, notes provide adequate documentation. Footnotes differ from endnotes only in their placement in the text. Footnotes are placed at the bottom of the page—the same page on which the citation is found. Endnotes are consolidated in one list and placed at the end of the paper.

Number notes consecutively throughout your paper, beginning with 1. Place the number at the end of a phrase, sentence, or paragraph, or immediately following any quoted material, even if only a single word. Raise the number slightly above the line; such numbers are called superscripts.

The form used for notes is slightly different from that of a list of sources. For example, an author's first name is given first since notes are not listed alphabetically. There are also variations in punctuation and indentation. Compare the bibliographic citation below with the note that follows.

Bibliographic Citation

Lash, Joseph P. <u>Eleanor: The Years Alone</u>. New York: Norton, 1972.

Note Citation

[1]Joseph P. Lash, <u>Eleanor: The Years Alone</u> (New York: Norton, 1972) 220.

Documentary Notes (Endnotes and Footnotes)

The following models, using the MLA style, will help you design documentary endnotes, footnotes, and content notes. For the APA style and the citation-sequence system mentioned above, see chapters 12 and 13.

BOOKS

A Book with One Author

²Stanley Fish, <u>Is There a Text in This Class?</u> (Cambridge: Harvard UP, 1980) 103.

Note: For two or more books by the same author, give the author's complete name in each note.

A Book with Two Authors or Editors

³Paul R. Ehrlich and Anne H. Ehrlich, <u>Healing the Planet</u> (Reading: Addison, 1991) 171.
⁴Marjorie Pryse and Hortense J. Spillers, eds., <u>Conjuring: Black Women, Fiction, and the Literary Tradition</u> (Bloomington: Indiana UP, 1985) 133.

A Book with Three Authors

⁵Herman Kahn, William Brown, and Leon Martel, <u>The Next 200 Years</u> (New York: Morrow, 1976) 84.

A Book with More Than Three Authors

⁶Bernard Bailyn et al., <u>The Great Republic: A History of the American People</u> (Lexington: Heath, 1977) 959.

Note: The abbreviation "et al." stands for "and others."

A Book with a Corporate Author

⁷U.S. Department of Energy, <u>An Assessment of Thermal Insulation Materials</u> (Washington: GPO, 1978) 57.

Note: GPO is an abbreviation for Government Printing Office.

A Book with an Anonymous Author

[8]<u>Writers' and Artists' Yearbook, 1980</u> (London: Adam and Charles Black, 1980) 93.

A Book with an Author Who Uses a Pseudonym (a Fictitious Name)

[9]Michael Innes [J. I. M. Stewart], <u>Going It Alone</u> (New York: Dodd, 1980) 23.

Note: The author's real name may be supplied in brackets.

A Scholarly Edition

[10]Charles Dickens, <u>Oliver Twist</u>, ed. Kathleen Tillotson, The Clarendon Dickens (Oxford: Clarendon, 1966) 211.

Note: If the work of the editor is being discussed or cited, the editor's name comes first:

[11]Kathleen Tillotson, ed., <u>Oliver Twist</u>, by Charles Dickens, The Clarendon Dickens (Oxford: Clarendon, 1966) 211.

A Work in a Series

[12]Donald H. Reiman, <u>Shelley's "The Triumph of Life": A Critical Study</u>, Illinois Studies in Lang. and Lit. 55 (Urbana: U of Illinois P, 1965) 34.

A Single Work Published in More Than One Volume (with Continuous Pagination)

[13]Edgar Johnson, <u>Sir Walter Scott: The Great Unknown</u>, 2 vols. (London: Hamilton, 1970) 117.

A Book That Is Part of a Multivolume Work with a Single Title

[14]Arnold Kettle, <u>An Introduction to the English Novel</u>, vol. 2 (London: Hutchinson U Library, 1953) 74.

A Book That Is Part of a Multivolume Work by One Author When Each Volume Has a Separate Title

[15]Robert Coles, <u>Privileged Ones</u>, vol. 5 of <u>Children of Crisis</u> (Boston: Little, 1977) 506.

A Book That Is Part of a Multivolume Work When Each Volume Has a
Separate Title and Author

[16]J. I. M. Stewart, <u>Eight Modern Writers</u> (Oxford: Oxford UP, 1963) 519, vol. 12 of <u>Oxford History of English Literature,</u> ed. John Baxton and Norman Davis, 1945-86.

A Book with Different Authors for Each Chapter and a Single Editor

[17]Daniel Hoffman, ed., <u>Harvard Guide to Contemporary American Writing</u> (Cambridge: Harvard UP, 1979) iv.

A Reprint of an Older Edition

[18]Zora Neale Hurston, <u>Their Eyes Were Watching God</u> (1937; Urbana: U of Illinois P, 1978) 119.

Note: The date, but not the publisher, of the first edition is given immediately after the title.

A Paperback Reprint of a Hardback Edition

[19]Jill Ker Conway, <u>The Road from Coorain</u> (1989; New York: Vintage, 1990) 58-60.

A Revised Edition

[20]Richard Ellmann, <u>James Joyce,</u> 2nd ed. (New York: Oxford UP, 1982) 395.

A Revised Version of a Work of Literature

[21]John Fowles, <u>The Magus,</u> rev. version (Boston: Little, 1977) 245.

A Translation

[22]Homer, <u>The Iliad,</u> trans. Richmond Lattimore (Chicago: U of Chicago P, 1951) 142.

Note: If the work of the translator is being discussed, this should be cited as follows:

[23]Richmond Lattimore, trans., <u>The Iliad,</u> by Homer (Chicago: U of Chicago P, 1951) 142.

Sacred Writings

Citations from the Bible and other sacred writings are usually documented within parentheses in the text of the paper: (Gen. 20: 1–17). Sacred writings referred to in a note are neither underlined nor placed in quotation marks.

PARTS OF BOOKS

An Article, Essay, Chapter, or Other Part of a Book with a Single Author

[1]Doris Lessing, "The Temptation of Jack Orkney," <u>Stories</u> (New York: Knopf, 1978) 564.

An Introduction, Afterword, Preface, or Foreword to a Book Written by Someone Other Than the Book's Author

[2]Alice Walker, afterword, <u>I Love Myself: A Zora Neale Hurston Reader</u>, ed. Alice Walker (Old Westbury: Feminist Press, 1979) 297.

A Previously Published Essay or Article from a Collection of Writings by Different Authors

[3]Edward W. Said, "An Ideology of Difference," <u>Critical Inquiry</u> 12 (1985): 89–107, rpt. in <u>"Race," Writing, and Difference</u>, ed. Henry Louis Gates, Jr. (Chicago: U of Chicago P, 1986) 41.

An Essay or Article from a Collection of Works Not Previously Published

[4]Dennis Brutus, "English and the Dynamics of South African Creative Writing," <u>English Literature: Opening Up the Canon</u>, Selected Papers from the English Institute, 1979, ed. Leslie A. Fiedler and Houston Baker, Jr. (Baltimore: Johns Hopkins UP, 1981) 1–14.

A Short Story, Poem, or Essay from an Anthology

[5]George Herbert, "The Flower," <u>Seventeenth-Century Prose and Poetics</u>, ed. Alexander M. Witherspoon and Frank J. Warnke, 2nd ed. (New York: Harcourt, 1963) 857.
[6]Alexander Pope, "The Rape of the Lock," <u>The Norton Anthology of World Masterpieces</u>, ed. Maynard Mack et al., 6th ed., vol. 2 (New York: Norton, 1992) 306–26.

A Novel or Play from an Anthology

[7]Toni Morrison, _Sula_, _The Norton Introduction to the Short Novel_, ed. Jerome Beaty, 2nd ed. (New York: Norton, 1982) 581.

Afterword, Preface, Introduction, or Other Editorial Comment on Individual Pieces in a Collection

[8]Jerome Beaty, afterword to _Sula_, _The Norton Introduction to the Short Novel_, ed. Jerome Beaty, 2nd ed. (New York: Norton, 1982) 661.

An Unsigned Article in a Widely Known Reference Work

[9]"Solar Energy," _The New Columbia Encyclopedia_, 4th ed. (1975) 2556.

A Signed Article in a Widely Known Reference Work

[10]Howard Suber, "Motion Picture," _Encyclopedia Americana_, 1981 ed.

An Article in a Specialized, Less Familiar Reference Work

[11]D. H. Monro, "William Godwin," _The Encyclopedia of Philosophy_, ed. Paul Edwards, 8 vols. (New York: Macmillan, 1967) 3: 358.

[12]John W. Roberts, "James Baldwin," _Dictionary of Literary Biography_, ed. Thadious M. Davis and Trudier Harris, 134 vols. (Ann Arbor: Gale, 1984) 33: 14.

PERIODICALS

A Signed Article from a Daily Newspaper Divided into Sections Paginated Separately

[1]Milton R. Benjamin, "U.S. Is Allowing Argentina to Buy Critical A-System," _Washington Post_ 19 July 1982: A1+.

Note: Use " + " for an article that begins in one part of a periodical and continues elsewhere.

A Signed Article from a Daily Newspaper Paginated Continuously

[2]Peter Passell, "Czechs Tread Minefield on the Way to Capitalism," _New York Times_ 18 Apr. 1992, natl. ed.: 17+.

Note: Some newspapers are published in more than one edition, and the pagination varies from one to another. Indicate the edition if it is specified on the masthead.

An Unsigned Article from a Daily Newspaper

[3]"Soviet Group Presses for Broader Arms 'Dialog,'" <u>New York Times</u> 5 Sept. 1982, sec. 1: 16.

A Signed Article from a Weekly Magazine or Newspaper

[4]Bruno Bettelheim, "Reflections: Freud and the Soul," <u>New Yorker</u> 1 Mar. 1982: 52+.

[5]James Lewis, "Jobless Reality Fails to Impress Thatcher's Cabinet," <u>Manchester Guardian Weekly</u> 5 Sept. 1982: 3.

An Unsigned Article from a Weekly Publication

[6]"Computers," <u>Time</u> 2 Aug. 1982: 72.

A Serialized Article

[7]William J. Broad, "Science Showmanship: A Deep 'Star Wars' Rift," <u>New York Times</u> 16 Dec. 1985: 1+, pt. 2 of a series begun on 15 Dec. 1985.

A Signed Editorial

[8]Gerard Smith, "Toward Arms Control," editorial, <u>New York Times</u> 29 June 1982: A23.

An Unsigned Editorial

[9]"Tuition Subsidies Are Not Benign," editorial, <u>New York Times</u> 3 July 1982: 20.

An Article from a Monthly Magazine

[10]William Greider, "The Education of David Stockman," <u>Atlantic</u> Dec. 1981: 27.

An Article in a Journal with Pages Numbered Continuously Through Each Yearly Volume

[11]Blanche H. Gelfant, "Mingling and Sharing in American Literature: Teaching Ethnic Fiction," <u>College English</u> 43 (1981): 763.

Note: The numbers after the title of the journal refer to the volume number, the date, and the pages of the article cited.

An Article in a Journal That Numbers Pages Separately for Each Issue

[12]Peter Biskind, "Rebel Without a Cause: Nicholas Ray in the Fifties," Film Quarterly 28.5 (1974): 32.

Note: The numbers following the journal title refer to the volume (28) and issue (5).

[13]Claire Sprague, "Dialectic and Counter-Dialectic in the Martha Quest Novels," Journal of Commonwealth Literature 14 (1979): 39.

Note: Where there is no volume number, treat the issue number as though it were a volume number.

A Signed Review with a Title

[14]Peter L. Berger, "A Woman of This Century," rev. of Hannah Arendt: For Love of the World, by Elizabeth Young Bruehl, New York Times Book Review 25 Apr. 1982: 1, 20–21.

A Signed, Untitled Review

[15]John F. C. Harrison, rev. of The Age of Capital, 1848–1875, by E. G. Hobsbawm, Victorian Studies 20 (1977): 423.

An Unsigned, Untitled Review

[16]Rev. of The French Lieutenant's Woman, by John Fowles, Times Literary Supplement 12 June 1969: 629.

A Letter to the Editor

[17]R. W. Flint, letter, New Republic 18 Feb. 1957: 23.

A Response to a Letter or Letters

[18]Nicholas Lemann, reply to letters of Roger Williams and Virginia K. Williams, Atlantic Dec. 1984: 14.

A Speech or Address for a Special Occasion Printed in a Periodical

[19]Toni Morrison, "Address to the American Writers Congress," 9 Oct. 1981, in Nation 24 Oct. 1981: 396.

An Article from Dissertation Abstracts *or* Dissertation Abstracts International

[20]John Bryan Webb, "Utopian Fantasy and Social Change," DA 43
(1982): 8214250 (State U of New York at Buffalo).

An Article from a Volume of Abstracts

[21]John W. C. Johnstone, "Who Controls the News," American
Journal of Sociology 87 (1982): 1174-81, abstract from America:
History and Life 20.A (1983): 2120.

An Article from a Newsletter

[22]Douglas Cliggott, "Proposed Tax Reform Will Have Negative
Effect on Capital Investment," Business Executive Expectations Third
Quarter 1985: 2.

Note: Newsletters may not include volume and issue numbers, dates,
or even pagination. In cases where a publication does employ the usual
conventions needed for a citation, adapt what information you have to a
form as close as possible to that of a conventional periodical citation,
making sure that you provide enough information for readers to find the
source.

OTHER WRITTEN SOURCES

The Published Proceedings of a Conference

[1]Conserving the Historical and Cultural Landscape, proc. of the
Conference of the National Trust for Historic Preservation, Western
Region, 2-3 May 1975, Denver (Washington: Preservation Press, 1975)
54.

A Government Publication

[2]Office of the Federal Register, United States Government
Manual, 1980-81 (Washington: GPO, 1980) 37.

A Legal Reference

[3]Brown v. Board of Education of Topeka, 347 US 483 (US Supr.
Ct., 1954).

A Pamphlet

[4]Jules Saltman, Teenagers and Alcohol: Patterns and Dangers (New
York: Public Affairs Comm., 1983) 3.

A Letter Printed in a Volume of Collected Letters

[5]Edmund Wilson, "To William Faulkner," 25 Sept. 1956, Letters on Literature and Politics, 1912-1972, ed. Elena Wilson (New York: Farrar, 1977) 540.

An Unpublished Letter from a Collection

[6]Adlai E. Stevenson, letter to Ralph McGill, 11 May 1954, Ralph McGill Papers, Emory University, Atlanta.

A Personal Letter

[7]Grace Paley, letter to the author, 30 July 1981.

A Dissertation

[8]Donald Joseph Gray, "Victorian Verse Humor," diss., Ohio State U, 1956, 29.

A Document from an Information Service

[9]Paul V. Delker, Adult Education--1980 and Beyond, Occasional Paper No. 59 (Columbus: Ohio State U, 1979) 19 (ERIC ED 189 309).

A Manuscript or Typescript

[10]Hart Crane, The Bridge, ms., Hart Crane Collection, Columbia U, New York.

NON-PRINT SOURCES

A Lecture or Publicly Delivered Paper

[1]George Levine, "George Eliot's Scientific Ideal: The Hypothesis of Reality," The English Institute, Cambridge, MA, 1 Sept. 1979.

A Radio or Television Program

[2]The Doomsayers, prod. Brian Capener, PBS Special, 8 Sept. 1982.
[3]"Maya Angelou," narr. Bill Moyers, Creativity, PBS Special, WPBA, Atlanta, 8 Jan. 1982.

Note: When you want to refer to a particular individual (producer, director, narrator, or actor), cite that person's name first:

[4]Bill Moyers, narr., "Maya Angelou," _Creativity_, PBS Special, WPBA, Atlanta, 8 Jan. 1982.

A Performance of Music, Dance, or Drama

[5]Giacomo Puccini, _La Bohème_, cond. James Levine, with Teresa Stratas, Metropolitan Opera, Metropolitan Opera House, New York, 13 Jan. 1982.

Note: When you want to refer to a particular individual (conductor, director, choreographer), cite that person's name first:

[6]James Levine, cond., _La Bohème_, by Giacomo Puccini, with Teresa Stratas, Metropolitan Opera, Metropolitan Opera House, New York, 13 Jan. 1982.

A Film

[7]_Vietnam: An American Journey_, Films Inc., 1979.
[8]_Rebel Without a Cause_, dir. Nicholas Ray, with James Dean, Sal Mineo, and Natalie Wood, Warner Brothers, 1955.

Note: When you want to refer to a particular individual, cite that person's name first:

[9]Nicholas Ray, dir., _Rebel Without a Cause_, with James Dean, Sal Mineo, and Natalie Wood, Warner Brothers, 1955.

A Face-to-Face Interview

[10]Peter Vitousek, Professor of Biology, Stanford University, personal interview, 21 Jan. 1993.

A Telephone Interview

[11]Coretta Scott King, telephone interview, 1 Nov. 1982.

A Work of Art

[12]Paul Cézanne, _A Modern Olympia_, Louvre, Paris.

A Work of Art with a Cited Illustration

[13]Pierre Bonnard, _The Open Window_, The Phillips Collection, illus. in _Master Paintings from the Phillips Collection_, by Eleanor Green et al. (New York: Penghurst, 1981) 71.

A Musical Composition

[14]George Frideric Handel, _Messiah_, ed. Watkins Shaw, Novello Handel Edition (Sevenoaks, Eng.: Novello, n.d.).

Note: Use "n.d." (no date) for any undated material.

An Audio Recording

[15]Hammer, _Too Legit to Quit_, Capitol Records, CA-98151, 1991.

An Audio Recording from Which a Particular Song Is Referred to or Quoted

[16]The Beatles, "Revolution," _The Beatles/1967-1970_, Capitol, SEBX-11843, 1973.

An Audio Recording When the Work of the Performer or Performers Is Discussed

[17]Marilyn Horne, _Orfeo ed Euridice_, by Christoph Willibald Gluck, cond. by George Solti, Orchestra and Chorus of the Royal Opera House, Covent Garden, London, OSA1285, 1970.

A Videotape or Videorecording

[18]_The Nuclear Dilemma_, videorecording, BBC-TV, New York: Time Life Multimedia, 1974.

A Computer Program on Tape or Disk

[19]Richard J. Ward, _The Executive Game_, computer software, Bowling Green State U, Hewlett-Packard, A880-2232A.

Note: Computer programs vary considerably. For this reason you will have to adapt a citation to the information you have. When possible, you should include an author, title, place of production, company or organization that produces the program, identifying number, and date.

Material from a Computer Service

[20]"Salk, Jonas Edward," _American Men and Women of Science_, 15th ed. (Bowker, 1983) (_Dialog_ file 236, item 0090936).

Note: Cite material from a computer service such as _Dialog_ or _BRS_ like printed material found in books and periodicals, but add a reference to the service at the end of the citation, giving the name of the service and the numbers identifying the database and the particular item from that base.

If you are using documentary notes—as in the sample paper in this chapter—you should fully identify each source in the first citation, including, when appropriate, author, title, place of publication, publisher, date, and page. For each note after the first, indicate the source as briefly as possible and give the page for that reference. Follow these guidelines for references to a source after the first full citation note:

When Only One Work by an Author Is Listed, Cite the Author's Last Name and the Page Number

[1]Hareven 307.

When There Is More Than One Work by an Author, Use the Author's Last Name, a Shortened Title, and the Page

[2]Lash, *Love* 213.
[3]Lash, *E&F* 201.

For Citations Without an Author, Use an Abbreviated Title and the Page

[4]"Reflections" 52.

Selected Pages from a Sample Paper with Endnotes

The paper that Michael Gold turned in to his professor (see p. 237) was documented with the MLA style of parenthetical references in the text and a bibliography, or "Works Cited" list, at the end. Some teachers ask students to use endnotes (or footnotes) while others may require both notes and a bibliography. What follows are the last two pages of Michael's paper as they would look if the paper were documented with endnotes—as well as complete endnotes for the paper.

would insist today that James Dean lives, Rebel Without
a Cause is still alive in the minds of people who study
the history of film. In recent years, scholars have
tried to judge the film as a whole, rather than as a
showcase for the magic that Dean created. They are
studying its values, its art, and its place in American
film history. Peter Biskind, writing in Film Quarterly,
sees Rebel as a reflection of the conservative values of
mid-fifties America. He argues that the young
characters condemn their parents' weaknesses, but that
in the end the film affirms traditional family values
and remains "a profoundly conservative film."[30] David
Cook, on the other hand, in his History of Narrative
Film, sees the film as "a definitive statement of the
psychic and emotional ills that beset America during the
period."[31] Douglas McVay considers Rebel to be Nicholas
Ray's masterpiece and one of the four best films of the
fifties.[32] David Thomson, who thinks of Rebel as the
work of a director who was both a serious social critic
and a "great romantic" producing great art,[33] warns of
the difficulty of ever recreating that initial response:

> So Rebel is vibrant with yearning aspirations,
> and Ray's beautiful and brave venturing with
> space, decor, and faces lost in a night
> wilderness of screen. We can never regain the
> view we had of the film in 1955, when its
> rueful passion swept so many of us away.[34]

Even though almost thirty years have passed since
audiences first settled down to watch Rebel Without a

Cause, evaluating its place both in film history and in American society is still not easy. A profoundly conservative film, a tragedy in the classical sense, a high romance, or scathing social comment—which is the appropriate category for this still controversial film? When we consider the many different people who contributed to its creation, we may conclude that it is all of these. It is certainly not surprising to discover that the film that has what Kreidl calls "a disparate smattering of different vocabularies from different sources" should evoke such varied responses.[35]

Rebel Without a Cause was generated through conflict; it was finally realized when the community of people who wanted to bring it about discovered ways to compromise and cooperate. But the conflict that created Rebel is still alive in the minds of people who interpret it. A film more than a book exists in the minds of its viewers. Although some may have a videotape of the film, which they can study at their leisure, most people must rely on memory.[36] The community of interpreters—those who remember, study, and talk and write about Rebel—will probably always be fraught with conflict both because memories are highly personal and because the struggle between generations that Rebel explores is constantly being renewed.

Notes

[1] Jack Lusk, president, Swank Motion Pictures, letter to the author, 28 Feb. 1992.

[2] Ezra Goodman, "Delirium over Dead Star," _Life_ 24 Sept. 1956: 75.

[3] Sam Astrachan, "The New Lost Generation," _New Republic_ 4 Feb. 1957: 17-18.

[4] Herbert Mitgang, "The Strange James Dean Death Cult," _Films and Filming_ 23.2 (1979): 114.

[5] Goodman 78.

[6] "Fan," "Talk of the Town," _New Yorker_ 2 Aug. 1969: 22.

[7] Lusk.

[8] Mayberry, George, "Alternatives to the Novel," _New Republic_ 24 July 1944: 108.

[9] Edwin J. Lukas, rev. of _Rebel Without a Cause . . . The Hypnoanalysis of a Criminal Psychopath_, by Robert M. Lindner, _The Annals of the American Academy of Political and Social Science_ 236 (1944): 216.

[10] John Francis Kreidl, _Nicholas Ray_, Twayne's Theatrical Arts Ser. (Boston: Twayne, 1981) 91.

[11] Nicholas Ray, "Story into Script," _Sight and Sound_ 26 (1956): 70.

[12] Kreidl 94.

[13] Ray 71-72.

[14] David Dalton, _James Dean: The Mutant King_ (San Francisco: Straight Arrow, 1974) 225.

[15] Ray 73.

[16] Ray 73.

[17] Kreidl 93.

[18] Kreidl 86.

[19] Dalton 236.

[20] Dalton 232.

[21] Dalton 236, 253.

[22] Penelope Houston and John Gillett, "Conversations with Nicholas Ray and Joseph Losey," Sight and Sound 3 (1961): 184.

[23] Kreidl 208.

[24] Dalton 230.

[25] David Thomson, "Rebel Without a Cause," Take One Mar. 1979: 15.

[26] Kreidl 77.

[27] Ray 74.

[28] Kreidl 82.

[29] Dalton 227.

[30] Peter Biskind, "Rebel Without a Cause: Nicholas Ray in the Fifties," Film Quarterly 28.5 (1974): 37.

[31] David A. Cook, A History of Narrative Film, 2nd ed. (New York: Norton, 1990) 500.

[32] Douglas McVay, "Rebel Without a Cause," Films and Filming 23.2 (1979): 24.

[33] Thomson 15.

[34] Thomson 16.

[35] Kreidl 86.

[36] The availability of videotape makes it possible to study films the way scholars study written works of literature. Future responses to Rebel may be based more on careful critical analysis than on emotional response.

AN ANNOTATED LIST
OF SELECTED REFERENCE
WORKS

The following list of reference works represents only a small percentage of books available in the reference sections of even small libraries. By consulting this list, however, you should get a good idea about where to start researching almost any topic. If you find one reference work in a discipline, others will be shelved nearby.

It will be helpful if you understand the specialized vocabulary used to describe reference books. The word **bibliography** refers to lists of books or other material about a subject. There are very broad bibliographies that cover a whole field of studies (the humanities, for example), more limited ones that cover a discipline (psychology), and ones that list material on a very specific topic (the novels of William Faulkner). **Abstracts** are brief summaries of books, articles, research reports, dissertations, or speeches. **Indexes** are used to retrieve pieces of information from larger units— periodicals, parts of books, microform collections, or non-print materials. Some indexes include abstracts of the entries. Most **dictionaries** provide information about words, proper names, and phrases. **Encyclopedias** provide more detailed information, background, and explanations of people, places, things, events, and ideas. There is, however, often some overlap, since dictionaries may give more than definitions, and some encyclopedias include definitions of many specialized words.

Before you use a reference work, you should study the format and instructions for users. If you read the introduction or other explanation about how to use a given work, you should soon be able to use it success-

le, however, consult the reference librarian for

below are cited as they are usually referred to by arians: those usually identified by the name of the ith the author's name first; titles are noted first for dentified by title, as in the case of encyclopedias and volume works.

ace works are now produced both in book form and in compu... ases (on-line), and the number of sources available on-line is increasing rapidly. If you are planning to do a computer search, you may want to ask your computer librarian whether those reference works appropriate to your topic are available on-line.

General Reference Works

BIBLIOGRAPHIES

Bibliographic Index. New York: Wilson, 1938–.
This extensive listing by subject includes bibliographies that appear in books, pamphlets, and periodical articles. It also lists bibliographies published as individual books and pamphlets.

Books in Print. New York: Bowker, 1948–.
See page 63. Available on-line and on CD-ROM.

Cumulative Book Index. New York: Wilson, 1898–.
Lists books published in English by author, subject, and title.

Katz, Bill, and Linda Sternberger Katz. *Magazines for Libraries*. 5th ed. New York: Bowker, 1986.
Useful for students looking for information about the purpose, scope, and audience of a periodical. In some cases you can find out about a periodical's bias or value judgments.

BIOGRAPHICAL SOURCES

Contemporary Authors. Detroit: Gale, 1962–.
An up-to-date source of information on living authors of fiction and nonfiction in many fields. A good place to look for material on authors who are not well known.

Current Biography. New York: Wilson, 1940–.

Attempting to cover all important living people in all fields, this is a good source of information for popular figures such as entertainers.

Dictionary of American Biography (DAB). 21 vols. New York: Scribner's, 1927, with supplements.

Covers only people not living and provides authoritative signed articles on important Americans. Also cites further sources of information.

Dictionary of American Negro Biography. Ed. Rayford W. Logan and Michael R. Winston. New York: Norton, 1982.

Spanning some three centuries, this is an invaluable source of information about more than seven hundred black Americans in all fields. Covers only those who died before 1970.

Dictionary of Canadian Biography. Toronto: U of Toronto P, 1966, with supplements.

Includes native Canadians as well as people from other countries who have contributed to Canadian life. As with DAB and DNB, no living people are included.

Dictionary of National Biography (DNB). 22 vols. London: Oxford UP, 1908–1909, with supplements.

Provides substantial biographical material for notable individuals no longer living. Covers Great Britain and colonial countries.

The McGraw-Hill Encyclopedia of World Biography. New York: McGraw, 1973.

Includes information on the living and the dead. A good place to go for biographies of women and members of minority groups less represented in more traditional sources.

Who's Who. New York: St. Martin's, 1849–.

Begun in 1849 as a list of titled British aristocracy and still primarily a British source, since 1897 these annual volumes have provided biographical information and current addresses (and for authors, a list of works) for prominent people in many fields. A reliable source for information about the living. *Who Was Who* is a compilation of biographies of people no longer living selected from *Who's Who* 1897–1970.

Who's Who in America. Chicago: Marquis, 1899–.

Up-to-date biographical information about living Americans. The standards for selection are high, as people must be well-known for significant and reputable achievements. *Who Was Who in America* is a selection from previous volumes of people now deceased. *Note:* There are many specialized biographical sources that include *Who's Who* as part of their title. Some are published by Marquis Press of Chicago, and some are from other publishing houses. You may find one of these helpful when more general biographical sources fail. Available on-line as *Marquis Who's Who.*

DICTIONARIES

American Heritage Dictionary of the English Language. 2nd college ed. Boston: Houghton, 1982.
A good desk dictionary that includes new words used in business, science, and technology. It also contains valuable material on the history of the English language as well as guides to punctuation, grammar, and usage.

Oxford English Dictionary (OED). 20 vols. 2nd ed. London: Oxford UP, 1989.
Traces the historical development of English words. Dated quotations listed in chronological order illustrate the ways each word has been used, detailing how its meaning has changed. This is a fascinating work and an invaluable resource for finding out much of what is known about the history of words.

Random House Dictionary of the English Language. 2nd ed. New York: Random, 1987.
This unabridged dictionary is comprehensive, up-to-date, and fun to use.

Webster's New Collegiate Dictionary. 9th ed. Springfield: Merriam, 1983.
An authoritative desk dictionary for help in understanding the English language as it is actually spoken and written today. It includes both specialized terminology and new words.

Webster's Third New International Dictionary of the English Language. Springfield: Merriam, 1981.
An unabridged dictionary, this work gives brief definitions of words from both standard and spoken English. There are also quotations from contemporary sources.

ENCYCLOPEDIAS

Academic American Encyclopedia, Collier's Encyclopedia, Encyclopaedia Britannica, the *Encyclopedia Americana,* and the *New Columbia Encyclopedia* are discussed on pages 35–39.

Random House Encyclopedia. New York: Random, 1990.
A good, easy-to-use, readable reference work for a wide range of general topics. Comparable to the *New Columbia Encyclopedia.*

GEOGRAPHICAL SOURCES

Columbia Lippincott Gazetteer of the World. Ed. Leon E. Seltzer, with the cooperation of the American Geographical Society. New York: Columbia UP, 1952. Supplement 1961.
Lists places of the world alphabetically, including countries, parts of countries, cities, and towns, as well as major geographical features such as bodies of water, mountains, etc. It also gives information about industry, agriculture, size, and other details.

The Times Atlas of the World. Comprehensive (8th) ed. New York: Times Books, 1990.
Detailed maps and listings of most of the places of the world. Each item listed is coded so that you can easily find it on a map.

The Times Atlas of the World. 5 vols. London: The Times, 1955–59.
These outstanding volumes are known for the beauty and accuracy of their maps. Some of the material is, of course, out-of-date. Many of the African maps, for example, must be supplemented with more recent atlases.

The Times Index-Gazetteer of the World. London: The Times, 1965.
Lists almost three times as many communities and geographical features as *Columbia Lippincott.* It provides latitude and longitude along with map locations, but it does not include descriptions.

Webster's New Geographical Dictionary. Springfield: Merriam, 1972.
Provides brief, basic information such as location, size, population, history, and economy for many places. Not as extensive as *Columbia Lippincott,* but more up-to-date.

INDEXES

Biography Index. New York: Wilson, 1946–.
You will often save time searching for biographical material by beginning with this index, as it will lead you to particular volumes or editions of reference books as well as to book-length biographies and biographical information in periodicals. It also contains a listing by profession or occupation of all the people included so that a student looking for names of important people in various fields—animal train-

ers, criminologists, hermits, midwives, pacifists—can easily find them.

Biography and Genealogy Master Index. Ed. Miranda C. Herbert and Barbara McNeil. Detroit: Gale, 1980–.

A consolidated index to more than 3,200,000 articles in over 350 dictionaries of biography. Material in annual volumes is accumulated every five years. Does not cover book-length biographies or biographical material in periodicals. A good place to go when you want basic information about people's lives: birth date, dates of major accomplishments, or educational background. Available on-line.

Book Review Digest. New York: Wilson, 1906–.

Cites selected reviews of works of literature and nonfiction books in all fields. The citations are alphabetized by the author of the book reviewed, and each includes a brief description of the book, quotations from selected reviews, and references to other reviews.

Book Review Index. Detroit: Gale, 1965–.

Covers more than three times as many periodicals as *Book Review Digest,* but does not provide excerpts or summaries. Publication was suspended from 1969 to 1977. Available on-line.

Essay and General Literature Index. New York: Wilson, 1900–.

Published three times a year, this index emphasizes material in the humanities and social sciences. Indexed by author, subject, and some titles, this work will lead you to individual essays and portions of books on topics that you would not be able to find in card catalogs or standard periodical indexes. For example, a general work on twentieth-century British novelists may have an important chapter on D. H. Lawrence; such a chapter would be indicated here, but not in a card catalog.

The Magazine Index. Menlo Park: Information Access, 1977–.

See page 43. Available in microform and on CD-ROM.

Monthly Catalog of United States Government Publications. Washington: GPO, 1895–.

The most comprehensive index to government-generated materials. Indexed by author, subject, key words, title, and other categories. Before you use this index, find out—ask a librarian—if there are more specialized indexes to government publications treating your subject. Available on CD-ROM.

The New York Times Index. New York: The New York Times, 1913–.

See page 44. Volumes covering the years from 1851 through 1912 have been published in ten volumes as *The New York Times Index, Prior Series.*

Personal Name Index to the New York Times Index. 22 vols. Succasunna: Roxbury, 1976–1983.
   Consolidated index to name entries appearing in *The New York Times Index* from 1851 to 1974. An excellent index for finding articles on individual people. Includes obituaries.

Readers' Guide to Periodical Literature. New York: Wilson, 1900–.
   See pages 42–43. Also available on CD-ROM and on-line.

YEARBOOKS

Facts on File: A Weekly World News Digest. New York: Facts on File, 30 October 1940–.
   A good source for a brief overview of events and information reported in newspapers. You could start here for the basic facts about an international crisis, the highlights of sports events, or a list of the best-sellers. The cumulative five-year index can be very useful for identifying the dates when long-term news events were covered. Available on-line.

Whitaker's Almanac. London: Whitaker, 1868–.
   Contains valuable statistical information on government, finance, population, commerce, and general statistics of countries all over the world, with special emphasis on the British Commonwealth. A good place to go if you want information on a wide range of topics from the activities of the royal family to the winners of the London Film Festival.

The World Almanac and Book of Facts. New York: Newspaper Enterprise, 1868–.
   A good source for factual material in many fields. Valuable both for current and for historical topics.

Humanities

GENERAL

Directory of American Scholars. 8th ed. New York: Bowker, 1982.
   An excellent source for information about American scholars in the humanities who are currently active in teaching, research, and pub-

lishing. The directory is arranged in four subject volumes—History (I), English, Speech, and Drama (II), Foreign Languages, Linguistics, and Philology (III), and Philosophy, Religion, and Law (IV). Turn here to find out about the education and professional history of important figures in these fields.

Humanities Index. New York: Wilson, 1974–. (Formerly *International Index,* 1907–65; *Social Sciences and Humanities Index,* 1965–74.)
Indexes articles in periodicals by author and subject in the following fields: archeological and classical studies, area studies, folklore, history, language and literature, literary and political criticism, performing arts, philosophy, and religion and theology. A separate book review section is organized by author of the book reviewed. Available on-line and on CD-ROM.

ART

Art Index. New York: Wilson, 1930–.
An excellent index to periodicals that publish articles on archeology, architecture, art history, fine arts, crafts, and related fields. There are subject and author entries, and there is a separate section of book reviews alphabetized by the author reviewed. Available on-line and on CD-ROM.

McGraw-Hill Dictionary of Art. 5 vols. London: McGraw, 1969.
An encyclopedia despite its title, this is a useful source for basic information about artistic movements, schools of art, periods, and individual artists. The articles are signed and include bibliographies.

FILM

Film Literature Index. Albany: Filmdex, 1974–.
Indexes selected articles about films in some three hundred various periodicals not all chiefly concerned with film. There is also an index of reviews of books about films.

The Filmgoer's Companion. 7th ed. By Leslie Halliwell. New York: Hill and Wang, 1980.
Emphasis is on details about actors and movies rather than serious critical evaluations. Intended for the general reader rather than the student, this book is mainly useful for quickly finding the date, director, and actors of a given film or for identifying the names of films in

which particular actors have played. The index is invaluable for identifying even the most obscure person associated with a film.

International Index of Film Periodicals. New York: Bowker, 1973–.
Indexes some sixty periodicals devoted exclusively to film. The best index for serious studies of films.

The New York Times Film Reviews, 1913–1968. 5 vols. New York: The New York Times and Arno, 1970. (Subsequent volumes update the collection.)
Reproduces film reviews in chronological order exactly as they first appeared in the *Times,* including photographs. These volumes provide critical discussion of thousands of movies, and they also serve as a fascinating history of film.

HISTORY

America: History and Life. Santa Barbara: Clio, 1964–.
Cites articles in over two thousand periodicals. Volumes published from 1974 on include a brief abstract of each article. As with other complex indexes, you should study the format before you begin to use it, but you may find this one more cumbersome than others. Available on-line and on CD-ROM.

An Encyclopedia of World History. Ed. William L. Langer. Boston: Houghton, 1972.
A chronological listing of world events from the time of the first historical records through 1970. The *New Illustrated Encyclopedia of World History* is the same work except for the correction of a few errors and the addition of illustrations.

Harvard Guide to American History. 2 vols. Ed. Frank Freidel. Cambridge: Harvard UP, 1974.
An invaluable bibliography covering all periods of American history. The first volume also includes an introduction to the methods and materials of historical research.

Historical Abstracts. Santa Barbara: Clio, 1955–.
Brief summaries of periodical essays on the history of the world from 1450 to the present; 1955–72 cover 1775 to present; 1973 on covers 1450 to present. After 1964 *Historical Abstracts* excluded the history of the United States and Canada, which has since been treated in the companion, *America: History and Life.* Available on-line and on CD-ROM.

Morris, Richard, et al. *Encyclopedia of American History.* New York: Harper, 1982.

This valuable single-volume work is divided into three parts: a narrative of events from the founding of the colonies through the 1970s, a section treating various topics in American history, and an alphabetical listing of brief biographies of five hundred notable Americans in several different fields. The second section is useful for students who want a chronological overview of a broad subject such as American music or developments in medicine.

New Cambridge Modern History. 14 vols. Cambridge: Cambridge UP, 1957–.

Authoritative discussion of world history from the Renaissance through the mid-twentieth century. The first twelve volumes are arranged chronologically, with chapters—each written by a renowned authority—focusing on nations and geographical regions and subheadings treating political, religious, economic, and cultural events. Volume 13 consists of twelve essays—each written by an expert—on broad subjects such as industry, revolution, or warfare, providing a good historical overview. Volume 14 is an historical atlas.

Shepherd, William. *Historical Atlas.* New York: Barnes, 1964.

Provides maps for world history from 1450 B.C. to the early 1960s. A useful supplement to the study of many historical topics such as the territorial expansion of the Roman Empire, the countries that remained neutral during World War II, or the original members of the United Nations.

LITERATURE

Altick, Richard, and Andrew Wright. *Selective Bibliography for the Study of English and American Literature.* 6th ed. New York: Macmillan, 1979.

A highly selective, up-to-date list of the best materials available to students of English and American literature. Students doing research on almost any topic in these fields will find valuable help here. Many of the 636 items are books in related fields—philosophy, history, religion—that are important to the study of literature.

Articles on American Literature, 1900–1950. Comp. by Lewis Leary. Durham: Duke UP, 1954. (Separate volumes for 1950–67 and 1968–75.)

These three volumes include an extensive—though admittedly incomplete—listing of articles on major and minor American authors.

Cambridge Bibliography of English Literature. 5 vols. Ed. F. W. Bateson. Cambridge: Cambridge UP, 1940–57.

Covers significant literary works from the Old English through the modern periods. Arranged both by genre (poetry, drama, novel) and chronology. Cites books and articles that treat each work listed.

Kolb, Harold. *A Field Guide to the Study of American Literature.* Charlottesville: U of Virginia P, 1976.
A useful introduction to selected works on American literature. The annotations indicate the content and value of each citation. This is a good book to consult if you want to do research on some aspect of American literature or culture.

Literary History of the United States. 2 vols. Ed. Robert E. Spiller et al. New York: Macmillan, 1972 and 1974.
Volume 1 is a comprehensive history of American literature presented chronologically. Separate essays feature major writers, individual genres (poetry, fiction, drama, folklore, etc.), and various literary phenomena and types. Also includes a selected list of books. Volume 2 is a cumulative bibliography of books and articles organized by type, period, topic, and author.

The MLA International Bibliography of Books and Articles on the Modern Languages and Literatures. (Formerly *American Bibliography,* 1921–55, *Annual Bibliography,* 1956–62.) New York: MLA, 1963–.
Divided by national literatures and subdivided by literary periods, this index is comprehensive and thorough. Since the index has gradually expanded to include more periodicals, it is important that you study the table of contents and the format of each volume that you use. An indispensable index for topics that focus on a given author. Available on-line and on CD-ROM and on tape.

The New Cambridge Bibliography of English Literature. 5 vols. Ed. George Watson. Cambridge: Cambridge UP, 1969–77.
An updated version of the original *Cambridge Bibliography.* Along with the original, this work provides a comprehensive overview of English literature and indicates the scope of materials available on each literary figure.

Oxford History of English Literature. 12 vols. Ed. F. P. Wilson and Bonamy Dobrée. Oxford: Oxford UP, 1945–.
A continuous history of English literature from the earliest times to the modern period, aimed at both the scholar and the general reader. Includes treatment of other fields—the arts, philosophy, science—where they relate to literature. Bibliographies accompany each volume.

Patterson, Margaret. *Literary Research Guide.* 2nd ed. New York: MLA, 1983.
A very helpful guide for all areas.

Year's Work in English Studies. London: Murray, 1919/20–.
Articles and books on a selective survey of English literature. There is a brief description and usually a critical evaluation of each work cited. A good source to use to learn what kind of studies were published on authors during specific years. If you are studying an author's changing reputation, for example, you will find a record of that change here. Each volume published since 1954 contains a chapter on American literature.

MUSIC

New Harvard Dictionary of Music. Rev. ed. By Willi Apel and Don Michael Randel. Cambridge: Harvard UP, 1986.
A storehouse of valuable information on all aspects of music, this is a classic work of music literature. Here you can learn about instruments, composers, types of music, and specific compositions, as well as definitions of musical terms. Many items are placed historically. You will find, for example, a brief history of the cello and the guitar.

Music Index. Detroit: Information Coordinators, 1949–.
Indexes periodicals that specialize in music and articles on musical topics published in more general publications. There are citations to articles on all kinds of music, including popular, jazz, opera, dance, and many others.

The New College Encyclopedia of Music. By J. A. Westrup and F. Ll. Harrison, rev. by Conrad Wilson. New York: Norton, 1976.
This useful work contains six thousand entries on musical terms, composers, compositions, instruments, and so on. Beginning students should find the many brief bibliographies particularly helpful.

The New Grove Dictionary of Music and Musicians. 20 vols. Ed. Stanley Sadie. London: Macmillan, 1980.
An excellent source of authoritative information on all aspects of music. There are substantial signed articles on topics ranging from music in ancient times to the contemporary world. Most include bibliographies.

A Dictionary of Comparative Religion. Ed. S. G. F. Brandon. New York: Scribner's, 1970.

This one-volume work includes short informational entries and twenty-eight longer, more comprehensive articles on world religions. Good bibliographies and a helpful system of cross-references make this an excellent place to begin research, especially for quick identification of key figures and concepts.

Encyclopedia of Bioethics. 4 vols. Ed. Warren T. Reich. 1978. New York: Free Press, 1982.

A comprehensive, detailed, and easy-to-use encyclopedia that covers all aspects of a new and exciting field. Written by a large team of experts from many traditions, this work is useful both for an overview and for detailed investigation. Includes bibliographies and an index.

Encyclopedia of Philosophy. 8 vols. Ed. Paul Edwards. New York: Macmillan, 1967. (Reprinted 8 vols. in 4 vols., New York: Macmillan, 1972.)

This is the most authoritative and comprehensive reference work on philosophy available in English. Each signed article has its own bibliography. There are articles on concepts and systems in philosophy, historical essays, and over nine hundred articles on individual thinkers.

Encyclopedic Dictionary of Religion. 3 vols. Ed. Paul Kevin Meagher et al. Washington: Corpus, 1979.

This is the most up-to-date and comprehensive work of its kind available in English. Signed entries by experts in the field cover a wide range of facts, events, persons, issues, and concepts. Focuses on Western religions, but includes Eastern religions as well. Especially good on important figures in religious thought and history. Includes a bibliography and cross references for each entry.

The Philosopher's Guide to Sources, Research Tools, Professional Life, and Related Fields. Ed. Richard T. DeGeorge. Lawrence: Regents Press of Kansas, 1980. (Replaces DeGeorge's *Guide to Philosophical Bibliography and Research*.)

This well-organized companion to philosophical research should also be helpful to students in religion, social science, the fine arts, literature, and other allied fields. In twenty-two chapters, it lists thousands of guides, handbooks, indexes, overviews, summaries, biographies, and so on. Turn here for a guide to the standard works in philosophical research.

The Philosopher's Index. Bowling Green: Philosophy Documentation Center, Bowling Green State U, 1967–.

This comprehensive index to periodicals and books in philosophy and closely related fields consists of a subject index, an author index with abstracts of articles and books, and a book review index. If you are looking for a work in philosophy, it's here. Available on-line.

A Reader's Guide to the Great Religions. Ed. Charles J. Adams. New York: Free Press, 1977.

A rich and authoritative guide to the best materials on the history and traditions of the world's major religions. Each chapter, written by an expert, provides a good introduction to a particular religion and discusses the usefulness and value of the works cited.

Religion Index I: Periodicals. Ed. G. Fay Dickerson. Chicago: American Theological Library Association, 1977–. (Formerly *Index to Religious Periodical Literature,* 1949–77.)

This major and indispensable index for religious periodicals provides a cumulative guide to over three hundred major journals. It contains a subject index with extensive cross-references and an author index with abstracts of most articles. Thus it not only locates material, but also saves time in that it allows you to judge whether an article seems appropriate for a given research topic. (*Religion Index II* covers multi-volume works not generally useful to the beginning student.)

Social Sciences

GENERAL

American Men and Women of Science: Social and Behavioral Sciences. 13th ed. Ed. Jaques Cattell Press. New York: Bowker, 1978.

Excellent source for information about people currently active in the social sciences.

Encyclopaedia of the Social Sciences. 15 vols. Ed. Edwin R. A. Seligman. New York: Macmillan, 1930–35.

An invaluable work, particularly useful for learning how the social sciences were understood in the 1930s. Want to know what the established view of Freud was in the 1930s? It is here. About half the articles are biographical. Provides excellent historical information on many topics such as abortion, adoption, segregation, and unemployment.

International Encyclopedia of the Social Sciences. 8 vols. Ed. David L. Sills. New York: Free Press, 1977.

Intended to complement rather than replace the *Encyclopaedia of the Social Sciences.* The articles, which are signed and include bibliographies, are mainly analytical and comparative, rather than historical and descriptive.

PAIS International in Print. New York: Public Affairs Information Service, 1991–. (Formerly *Public Affairs Information Service Bulletin* [PAIS]. New York: Public Affairs Information Service, 1915–1990.)

An outstanding general index, *PAIS* covers all aspects of public affairs: copyright laws, interest rates, taxes, international affairs, education, social movements, political issues, and much more. Excellent for finding information and sources on current events and issues of current concern such as nuclear nonproliferation. Available on-line and on CD-ROM as *PAIS International.*

Social Sciences Index. New York: Wilson, 1974–. (Formerly *International Index,* 1907–65; *Social Sciences and Humanities Index,* 1965–74.)

Indexes articles and periodicals by author and subject for all the social sciences. A separate book review section is organized by author of the book reviewed.

Webb, William, and Carl M. White. *Sources and Information in the Social Sciences.* 3rd ed. Chicago: American Library Association, 1985.

An excellent introduction to reference materials for all areas of social science, including economics, sociology, anthropology, psychology, and political science. Disciplines that overlap with these subjects— education, business administration, geography, and history—are also included. Much more than a descriptive list of sources, each chapter serves as an introduction to the discipline. Any student would do well to browse through this valuable book both to learn how information in the social sciences is organized and to discover reference tools for specific research topics.

ANTHROPOLOGY, PSYCHOLOGY, AND SOCIOLOGY

Frantz, Charles. *The Student Anthropologist's Handbook.* Cambridge: Schenkman, 1972.

An interesting overview of the discipline, including a discussion of the training required to become an anthropologist, the kinds of activities professional anthropologists engage in, and an introduction to research materials and institutions.

Kottak, Conrad Phillip. *Researching American Culture: A Guide for Student Anthropologists*. Ann Arbor: U of Michigan P, 1982.
This interesting work focuses on anthropological studies in the United States.

McInnis, Raymond G. *Research Guide for Psychology*. Westport: Greenwood, 1982.
A guide to some 1,200 information sources in psychology, including general works, handbooks, encyclopedias, etc.

Psychological Abstracts. Washington: American Psychological Association, 1927–.
Covering more than those subjects strictly considered part of psychology, this work provides brief summaries (abstracts) of articles from journals and chapters from books in all the social sciences. This important index is not as easy to use as the *Social Science Index,* but it is more specialized and provides more information about each reference. To find material in the volumes from 1973 to the present, consult the *Sources of Psychological Index Terms.* As with any reference work, you should study the introductory material (instructions for the user) of the volume actually used since the format for citations may vary. Available in CD-ROM as *PsychLIT* and on-line as *PsycINFO*.

Sociological Abstracts. New York: Sociological Abstracts, 1953–.
Like *Psychological Abstracts,* this work is useful for many disciplines within the social sciences. To use it, however, you will find it necessary to study the table of contents and the indexing system. If you find a source cited in this or other abstract volumes, you can study the abstract to decide whether you want to look for the original. The latest studies on child care, alcohol abuse, and sexism are among the thousands of sociological topics indexed here on CD-ROM as *Sociofile* and on-line.

BUSINESS AND ECONOMICS

Business Index. Menlo Park: Information Access, 1979–.
Available on microform, this index is especially useful for finding very current material on business topics in general magazines, business periodicals, and newspapers (including the *Wall Street Journal*). Since the listings are cumulative, you will be able to locate material on many business topics efficiently and easily. This index is constantly updated, and older material is dropped as new listings are added. Available on CD-ROM (through *InfoTrac*).

Business Periodicals Index. New York: Wilson, 1958–.

Indexes articles in the following fields: accounting, advertising, automation, banking, communications, economics, finance and investments, insurance, labor, management, marketing, taxes, etc. An overview of articles in the significant journals. Book reviews are in a separate section. Available on CD-ROM.

Daniels, Lorna M. *Business Information Sources.* Berkeley: U of California P, 1985.

The best guide to sources in all aspects of business and economics. Any student interested in studying a topic related to these fields should consult this book first to learn about the available sources.

Encyclopedia of Management. 2nd ed. Ed. Carl Heyel. New York: Van Nostrand, 1982.

A very good encyclopedic dictionary on a variety of topics such as consumer protection, data communications, motivation, and trade shows. Substantial articles on these and many other topics include references that direct the reader to important texts and articles on the subject.

McGraw-Hill Dictionary of Modern Economics: A Handbook of Terms and Organizations. 3rd ed. New York: McGraw, 1983.

A very useful dictionary; each entry includes a definition as well as at least one other source that provides more information.

MIT Dictionary of Modern Economics. 3rd ed. Cambridge: MIT Press, 1986.

Students interested in economics will enjoy browsing through this valuable source of information.

Moody's Manuals. New York: Moody's Investors Service.

Moody's Manuals provide comprehensive financial information in seven annual publications, six devoted to U.S. companies, one to leading foreign companies. If you want financial information about a particular company, begin with *Moody's Complete Corporate Index,* which will lead you to the appropriate manual. Students doing substantial research on business topics should be familiar with all Moody's publications. *Moody's Corporate Profiles* is available on-line; it provides access to information in other Moody's publications.

Standard and Poor's Corporation Records. New York: Standard and Poor's.

A widely used reference for information on more than 10,000 U.S. companies. Basic information on companies is revised regularly and latest developments are reported in daily updates. If you are looking for particular topics, begin with the topical index. Students doing substantial research on business topics should be familiar with all *Standard and Poor's* publications. *Standard and Poor's Corporation Records Online* provides access to current and historical business information.

Value Line Investment Survey. New York: A. Bernhard.
Provides objective, authoritative information on some 1,700 companies. Excellent source for investment information.

EDUCATION

Current Index to Journals in Education (CIJE). Phoenix: Oryx, 1969–.
An index to almost eight hundred educational and education-related materials. The place to turn for a thorough review of the literature on a topic. Produced by the Educational Resources Information Center *(ERIC)*, *CIJE* uses the same subject headings (descriptors) as *Resources in Education*, described below. Available on CD-ROM and on-line through *ERIC*.

Education Index. New York: Wilson, 1929–.
Includes fewer periodicals than *CIJE*, but covers a much longer period of time. You may prefer to use this more selective index, since you will not find many of the periodicals indexed in *CIJE* in small or even medium-sized libraries. Available on CD-ROM and on-line.

The International Encyclopedia of Education: Research and Studies. New York: Pergamon, 1985 (Supplement, 1988).
Excellent up-to-date overview of scholarship on educational systems throughout the world.

Resources in Education (RIE). [Known as *ERIC*] Washington: GPO, 1975. Formerly *Research in Education*, 1966–74.
An index to many documents not published in journals. Contains an order form for obtaining copies of documents. These documents are stored on microform in many libraries. Copies can usually be made with a microform reader-printer. Like *CIJE*, *RIE* is produced by the Educational Resources Information Center; this index and the collection of documents it catalogs are often referred to by librarians and researchers as *ERIC*. Available on CD-ROM and on-line as *ERIC*.

World of Learning. London: Europa, 1947–.
Gives basic information about a variety of educational institutions throughout the world, including libraries, research institutes, colleges, and universities, as well as learned societies and museums. This is a good place to find the address, telephone number, and purpose of an institution. You will also find general information on when and how

an institution was founded; the number of students; and for large or prestigious schools, the names of chief officers.

POLITICAL SCIENCE AND GOVERNMENT

The Almanac of American Politics. By Michael Barone and Grant Ujifusa. Washington: Barone, 1972–.
The subtitle of this delightful book tells you what you will find in it: almost anything you ever wanted to know—and then some—about "The President, the Senators, the Representatives, the Governors: Their Records and Election Results, Their States and Districts."

Brock, Clifton. *The Literature of Political Science.* New York: Bowker, 1969. An introduction to library materials and research methods in political science. It includes descriptions of various indexes and abstracts to help you find material in periodicals. An excellent introduction to government publications and the many publications of public organizations.

Congressional Quarterly Almanac. Washington: Congressional Quarterly, 1945–.
Summarizes congressional activity every year. Here you will find concise information about committee hearings, voting records, investigations, texts of presidential addresses, and lobbying efforts, as well as details of major legislation.

Congressional Quarterly's Guide to Congress. 3rd ed. Eds. Robert A. Diamond and Patricia Ann O'Connor. Washington: Congressional Quarterly, 1982.
Periodically revised, this comprehensive overview of the workings of Congress is placed in a large historical context; it explains the powers, procedures, and structures of Congress; and it discusses the relationship of Congress to the society at large.

Congressional Quarterly's Politics in America. Washington: Congressional Quarterly, 1989–.
Similar to the *Almanac of American Politics,* this work provides information about Congressional Committees, election districts, and election manuals and handbooks.

Congressional Quarterly Weekly Report. Washington: Congressional Quarterly, 1943–.
Gives a comprehensive summary of congressional activity for each week. If you are researching a specific legislative act—the Civil Rights

Act of 1964, for instance—you may want to go to the *Weekly* for a summary of all the activities and debate leading to its passage.

Holler, Frederick L. *Information Sources of Political Science.* Santa Barbara: Clio, 1981.
More up-to-date and comprehensive than *The Literature of Political Science* (see above), this work describes the important reference works in related fields such as psychology and philosophy. A pleasure to read, this guide will be very useful to students doing research on topics concerning the public aspects of social science.

The United States Government Manual. Washington: GPO, 1935–.
An up-to-date source of information on all aspects of the organization of the federal government. Published every year, it includes names, addresses, and telephone numbers of public officials in all branches of government; explanations of the function of all government departments; and basic information about domestic and international organizations that are allied to the United States. Want to know the names of the Supreme Court justices, how to obtain information from the Environmental Protection Agency, or how the Department of Health and Human Services is organized? To answer these and many other questions, check the *Government Manual.*

York, Henry E. *Political Science: A Guide to Reference and Information Sources.* Englewood: Libraries Unlimited, 1990.
This up-to-date research guide includes bibliographical references and indexes.

Natural and Applied Sciences

GENERAL

American Men and Women of Science: Physical and Biological Sciences. 7 vols. 15th ed. Ed. Jaques Cattell Press. New York: Bowker, 1982.
The best source for information about living scientists who are currently active. Available on-line.

Dictionary of Scientific Biography. 16 vols. New York: Scribner's, 1970–81 (Supplement, 1977; Index, 1981).
A valuable source for the history of science. The articles provide reliable information on the professional lives of thousands of scientists

from classical antiquity to modern times. The twentieth-century figures have all been dead for some years, and all achieved considerable distinction.

General Science Index. New York: Wilson, 1978–.
This cumulative subject index to general science periodicals is commonly found in public libraries. It is a good source for beginning science students to use. Available on CD-ROM and on-line.

McGraw-Hill Encyclopedia of Science and Technology. 15 vols. 5th ed. New York: McGraw, 1982.
This high-quality, up-to-date work provides excellent background reading in almost all scientific and technological topics. It is appropriate for the sophisticated student of science as well as for the beginning researcher who is investigating a scientific topic.

McGraw-Hill Yearbook of Science and Technology. New York: McGraw. Published annually.
Updates the latest edition of the *Encyclopedia*. A good source for a summary of scientific development in recent years.

Science Citation Index. Ed. Eugene Garfield. Philadelphia: Institute for Scientific Information, 1982.
An interdisciplinary index to scholarly journals in the sciences and to books since 1977. It links each publication listed with all others that cite it. Once you learn to use the *Science Citation Index*, you will find that it provides a relatively easy way to find the important information on a given topic. Available on-line as part of *Scisearch*.

ASTRONOMY

The Cambridge Encyclopaedia of Astronomy. Ed. Simon Milton. Cambridge: Institute of Astronomy, 1977.
A well-illustrated, topically arranged survey of astronomy, this work provides an authoritative introduction to many aspects of the field.

BIOLOGY, MEDICINE, AND NURSING

Biological Abstracts. Philadelphia: BioSciences Information Service of Biological Abstracts, 1926–.
The basic research tool for research in biology and biomedicine. Excellent abstracts give you a summary of each citation. Available on CD-ROM and on-line as *Biosis*.

Cumulative Index to Nursing and Allied Health Literature. Glendale: Glendale Advertisement Medical Center, 1977–. (Formerly *Cumulative Index to Nursing Literature,* 1956–1976.) Available on CD-ROM as *CINAHL*. Organized by both subject and author, this comprehensive index will lead you to articles on all aspects of nursing and allied health sciences.

The Encyclopedia of the Biological Sciences. 2nd ed. Ed. Peter Gray. New York: Van Nostrand, 1970.
This single-volume work provides accurate information on biological topics for nonexperts.

Grzimek's Animal Life Encyclopedia. 13 vols. Ed. Bernhard Grzimek. New York: Van Nostrand, 1972–75.
This is an informative and fascinating reference work. Each volume treats its subject—fishes, birds, mammals, reptiles, and so on—with authority and style. Generous use of color plates and photographs enhances the readable text. International in scope, this is a good place to turn for an overview of the animal kingdom. Each volume has a good index and a list of suggested readings.

Index Medicus. U.S. Department of Health and Human Services. N.I.H. Publications. Washington: National Library of Medicine, 1960– (monthly).
This is the authoritative index to periodical literature in medicine and related fields. Biological literature is well represented. Although many of the articles cited are technical and intended for experts, you may find this index helpful if you are researching general topics in medicine or biology. Available on CD-ROM and on-line as *Medline*.

CHEMISTRY AND PHYSICS

The Condensed Chemical Dictionary. 10th ed. New York: Van Nostrand, 1981.
In addition to providing definitions of chemical terms, this is a useful source for concise information about commercial and trade market products and for pharmaceuticals and drugs.

The Encyclopedia of Physics. Eds. Rita G. Lerner and George L. Trigg. Reading: Addison, 1981.
This single-volume work is an authoritative source for background information and for an overview of the major principles and problems of physics. More than this, it contains speculative articles on contro-

versial developments, written by experts engaged in current research. Extensive bibliographies and clear charts and diagrams make this a useful and usable source.

Handbook of Chemistry and Physics. 58th ed. Cleveland: Chemical Rubber, 1913–.
This is the most useful single-volume reference work available to the undergraduate and graduate student in chemistry and physics. It is divided into six parts with a good index and constitutes, as its subtitle indicates, "A Ready Reference Book of Chemical and Physical Data." Turn here for the facts, and go to the sources listed above for the explanations.

COMPUTER SCIENCE

Computers and Control Abstracts. Piscataway: Institute of Electric Engineers with The Institute of Electrical and Electronic Engineers, 1969–.
Part C of the three-part *Science Abstracts.* Published twice monthly, this excellent index provides sources for information on all aspects of computer science, including computer languages, equipment, software, hardware, new terminology, and latest developments in the field. Available on-line as *Inspec.*

The Directory of On-line Databases. Cuadra Associates, 1980–.
Updated quarterly, this excellent directory provides accurate, concise, and useful information about databases in all fields.

ENGINEERING

Applied Science and Technology Index. Ed. Rose Manofsky. New York: Wilson, 1958–.
A multidisciplinary subject index covering a wide range of topics including several kinds of engineering, as well as the applied aspects of chemistry, geology, and physics. If you are researching general science topics, you will want to browse through this index to get an idea of the scope of its coverage.

Engineering Index. New York: Engineering Index, 1906–.
Worldwide coverage of the journal literature, publications of engineering societies and organizations, and selected government books. Available on CD-ROM and on-line as *Compendex.*

Allaby, Michael. *Dictionary of the Environment*. New York: New York UP, 1989.
Provides definitions of extensive list of terms related to environmental concerns. Here is a place to get brief definitions of chlorofluorocarbons, the greenhouse effect, or desertification.

Burke, John Gordon. *Guide to Ecology Information and Organizations*. New York: Wilson, 1976.
For research on environmental issues before 1976 this work is a useful source, but it would be out-of-date for recent topics.

Burton, John A. *The Atlas of Endangered Species*. New York: Macmillan, 1991.
An overview of selected species threatened by extinction. A good general discussion of factors that have caused the crisis. Excellent photographs and a good index.

Grzimek's Encyclopedia of Ecology. Ed. Bernhard Grzimek. New York: Van Nostrand, 1976.
A comprehensive approach to the study of ecology. Beautifully illustrated and a pleasure to read, this work is a valuable source of general and detailed information on ecological topics.

McGraw-Hill Encyclopedia of Environmental Science. 2nd ed. Ed. Sybil P. Parker. New York: McGraw, 1980.
Concerned with the complex interaction between living things and environmental phenomena, this specialized encyclopedia focuses on many aspects of the earth and the ways it has been used.

PERMISSIONS
ACKNOWLEDGMENTS

Pp. 36–38: "jungle and rain forest" article from the *Academic American Encyclopedia,* 1990 Edition. Copyright © 1990 by Grolier Incorporated. Reprinted by permission.

Pp. 40–41: Excerpt from index to the *Encyclopedia Americana,* 1980 Edition. Copyright © 1980 by Grolier Incorporated. Reprinted by permission.

Pp. 42–43: Excerpt from the *Readers' Guide to Periodical Literature.* Reprinted by permission of The H. W. Wilson Company.

P. 44: Excerpt from the *New York Times Index,* 1981. Copyright © 1981 by the New York Times Company. Reprinted by permission.

P. 50: Excerpt from the computer version of the *MLA International Bibliography.* Reprinted by permission of the Modern Language Association of America.

P. 50: Excerpt from *InfoTrac* database. Copyright © 1991 by the Information Access Company. Reprinted by permission.

Pp. 78–79: Excerpts from the *PsycINFO* database. Copyright © 1986–1993 by the American Psychological Association. Reprinted with permission of the American Psychological Association, publisher of *Psychological Abstracts* and the *PsycINFO* database.

INDEX

bibliographies in, 39–40
described, 357
excerpt from *Americana* index, 40–41
general, 35, 39
indexes to, 39–40
list of, 35, 39
recommended, 360–61
specialized, 41
engineering, recommended sources on, 379
environmental science, recommended sources on, 380
ERIC database, 49, 53, 77, 374
exclamation point
spacing, 226
uses, 221
exploring, 2–5

F

Facts on File database, 52
film, citing
in bibliography (MLA), 203
in notes (MLA), 350
in reference list (APA), 358
in reference list (CBE), 286
film, recommended sources on, 364–65

G

general knowledge
distinguishing, 134–35
recording, 133
General Periodicals Index, 43, 49
General Science Index
described, 48
Lisa Lee using, 48, 72
geographical sources, recommended, 361
Gold, Michael
choosing and focusing his topic, 23–25
consulting the reference librarian, 34
documentation style used, 131
his bibliography, 249–50
his final paper, 237–50
his outlines, 152–54
his search strategy, 75
his thesis statement, 146
interpreting, 128
organizing note cards, 141
paraphrasing, 125–26
questionnaire, 100
revising his draft, 171–73, 174

sample paper with endnotes, 352–56
steps leading to his paper, 235–36
writing a letter, 101
writing a thesis statement, 144
government
approaches to, 252
recommended sources on, 375
government publications, citing
in bibliography (MLA), 201
in notes (MLA), 348
in reference list (APA), 258
Guide to Reference Books, 63

H

Handbook for Authors of Papers in American Chemical Society Publications, 187
Harris, David
consulting indexes, 66
documentation style used, 185
focusing his topic, 27
his abstract, 290
his computer search, 77–79
his final paper, 261–78
his outline, 155–56
his references, 276–78
his thesis statement, 145–46
revising his draft, 175
steps leading to his paper, 260
Historical Abstracts database, 53
history
approaches to research in, 233
recommended sources on, 365–66
humanities
approaches to research in, 232–35
documentation for, 185–214
recommended sources on, 363–70
sample papers, 178–83, 237–50
Humanities Index, 45
hyphen
spacing, 226
uses, 223
hypothesis, testing, 142–43

I

idea, controlling, *see* thesis statement
ideas
discussing with others, 15
letting them brew, 15
illustrations, citing, 207
indentation, 228

quotation marks
  spacing, 226
  uses, 223
quotations
  indenting, 167
  integrating into text, 166–67
quoting, 120–21

R

radio programs, citing
  in bibliography (MLA), 202–03
  in notes (MLA), 202–03
Readers' Guide Supplement and International Index, 45
Readers' Guide to Periodical Literature
  description, 42–43
  excerpt from, 42–43
  using, 33
reader, imagining, 160–61
reading effectively, 92–93
reference department, library, 33–34
reference works, annotated list, 357–80
religion, sources on, 369–70
Religion Index database, 53
reporting research findings, 5–6
research
  about new topics, 14
  about topics you know something about, 14
  as vocation, 10–11
  definition, 1
resources
  academic, 6–8
  community, 8–9
  human, 9–10
  introduction to, 6–7
revising
  checklist, 174
  eliminating unnecessary words, 170–71
  examples of, 171–75
  final revision, 173–74
  organization, 168–69
  paragraphs, 171
  sentences, 171–73
RLIN, 63, 80

S

sample papers
  about literature (Carla Medina), 308–17, 339

a short paper (Linda Orton), 178–83
  in humanities (Michael Gold), 237–50
  in natural and applied sciences (Lisa Lee), 289–303
  in social sciences (David Harris), 261–78
  using endnotes (Michael Gold), 353–56
science, *see* natural and applied sciences or social sciences
Scientific American, 279
Scisearch database, 54
search strategy
  an example (Carla Medina), 318–19
  planning, 74
semicolon
  spacing, 222, 226
  uses, 222
sexist language, 90, 162
social sciences
  approaches to research in, 251–53
  checklist for reference list, 284
  citing references in text of paper, 259
  documentation for, 253–59
  recommended sources on, 370–76
  sample paper in, 261–78
  sources for individual disciplines, 371–76
Social Sciences and Humanities Index, 45
Social Sciences Index, 45
sociology
  approaches to, 252
  recommended sources on, 371–72
source cards
  checklist for, 84
  examples, 83–85
  making, 82–85
  uses, 83–85
sources
  citing in text (APA), 259
  citing in text (MLA), 164–65
  citing material from secondary source, 205–06
  citing while composing, 164–65
  classifying, 86–87
  collecting, checklist for, 73
  evaluating, 87–90
  integrating into paper, 166–67
  primary, 234
  reading, 91–92
  recording on a computer file, 85
  reviewing possibilities, 72
  samples, 86
  secondary, 234